The Rise of Global Health

The Evolution of Effective Collective Action

JOSHUA K. LEON

D1598151

PRESS

Cover photo: *World Health Organization Executive Board Room,* by Thorkild Tylleskar, uploaded to Creative Commons by Thorkild Tylleskar, December 6, 2013

Published by State University of New York Press, Albany

For information, contact State University of New York Press, Albany, NY
www.sunypress.edu

Production, Eileen Nizer
Marketing, Michael Campochiaro

Library of Congress Cataloging-in-Publication Data

Leon, Joshua K., 1980–
 The rise of global health : the evolution of effective collective action / Joshua K. Leon.
       pages cm
 Includes bibliographical references and index.
 ISBN 978-1-4384-5517-4 (hardcover : alk. paper)
 ISBN 978-1-4384-5516-7 (pbk. : alk. paper)
 ISBN 978-1-4384-5518-1 (ebook)
 1. World health.   2. Public health—International cooperation.   3. Medical policy—International cooperation.   I. Title.

 RA441.L46 2015
 362.1—dc23   2014013127

10 9 8 7 6 5 4 3 2 1

*This book is dedicated to anyone in the world
denied the right to health.
And especially to the
Leon and Kremer families
for their immeasurable support.*

Contents

Illustrations

Figures

Tables

Acknowledgments

Karl-Orfeo Fioretos, my doctoral advisor at Temple University and academic mentor, provided innumerable insights into this project, devoting valuable time to reading and commenting—far more than his job description could ever fairly require. He is thorough, creative, and professional, and imparted all of these virtues through his advice on this project. Mark Pollack also provided extensive advice and feedback. His inputs on the project go back to its very early stages. In fact, this book really got started as a series of brainstorms in Pollack's prospectus seminar. Richard Deeg, currently chair of the Department of Political Science at Temple University, provided invaluable advice on early drafts. Clara Haignere from Temple's Public Health department provided much-needed insights from that very important disciplinary perspective. Two anonymous reviewers clearly devoted a great deal of their valuable time to providing extensive, insightful feedback for this project. They remain unnamed, but not unappreciated.

Special thanks also to Miguel Glatzer at LaSalle University for reading an important chapter draft at the Northeastern Political Science Association annual conference in 2011. A. Burcu Bayram of the University of Texas at Arlington gave encouraging feedback on a chapter draft at the 2013 Western Political Science Association Conference. I also owe a debt to students at Drexel University and Iona College, where I have taught a course called "The Politics of Global Health." At various stages they were force-fed readings from this project, and enthusiastically provided lively conversation and new ideas. Joel Oestreich of Drexel's International Area Studies made this possible by first proposing that I design the course.

Erin Leon did a very thorough job proofreading draft manuscripts, as she does with virtually everything I write. Not only did she help

omit embarrassing typos from later drafts, she read through the project critically and pushed me to clarify my most important ideas. Kind
appreciation to Eileen Nizer, Senior Production Editor at SUNY Press,
for thoroughly proofreading my final draft. I also owe additional grati-
tude to Karl-Orfeo Fioretos and Michael Hagen, the former graduate
chair at Temple University's Department of Political Science. Both were
instrumental in helping me attain the grant that enabled me to work
on this project full time.

Faculty mentors at California State University, Sacramento, where I
began graduate school in the master's level International Affairs program,
have also contributed to the intellectual development of this project in
many important ways. Patrick Cannon influenced my thinking on the
broader topic of poverty and development—and still helps point me in so
many important directions. Bahman Fozouni, my master's thesis advisor,
also provided much intellectual guidance over my career. My work has
changed direction since then, but their guidance was and is invaluable.

I owe a great thanks to Tricia Mulligan, chair of the Department
of Political Science and International Studies at Iona College, who also
welcomed my efforts to bring global health into the classroom. As with
Dr. Mulligan, Robert Lacey, Mary Hagerty, and Jeanne Zaino were also
been uncommonly welcoming, warm, collegial, and intellectually stimulating in my time at Iona College.

Even with this generous help, I wouldn't get far without Erin Leon's
moral support.

Portions of chapter 4 appeared in my article "Confronting Catastrophe: Norms, Efficiency and Evolution of the AIDS Battle in the UN"
from *Cambridge Review of International Affairs*.

Abbreviations

AAI	Accelerating Access Initiative
ACP	Africa, Pacific and Caribbean states
ADB	Asian Development Bank
AfDB	African Development Bank
ARV	Antiretroviral Medicine
BMG	Bill and Melinda Gates Foundation
CDC	Center for Disease Control
CGD	Center for Global Development
CIDA	Canadian International Development Agency
CRS	Creditor Reporting System
DAC	Development Assistance Committee
DARA	Development Assistance Research Associates
DCPP	Disease Control Priorities Project
EC	European Commission
EU	European Union
GAIN	Global Alliance for Improved Nutrition
GAVI	Global Alliance for Vaccine Immunization
GFATM	Global Fund to fight AIDS, Tuberculosis, and Malaria
GPA	Global Program on AIDS

GTT	Global Task Team on Improving AIDS Coordination Among Multilateral Organizations
HAART	Highly Active Antiretroviral Treatment
HHS	Department of Health and Human Services
HNP	Health, Nutrition and Population
IDA	International Development Administration
IDI	Infectious Disease Initiative
JICA	Japan International Cooperation Agency
MAP	Multi-country AIDS Program
MCA	Millennium Challenge Account
MDGs	Millennium Development Goals
MOFA	Japan Ministry of Foreign Affairs
MSF	Medicines Sans Frontieres (Doctors Without Borders)
NIH	National Institutes of Health
ODA	Official Development Assistance
OECD	Organization for Economic Cooperation and Development
PEPFAR	President's Emergency Program on AIDS Relief
RBMI	Roll Bank Malaria Initiative
SIDA	Swedish International Development Agency
TAN	Transnational Action Network
TRIPS	Agreement on Trade-Related Aspects of Intellectual Property Rights
UNAIDS	Joint United Nations Program on HIV/AIDS
UNDP	United Nations Development Programme
UNESCO	United Nations Educational, Scientific and Cultural Organization
UNICEF	United Nations Children's Fund
USAID	United States Agency for International Development

WASABI   Water Sanitation Broad Partnership Initiative

WFP   World Food Program

WHO   World Health Organization

CHAPTER 1

The Rise of a Regime Complex
for Global Health

Global public health has emerged as a central concern of the international development effort. The tenfold increase in international resources devoted to combating epidemics since 1974 has led to a potentially unwieldy "regime complex" that some have criticized for its inefficiency and overlap. In line with regime complex theory, the global health regime is decentralized with agencies nominally overlapping in mission, "governing" global health with no command hierarchy. In short, this is the type of regime that has generated increasing discussion—and lamentation—within the international relations literature. At the same time, the decentralized nature of global health governance poses a central problem for global public health: How to improve, if not fully coordinate, collective action as the regime expands? This is a primary problem that has engendered contentious debate within the fields of international relations, development, and global public health.

This book revisits prevailing understandings of how resources are allocated in the area of public health, identifying outcomes in global health's rise that we miss by applying the regime complex literature's narrative of overexpansion. It provides an analytical lens through with we may glean insights into the regime complex for global health, thereby offering insights into the larger challenge of decentralized collective action in global health governance. Drawing from international relations theory, this book explores the complex constellation of actors—states, multilateral institutions, civil society organizations, foundations, multinational corporations, and so on—whose collective activities constitute the transnational governance of public health. From the perspective of an author with an expertise in international relations, this book seeks to glean important generalizations that are valuable to students and scholars across the spectrum of political science, health, and development—while fully understanding the daunting challenge of merging the languages of these disparate disciplines. Applying these respective disciplinary debates is nevertheless a worthy undertaking as empirical lines between them become blurred, and the case of the regime complex for global health speaks loudly to many disciplines.

This book aims to generate meaningful understandings of an important aspect of global governance writ large, and to address a larger problem confronting global health, namely that of collective action among increasingly decentralized, independent sets of actors.

Global health governance is charged with managing public well-being by way of collective action. The global public health regime, the multifaceted locus of this collective action, is notable for increasingly specialized approaches among actors. This is a development intended to reduce inefficiencies and institutional overlap. Nevertheless there is a conventional prediction that regimes grow more stilted and inefficient as they increase in size and overlapping mandates. A 2009 symposium in *Perspectives on Politics* on the consequences of greater regime complexity found this to be true across a variety of issue areas—ranging from trade, human rights, intellectual property, security, and election monitoring.[1] We have much to worry about if the symposium's analysis amounts to a general rule about the consequences of the expansion of formal international cooperation in the twenty-first century. If greater complexity means that the global health regime is unable to expand without minimizing attendant inefficiencies, then the immediate future looks bleak for those individuals that the regime is intended to help. This also calls into question the current global agenda to expand development assistance channels toward other pressing global problems, most notably climate change, for which new north-south transfers figure centrally in the 2011 Durban plan.

If growth in resources, mandates, and aid producers is a source of inefficiency, nowhere should this be more apparent than in the arena of global health. The global health regime has grown remarkably over the past two decades and is now composed of a vast network of states, multilateral institutions and non-governmental organizations. It has origins in the creation of the World Health Organization in 1948, a specialized UN agency mandated to pursue, as stated in its constitution, "the attainment of all peoples of the highest possible level of health." It is a vast mandate, though the means and power by which the WHO can pursue this varies. In addition to monitoring epidemics, coordinating international responses to them, collaborating with a multitude of actors, and promoting health equality, the WHO plays a central role in fostering governance structures for global health activity in the twenty-first century. Today the regime encompasses a large number of creditor states, bilateral and multilateral programs, non-governmental organizations, and amorphous "public-private partnerships." In addition to the "big-bang" of new agencies created in the late 1990s and 2000s, the regime's growth is apparent in the sheer volume of new financial resources devoted to combating disease around the world.

Much of this dramatic increase in financial resources has come in the form of Official Development Assistance (ODA) devoted to health, making health one of the fastest growing sectors of international aid. In 1974, aid to global health totaled only $1.9 billion, according to the OECD. By 2006 aid to global health increased tenfold to a record $19.6 billion. During the same period, aid to health expanded from 5 percent of all development assistance to a record 16.5 percent. This remarkable expansion includes the creation of high profile agencies such as UNAIDS, the Global Fund, and the President's Emergency Program for AIDS Relief (PEPFAR). Just as significant has been the increased number of existing agencies that have prioritized health. The World Bank has become a central multilateral player in the global public health regime, and has altered the regime's fabric considerably.[2] Growing philanthropic foundations such as the Bill and Melinda Gates Foundation are adding further to this patchwork.

A large literature in the area of global health points toward increasingly disjointed global health activity as the regime has expanded. The new money the rich world has poured into global health coffers, it argues, does not mirror the actual patterns of disease in the developing world. Laurie Garrett's provocative article in *Foreign Affairs*, "The Challenge of Global Health," caused a stir in the development community by contending that funds for global health are misallocated. Garrett notes:

> [B]ecause the efforts this money is paying for are largely uncoordinated and directed mostly at specific high profile diseases—rather than at public health in general—there is a grave danger that the current age of generosity could not only fall short of expectations but actually make things worse on the ground.[3]

Just as much current thinking in the international relations literature would predict, Garrett's critique reflects a widespread perception that
the global health regime has become dollar-for-dollar increasingly inefficient over time. This book reaches a different conclusion. When viewed
in its totality, the global health regime has promoted efficiency in key
ways. As the global public health regime has seen its bureaucracy expand,
it has also seen high levels of specialization. As the bureaucracies within
the regime complex have grown larger and arguably more tangled, actors
within the regime have shown a greater inclination toward reducing
inefficiencies and better meeting the requirements of the global burden
of disease through the development of niche activities. Specialization
occurs according to issue area, as well as geography. One effect of this has
been to reduce the overlapping tasks associated with regime complexity.

As the regime complex literature illustrates, the rise of a regime
complex for global health—replete with numerous overlapping legal
forums and actors lacking central coordination—creates serious challenges for the future of global economic redistribution. This global governance arrangement also creates opportunities that are all too belatedly
gaining scholarly recognition. Evidence presented in this book suggests
an important development that is often overlooked: Under conditions
of regime complexity there is a surprising degree of complementarity
between actors despite a lack of formal cooperation. Formal multi-
sectoral cooperation between states, development agencies, and private actors proliferated during the rise of global health. Less discussed
has been the informal complementarity that actors have engaged in
through specialization. Underlying patterns of development assistance
shown throughout this book are individual actors within the regime,
whose roles and priorities vary starkly. Even though aid distributors have
increased global health outlays, they have also narrowed their range of
priority issues. Most choose to specialize in just one or two areas. Smaller
actors, correspondingly, also adopt highly specialized roles such as advocacy, ground level partnerships, or resource coordination. To understand
these important developments, factors hitherto under-explored in public health deserve greater attention, including emergent coordination
between development and health agencies, specialization among these
actors, and the emergence of a normative consensus among key actors
on economic approaches to development.

In sum, these developments portend opportunities as well as challenges when it comes to the specific question of how the global public
health regime allocates resources. The regime complex for global health

offers a critical empirical case for the new thinking in the IR literature that emphasizes overgrowth and inefficiency. The expansion of global governance in health did not insurmountably jeopardize resource maximization, and even encouraged efficiency. This is by no means the end of the story. By economizing health, the major institutions that have fueled its rise have also commoditized it. While formal and informal forms of complementarity emerged out of necessity during the rise of global health, this has not resolved the danger of health being subordinated to the imperatives of growth and profit.

Another hope for this book is that it will generate cross-disciplinary insights for scholars of public health alongside the expected international relations audience. Students and scholars of international relations unacquainted with public health may nevertheless find themselves unfamiliar with its basic disciplinary meanings. By "health," we are not referring merely to battling epidemics or the "absence of disease or infirmity," but "a state of complete physical, mental and social wellbeing" as the WHO constitution conceptualizes it.[4] This notion includes a wide range of epidemiological concerns—including those largely neglected by the regime. "Global public health" is itself distinct from "biomedicine," which is grounded largely in the health of the individual, and has been cited as a technologically oriented approach to individual diseases.[5] Public health, in Lee's words, "addresses the health of populations."[6] From there, the definition of public health encompasses the range of activities used to improve collective health. For many, public health emphasizes health as a non-excludable public good, and a fundamental human right.[7] Public health entails the political, social, and economic as well as biological determinants of health. It encapsulates mental as well as physical wellbeing, and the collective realization of our full human potential (though as we will see, this has been defined down to "economic" or "productive" potential by an elite consensus within the global public health regime). "Global health" departs from "international health" in regards to the reduced centrality of the nation state territory as a central driver of public health concern. Public health has "globalized" as increased political, social, and economic integration makes the issues driving public health increasingly transnational. Attendant global economic, environmental, and social forces more greatly impact global patterns of illness. Inequalities in a more competitive economy correspondingly underscore inequalities in physical wellbeing, social inclusion, and isolation.

Table 1.1 describes these key terminologies, which are persistently debated in the global health literature. Therefore these definitions include key debates, such as that concerning the scope of the human rights orientation of public health, and health's place as a public good. The term "global health governance," discussed further below, is itself subject to these debates. The very globality of health governance is itself both endlessly expansive and frustratingly delimiting. While the definition of global health governance may be interpreted as encompassing all the world's public health crises, many crises are locally defined and do not threaten transnational activity. Hence according to predominate understandings of global health, these conditions are likely to fall under the category of neglected diseases. By contrast, conditions thought to possess globality more loudly demand governance. This "global" logic

Table 1.1. Key Public Health Terminologies and Distinctions

Biomedicine	Concerns the physical well-being of the *individual*, and emphasizes technological approaches to confronting specific epidemics.
Public Health	Addresses the health of an entire *community*, including mental and physical well-being, the realization of full human potential, and health as a public good, in addition to a fundamental human right. Perspectives differ on the normative expansiveness of public health, and how far it should extend.
International Public Health	*State-centered* logic of public health, problem definitions and solutions centrally rooted in the state. Collective action centered on bargaining among states, and state-based organization is the primary driver of regime activity.
Global Public Health	States concerned increasingly with *transnational* issues relating to globalization. Decreased emphasis on national boundaries as the primary logic behind regime action.
Global Health Governance	Collective transnational action to address public health concerns across borders. Bias toward transnational threats despite potential expansiveness.

of governance in health is hotly contested, particularly by those who see health as a fundamental human right, yet the elite consensus under discussion in this book clearly emphasizes the emergent imperatives of liberal globalization in health governance, coupling a functioning global system with combating existential threats, and fostering individual productivity.

The remainder of this chapter proceeds in three parts. The first part identifies both broader and more nuanced patterns in the development of the global health regime. This section illustrates two key findings that have thus far been under-explored: the high propensity for specialization in global health and the general proximity of global health resources with actual global need. The second part examines formal cooperation and informal complementarity that underlies specialization patterns. Through this system development agencies are effectively coordinating the distribution of resources toward global health. Conditions of increased regime density have resulted in a highly enmeshed division of labor with persistent specialization patterns among creditors. Aid producers seek to maintain their value-added, and potentially their bureaucratic relevance, by playing specialized, complementary roles. This emerges in the context of economism that pervades the global north-led international development effort. This illustrates a global consensus encouraging specialization as well as cost-effectiveness within the regime. Global health, moreover, has itself become a precondition for economic growth espoused by major figures such as the World Bank and WHO. The final part provides an overview of the data and methodological approaches taken in this book.

Is Bigger Worse?

While the international relations discipline has long studied the vast increase in international organization since 1945, regime complex studies initiated a timely exploration of the unintended consequences of a multilateral architecture in seemingly terminal expansion by the twenty-first century. As the institutions and legal frameworks that constitute global governance have grown more complicated, scholars have increasingly devoted attention to the consequences of increased size and complexity. Karen Alter and Sophie Meunier's influential study sees "nesting" as a significant reason behind the unusual continuity of what should have been a relatively modest trade dispute involving the banana industries of the European Union and the United States.[8] Regional and bilateral commitments are "nested" when the parties to them are also bound by other, overarching legal agreements. The ensuing amalgamation of rules can potentially add complication to otherwise straightforward legal disputes. For Alter and Meunier, "institutions are imbricated one within another, like Russian dolls."[9] Their findings suggest that increasing additions of non-hierarchical frameworks—as states enter into bilateral agreements that may complicate existing multilateral ones, and vice versa—threaten an increase in suboptimal outcomes. By implication these changes are likely to increase the cost of international transactions.

The term "regime complex" was introduced by Raustiala and Victor whose study of the international legal frameworks for plant genetic resources sought to conceptualize the expansion of global governance over time and the consequent emergence of increasingly dense, complex networks of regimes.[10] For Raustiala and Victor, singular, or "elemental," regimes overlap in relationship to a single issue area, with none assuming official hierarchical authority over existing actors. There is, in their estimation, a "growing concentration and interconnection of institutions."[11] Regime complexes, they contend, "will become much more common in coming decades as international institutions proliferate and inevitably bump against one another."[12] This has sparked considerable discussion in the IR field. While new institutions are being formed, and others expand into new territory, existing agencies and bureaucracies are unlikely to simply disappear. The logical increase in institutional density will undoubtedly affect how existing regimes operate.

These studies generally reflect a pessimistic view of regimes as they expand. Indeed, new institutions created within regimes are often not hierarchical, leaving significant procedural ambiguities. This is the case in global health, which has seen a tremendous proliferation of new agencies that often serve similar functions. A variety of existing development institutions adopted responsibilities toward public health, thus blurring the line between health and economic development functions. This is likely to have far-reaching consequences according to the regime complex literature. With multiple, non-hierarchic forums, states strategically seek out those which are more favorable to their interests. The more channels that exist, the more costly navigating the regime will become for developing countries with scarce managerial resources.

Decentralization within growing international regimes has received increasing attention in the scholarly literature, with case studies finding varying results on its role in creating inefficiencies. Stephanie Hofmann's study of the relationship between NATO and the European Security and

Defense Policy—though not entirely competitive—suffers from having few incentives to cooperate, but considerable overlap in missions. This, she argues, has "clearly impeded the development of an efficient division of labor between the two institutions."[13] Judith Kelley deals directly with the case of competition among increasing numbers of agencies in election monitoring. Increased density, she argues, has a series of beneficial effects. The existence of multiple institutions can overcome deadlock, offering alternative agencies for states who may feel that existing agencies are biased against them. Moreover, the presence of multiple election monitoring agencies may increase legitimacy by reinforcing election results. But added inefficiencies are a cost of increased density. Competition creates a disincentive for cooperation. A lack of information sharing between agencies, or unwillingness to pool resources, can lead to costly overlapping and sub-optimal outcomes. Or, as Kelley puts it, "redundancies, communication failures, and waste."[14] Differing organizational biases, methods, or standards may cause these organizations to contradict each other or otherwise work at cross purposes. The regime complex literature raises important strategic questions for developing states that incorporate aid into governance: From which wealthy aid distributors do they seek support? Do they solicit input from the World Bank, UNDP, or WHO? Do prospective aid partners apply to PEPFAR or the Global Fund for assistance? Moreover, coordinating tasks should become more difficult between aid distributors, creating hard choices over which tasks to pursue when most spheres of activity already have numerous participants.

The complexity of the global public health regime extends to the types of transnational actors cooperating to address public health concerns. While this chapter shows that "traditional" nation-state actors and multinational organizations are more concertedly devoting resources to health, a diverse array of non-state actors are participating both within and outside of state-led health initiatives. In some cases, private actors are the catalysts for global health action. What the World Bank prizes as multi-sectoral approaches to health have blurred the line between public and private action in global health governance. While states have been thought to wield "hard" power in international affairs, the non-hierarchical nature of global health has meant that private actors are initiators of as well as participants in global health action.

The institutional arrangements depicted by regime complex theorists are far from perfect. Yet Victor and others have argued that conditions of regime complexity, if unavoidable, can be workable, and even effective due to their decentralized nature. According to Victor and Keohane, the regime complex for climate change may be a disguised blessing in the absence of "any politically feasible comprehensive regime."[15] While the international community has tried and so far failed to produce a single universal treaty on climate change, a decentralized regime complex offers considerable advantages. A wide ranging set of actors may be better able to address climate change's equally diverse sets of problems if unencumbered by centralized protocols. A regime complex may have long-term adaptability and flexibility that would be lost in an "institutional monopoly."[16] The "polycentricity" of twenty-first-century regimes, to use Elinor Ostrom's terminology, has also generated discussion in the study of institutions.[17] Also speaking to the halting efforts at establishing a climate regime that is "global" in character, Ostrom argues that a localized, "polycentric" climate regime enables independent actions that may in aggregate be more effective. Like Keohane and Victor she is skeptical of the express need for centralized global action to overcome collective action problems. The multitude of problems associated with global warming are more likely to inspire a multitude of solutions.[18]

Fidler calls this a "post-Westphalian" context for global health, in which "both states and non-state actors shape responses to transnational health threats and opportunities."[19] For Fidler, global health governance takes place not from central implementation, but through an "unstructured plurality" of actors. Sounding a theme similar to what we hear from Ostrom in regards to climate change, Fidler is skeptical of calls to revert to centralized, state-centered approaches to health governance. The WHO, for its part, has recognized this new reality through its 2005 International Health Regulations (IHR) and 2003 Framework Convention on Tobacco Control (FCTC) (the first international treaty negotiated under the auspices of the WHO). These two landmark agreements, explored further in chapter 3, integrated security, trade, and human rights principles, while at the same time creating key roles for non-state actors.[20] For Fidler, the quest for a centralized global architecture to coordinate regime activity is a misguided one.

Much of the academic and popular discussion concerning global health nevertheless laments the lack of any coordinating mechanisms to rationalize the explosion of new activity taking place. Largely for this reason, much of the regime complex literature, as well as an array of critical analysis in global public health, predicts the regime to grow less effective as it expands. A nuanced analysis of aid data suggests a mixed scenario in this regard. Increased complexity, volume, and density within a regime complex do not necessarily lead to the increased misallocation of resources. The global public health regime has grown substantially in size and complexity since the early 1990s. The most obvious of these changes is the dramatic increase in overall resources dedicated to health. The OECD's Creditor Reporting System, the main source of data for this project, collects data on aid to global health since 1974.[21] These data show that aid to health increased tenfold during that time, accelerating in the 1990s and 2000s. In the period from 2002 to 2006, total world ODA to health approached $72 billion, up from $43.7 billion over the previous five-year period. This amount is still less than what it would take to provide universally accessible care in the developing world, but has led to scaled-up responses on a variety of global health fronts.[22] Table 1.2 shows consistently rising levels of health assistance, and health's growing share of aid overall.

These patterns defied the dominant trend of declining aid in the 1990s. Once the Cold War period ended, levels of development assistance dropped off considerably. By 2000 Jean-Philippe Therien and Carolyn Lloyd declared development assistance to be "on the brink."[23] Yet even as aid declined there were also evident changes in how it was being viewed by wealthy actors. Results-based aid became increasingly important in the 2000s. Africa's economic decline in the 1990s, combined with its exploding AIDS crisis, put this region at the center of attention in international development. Economists and, increasingly, policymakers began to see reversing Africa's decline as germane to wealthy states' interests. Moreover, agencies such as the World Bank, the UNDP, and the WHO began producing reports that placed health at the center of international development. These agencies argue that improved societal health contributes to economic growth by making the workforce more productive

Table 1.2. Health's Share as a Percentage of World Aid by Five-Year Intervals

Year	Health ODA	Share
1977–1981	$13.5 billion	6.8%
1982–1986	$20b	8.4
1987–1991	$24b	8.3
1992–1996	$32.8b	12.7
1997–2001	$43.7b	13.5
2002–2006	$71.6b	13.7

Source: CRS Database, in millions of 2005 dollars.

and lifting the economic costs associated with disease. Additionally, the development community faced withering criticism associated with the structural adjustment policies of the 80s and 90s. As Therien and Lloyd argue, "after a decade dominated by the objective of structural adjust-ment, the much less controversial one of sustainable development has taken over as the new mantra of aid policies."[24]

Global health nevertheless became more central to international development during this time—defying the overall post-Cold War trend, also evident in table 1.2. While overall development assistance was declining, global health funding actually increased dramatically. Indeed it was during early post-Cold War years that health financing grew in both absolute and relative terms. In 1991, as the Cold War receded, overall development assistance topped $65 billion. During that year the total global health outlay was $5.3 billion, roughly 8 percent of over-all development assistance. By 1993 development assistance declined to below $50 billion overall, not eclipsing that level again until 1996. Health ODA by contrast rose to $6.7 billion by mid-decade, reaching $7.9 billion by the time the rest of the aid regime stabilized in 1996. By that year aid to health comprised a 15 percent share of world develop-ment assistance. By 2000 aid to health neared $11 billion, foreshadowing yet another surge in funding that happened later that decade.

The regime governing global health today is expansive, its end-point not entirely clear, overlapping with other spheres of global gover-nance. According to Sophie Harman:

> Global health is a unique area of governance that integrates scientists, medical practitioners, philanthropists, governments, and international institutions with grandmothers and local communities and self-styled celebrity advocates. Global health governance involves an amalgamation of various state, non-state, private and public actors and as such has developed beyond the institutional role of the WHO and state-based ministries of health. In the most basic sense of the term global health governance refers to trans-border agreement or initia-tives between states and/or non-state actors to the control of public health and infectious disease and the protection of people from health risks or threats.[25]

The overlapping "regime clusters" in global health prompted Fidler to equate global health governance to a regime complex. So many overlap-ping clusters manifest themselves, Fidler argues, because of a complex array of semi-related problems in global health.[26] For Jeremy Youde, global health governance has fundamentally changed in the globalization era, and must focus on factors that transcend state boundaries. Moreover, it must, according to Youde, include a wide range of multi-sectoral actors in the process of governance while maintaining transparency and accountability.[27] Kay and Williams, not uncritically, point out the political-economic context in which global health governance takes place, making note of the "hegemony of neoliberal ideology over health."[28] This has meant that at the same time global health imperatives have received greater attention than ever, the dominant elite consensus within the regime emphasizes individual responsibility over community values. The emphasis on "self-care" by implication undermines the notion of health as a fundamental right.[29]

The global health regime's transformation sparked fierce expert debate over resource allocation. As Kates, Morrison, and Lief argue, "investments in health seem to be uneven, raising cautionary notes about the global community's ability to meet, let alone sustain, financial needs over time."[30] New funds may be there, but priorities are awry. Science reporter Laurie Garrett—who sparked considerable debate over the issue in *Foreign Affairs*—states this position most forcefully. She contends that aid is "stovepiped" down to specific issue areas while ignoring broader health conditions:

> Stovepiping tends to reflect the interests and concerns of the donors, not the recipients. Diseases and health conditions that enjoy a temporary spotlight in rich countries garner the most attention and money. This means that advocacy, the whims of foundations, and the particular concerns of wealthy individuals and governments drive practically the entire global public health effort. Today the top three killers in most poor countries are maternal death around childbirth and pediatric respiratory and intestinal infections leading to death from pulmonary failure or uncontrolled diarrhea. But few women's rights groups put safe pregnancy near the top of their list of priorities, and there is no dysentery lobby or celebrity attention given to coughing babies.[31]

The new influx of funds, Garrett argues, does not correlate well with the global burden of disease. Instead of addressing in-country health issues holistically by boosting local health infrastructures, global aid producers rely too heavily on "vertical" disease-specific programs. This contention has been regularly reiterated in the global health literature. Shiffman's study of the effects of increased funding for HIV/AIDS found evidence of a "displacement effect" on other health issues, including general health infrastructure and population funding.[32] Mackellar's study of the CRS database's aid to health also noted disproportionate allocation toward communicable diseases characterized as "poor," such as respiratory illness, HIV/AIDS, and malaria. Drastically underemphasized by the global health regime, according to Mackellar, are non-communicable diseases like heart disease, cancer, and stroke, which receive no directly assigned development assistance.[33]

Into this debate have also emerged critics of aid itself, led by the popularity of William Easterly's *White Man's Burden* and Dambisa Moyo's *Dead Aid*. By this school of thought, aid is beyond reform—inevitably inviting waste, corruption, or dependency in developing countries.[34] The logical policy implication in that case would be to abolish rather than reform the project of global redistribution through public financing. In its place Moyo calls for a centrality of market principles far beyond that currently espoused by the development consensus. Recipient states should forego aid and instead engage the vicissitudes of creditors in capital markets, which Moyo argues would incentivize reform through market discipline.[35]

Along with a greater volume of aid has come greater bureaucratic complexity. There has been a massive merger between public health and economic development. This syncretism combines what are arguably separate regimes toward a common purpose: fostering growth by reducing the global burden of disease. A variety of development agencies have prioritized global health, particularly the World Bank and United Nations Development Programme (UNDP), with both playing a central role in shaping global health's political agenda. There was also a proliferation of altogether new actors as global health gained traction as a central development issue. This includes the creation of new agencies which are narrow in scope with a great deal of overlap, such as PEPFAR and the Global Fund to fight AIDS, Tuberculosis and Malaria.

Table 1.3 summarizes select major health agencies that emerged since the late 1980s, contributing to a denser global regime.[36] Table 1.3's partial display of an expanded regime suggests an element of truth to the case made by Garrett and other regime critics: There are a growing number of emergent actors whose activities are vertical, or narrow in scope, avoiding holistic approaches to public health. The 1990s and 2000s have witnessed a "big bang" of new agencies not seen since the post-war period, and a large number of them were vertical. This is indica-

Table 1.3. Select Emergent Global Health Agencies

Agency	Launched	Headquarters	Type	Purpose	Issue Breadth	Operating Budget
President's Emergency Program for AIDS Relief (PEPFAR)	2003	Washington DC	Bilateral	HIV/AIDS prevention and treatment, with particular emphasis on Africa.	Vertical	$6.9b
The Global Fund to Fight AIDS, TB, and Malaria (GFATM)	2002	Geneva	Multilateral, Public-private partnership	Addressing prevention and treatment, for HIV/AIDS, Malaria and Tuberculosis.	Vertical	$3.1b
Global Alliance for Improved Nutrition (GAIN)	2002	Geneva	Public-private partnership	Global support and advocacy for nutrition programs.	Vertical	$28.2m
Stop TB	2001	Geneva	Multilateral	Coordinating response to tuberculosis crisis, improving resource environment.	Vertical	$46.9m
Clinton Foundation	2001	New York	NGO	Broadly addresses public health, in addition to other development and diplomacy issues.	Broad	$297.5m
GAVI Alliance	1999	Geneva	Public-private partnership	Global immunization initiative.	Broad	$1b

continued on next page

Table 1.3. *Continued.*

Agency	Launched	Headquarters	Type	Purpose	Issue Breadth	Operating Budget
Roll Back Malaria	1998	Geneva	Multilateral (WHO sub-agency)	Anti-malarial activities.	Vertical	$17.2m
International AIDS Vaccine Initiative (IAVI)	1996	New York	Public-private partnership	AIDS vaccine development.	Vertical	$97.9m
Joint United Nations Programme on HIV/AIDS (UNAIDS)	1996	Geneva	Multilateral UN agency with some NGO governance	Coordinating AIDS response, improving resource environment.	Vertical	$182.4m
Bill and Melinda Gates Foundation	1994	Seattle	NGO	Development agency seeking high-tech market-based solutions with special emphasis on global health.	Broad	$2.6b
Partners in Health	1987	Boston	NGO	Promotes equality in health, clinic and hospital development, including treatment of communicable and non-communicable conditions in select poor countries.	Broad	$91.9m

tive of increased specialization—and also reflective of the "stovepiped" channels of aid lamented by Garrett.

Over time the global health governance has evolved from an elemental regime that is state-centric, or "international" in nature, to a "global" regime complex operating according to a transnational set of understandings. Harman contends that this evolution occurred simultaneously with the expansion of neoliberal globalization in the 1970s.[37] The evolution toward regime complex characteristics evolved gradually, accelerating in the 2000s as support for global health became enlarged and multifaceted. It is important to note at this point that a large number of actors and greater funds are likely but not sufficient conditions for a regime complex in global health. Table 1.4 notes these obvious elements

Table 1.4. The Regime Complex for Global Health

	Elemental Regime	Regime Complex
Issues	Public health/biomedical focus	Multiple: Trade, security, human rights, globalization, poverty, development, biomedical, etc.
Actors	"Westphalian" state-led hierarchy	"Post-Westphalian" absence of hierarchy among states and various private actors
Globalism	"International" health	"Global" health, neoliberal
Financing Channels	State-led, ODA	Varied, "partnerships," multiple forums
Leadership	State and multilateral organizations	Open ended: state leaders, development entrepreneurs, celebrities, "open source" participants
Centralization	Centralized, coordinated action	Decentralized action, but with formal cooperation and informal complementarity
Available Funds	Low	High
Number of Actors	Small	Large

of a changed regime, but makes note of other equally important criteria. An absence of hierarchy among actors is a critical characteristic, and in the "post-Westphalian" system of global health, this has manifested itself in several ways. Once established around the WHO as the central forum for global health activity, the regime has decentralized over time, with key decisions made by other actors including non-state entities. This shift has been actively encouraged by World Bank, whose approach to health has robustly promoted cross-sector approaches. In many cases, private actors such as the Bill and Melinda Gates Foundation take action independent of states or "Westphalian" actors.

Moreover, the sphere of issues connected to health has, to use the parlance of regime complex theory, come to overlap. Global health's rise has been tied to the transnational concerns of a rapidly globalizing world during the 2000s. Trade, security, urbanization, economics, and human rights serve as logics for global health governance.[38] Health has merged with other global logics in the realm as ideas as well as with complicated institutional realities. As the lines have blurred in this global constellation of actors, the regime has become what Fidler calls "open sourced."[39] A variety of actors act independently to impact global health, influencing the proceedings either through local action, global advocacy, or the independent direction of funds. The regime complex for global health is a chorus without a conductor.

Conformity with Disease Burden: Data and Limitations

In addition to using institutional theory to answer questions raised by three distinct literatures (those of international relations, global health, and development), this book adds key dimensions to the emergent debate over the use of international aid by further disaggregating the OECD's development assistance data—thereby offering fresh perspectives on the burning question of how aid is being used. In addition to analyzing aggregate distributions of official development assistance since 1974, this study generates surprising findings by looking at this data for individual OECD members, as well as specific development agencies. This reveals the hitherto underexplored patterns of specialization between aid producers, introducing a key nuance to interdisciplinary discussions on aid distribution.

As we have seen, great normative debate has ensued over how centralized the regime should be. The global distribution of resources, measured in terms of development assistance, reflects the burden of disease to a greater extent than that suggested by the regime's critics. Data for this book show that there are areas in which global funding allocations do not perfectly correlate with disease burden. The two areas where this is the case are child health and basic nutrition, which are two of the deadliest epidemics in the lesser developed world. Perinatal conditions are the leading cause of death among children under fifteen years of age, comprising 20 percent of all deaths in this age group.[40] They account for 6.4 percent of disease burden in low and middle income countries, more than HIV/AIDS (See table 1.5).[41] Maternal health and perinatal concerns have seen a marked decline in their share of health ODA, from a peak of 13.6 percent in the period from 1992–1996, to 9 percent between 2002 and 2006. Development assistance toward basic nutrition has undergone a similar, albeit less abrupt pattern. Aid in this category confronts arguably the most dangerous risk factors in the impoverished world, accounting for 14.2 percent of disease burden.[42] Yet aid to basic nutrition remains remarkably low, peaking at 1.7 percent in the period from 1997 to 2001 and dropping to 1.3 percent between 2002 and 2006.

Issues of general health infrastructure, thought to be under-prioritized, are actually a high priority for DAC members. Figure 1.1 shows the total world health ODA toward six major health issues addressed by the global public health regime. The graph shows the change over

Table 1.5. Leading Disease Burdens in Low and Middle Income Countries (2001)

Health Issue	Share of Disease Burden (%)
Perinatal Conditions	6.4
Lower Respiratory Infections	6.0
Heart Disease	5.2
HIV/AIDS	5.1
Cerebrovascular Disease	4.5
Diarrheal Diseases	4.2
Unipolar Depressive Disorders	3.1
Malaria	2.9
Tuberculosis	2.6
Chronic Obstructive Pulmonary Disease	2.4

Source: Disease Control Priorities Project

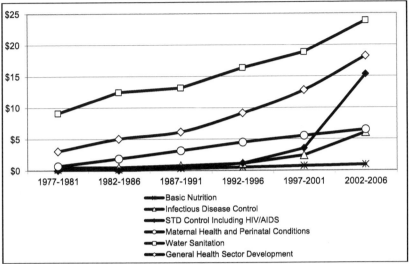

Source: CRS database. In billions of 2005 US dollars.

Figure 1.1. World Health ODA to Major Issue Areas

six five-year intervals reported by the OECD. These six health issues represent the majority of the disease burden in low- and middle-income countries (the combined recipients of all ODA), accounting for all health ODA during these periods. General health sector development and water sanitation have consistently been the regime's top priorities and both received significant gains in recent years despite the emergence of HIV/AIDS as a central priority. According to OECD calculations, aid to health infrastructure affects a variety of health emergencies. Just as importantly, it provides the only form of ODA within the CRS's categorization system that addresses non-communicable diseases (such as cancer, heart attack and stroke) which have become the largest sources of disease burden in low and middle income countries combined.[43]

Similarly, water sanitation addresses one of the largest concerns in the global public health regime. Its place as a high priority is consistent with its position as a leading detriment to health. Several key realities threaten to spread waterborne disease: 884 million people lack clean drinking water, while 2.6 billion lack access to basic sanitation, according to the UN.[44] After modest gains, however, HIV/AIDS was the largest overall beneficiary of new funding for global health during the last decade. During the period between 2002 and 2006 funding for HIV/

AIDS exceeded $15 billion, up from $3.5 billion during the 1997–2001 cycle.[45] This makes it the third largest statistical category behind general health infrastructure and water sanitation. It is apparently on pace to become the largest commitment. The second major category to see a sharp increase in funds in recent years is infectious disease control, which includes treatments for such major diseases as tuberculosis and malaria. Funding toward this category increased from $2.4 billion during the 1997–2001 cycle to more than $6 billion between 2002 and 2006. Despite broad criticism as an over-priority, the high prioritization of AIDS and other infectious diseases does in fact reflect their high impact, most particularly in areas that can be defined as "low" rather than "middle" income. This is especially the case in the priority regions of Africa where AIDS, tuberculosis, and malaria are among the highest disease burdens.

Critics contend that the public health regime has placed too great an emphasis on single issues, particularly AIDS, at the expense of the more holistic priority of global health development. However, as these figures show, general health sector development is the regime's second highest priority. This spending is substantially applied toward non-communicable diseases that comprise a growing share of disease burdens in low- and middle-income countries, as shown in figure 1.1. Water sanitation is also a leading risk factor in poor countries. Moreover, the emphasis on AIDS, tuberculosis, and malaria reflects a growing focus on Africa in the 2000s, which has become the central priority region of international development efforts. Table 1.6 shows the leading disease

Table 1.6. Leading Disease Burdens in Sub-Saharan Africa (2001)

Health Issue	Share of Disease Burden (%)
HIV/AIDS	16.5
Malaria	10.3
Lower Respiratory Infections	8.8
Diarrheal Diseases	6.4
Perinatal Conditions	5.8
Measles	3.9
Tuberculosis	2.3
Road Traffic Accidents	1.8
Pertussis	1.8
Protean Energy Malnutrition	1.5

Source: Disease Control Priorities Project.

burdens in Sub-Saharan Africa. This pattern of disease burden is distinct from the "low- and middle-income countries" designation often used by scholars. The vast majority of this region is officially low income and has not made the epidemiological transition toward non-communicable and chronic illness to the extent that middle-income countries have.

Figure 1.2 puts into sharper relief the overall prioritization in global public health by share. This chart shows funding for the six major global health issues as a percentage of total world health ODA. When viewed in terms of overall share, only infectious disease control and HIV/AIDS show gains, while the other four major categories decline, reflecting the crowding-out largely lamented by scholars. Patterns of distribution by share in world health ODA do reflect an over-emphasis on HIV/AIDS as public health scholars often contend. Yet, as figure 1.1 shows, absolute funding for most major health categories continued to rise steadily—and in much closer correspondence to the global burden of disease than the regime's intense critics indicate. This finding casts doubt on the premise that greater resources to global health invite the potential for even greater misallocation. As the OECD data suggest, the global public health regime has allocated development assistance in a manner closer

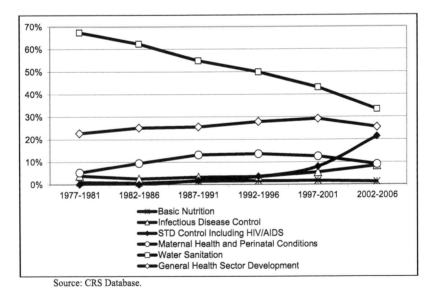

Source: CRS Database.

Figure 1.2. World Health ODA to Major Issue Areas by Percentage Share

to disease burden in *low-income countries* as the regime has expanded. Moreover, as the following subsection shows, these broad, well-remarked-upon trends obscure an equally important pattern, that of specialization.

These data show an important part of the story, but not the whole story. It is important to note their limitations. The data cover only up to 2006, making it difficult to discern with certainty the implications of the global financial crisis that began in 2008. Subsequent demands for austerity among many DAC members risk depressing global aid budgets in a similar manner to that of Japan (once the world's largest distributor of ODA) during the long-term economic slowdown of the 1990s. The data compiled for this book date back to 1974, offering important insights into trends over time, but without precise certainty. Records dating that far back are thought to be less complete then records on ODA in later years. In recent years, the OECD has compiled more comprehensive (though by no means complete) records, particularly on multilateral organizations and some non-state actors. This makes comparison between years difficult. The OECD data presented here include only public sources, not private philanthropy.

One interesting finding in the data suggests that purportedly overlooked areas such as general health sector development and water sanitation have received more attention over time than commonly thought by the regime's critics. However, among the wealth of funds dedicated to the general health sector, it is impossible to discern how much is allocated to specific "neglected diseases" such as cholera, river blindness, sleeping sickness, parasitic worms, and leprosy.[46] These diseases are characterized by their impact in dispersed, globally disconnected areas of little concern to powerful health financiers. Similarly, the data do not offer allocation amounts on specific non-communicable diseases such as cancer, heart disease, or road traffic accidents, which are responsible for increasing shares of mortality and disability in developing countries. Harman and others have argued that neglected diseases receive little global attention because they are less transnational or geopolitically destabilizing, and receive little global media attention.[47] For these reasons they are less of a threat to powerful northern countries operating according to security and economic logics.

These challenges make global health priorities difficult to estimate with precision. Other efforts at data collection have, however, shown similar trends to the ones identified above. Data by Ravishakar et al. published in *The Lancet* indicate similar growth over time, showing increases in aid to health growing nearly fourfold between 1990 and

2007.[48] The pace of increased funds accelerated in the 2000s. While the growth in overall funds was powered in part by new funds for HIV/AIDS, other issue areas saw growth as well. As with the data set developed for this book, Ravishankar et al. find correlations between aid distribution and the burden of disease. *The Lancet* data likewise show that aid is increasingly reaching the poorest areas.[49] More recent data published in *The Lancet* showed a continued (albeit apparently slowing) expansion through 2010.[50] As we will see below, and in subsequent chapters, this book adds to this discussion by analyzing patterns of health specialization by individual actors in the global health regime.

While data quantifying global aid patterns across time are inevitably incomplete, data on disease burden have been met with deeper controversy. Disease burden data produced by the Disease Control Priorities Project, a collaboration with the World Bank, WHO, National Institutes of Health, and academia, has become one of most widely used sources measuring health impacts. Consistent with the broader neoliberal context of global health governance, this key component of public policy has also been accused of commoditizing human welfare. Its measure of "disability adjusted life years" assigns higher value to economically productive years, thereby devaluing the young and elderly. While the World Bank and others utilize these data on the basis of cost efficiency, critics contend it subordinates fundamental health principles to cold economic rationalism.[51]

Formal Cooperation and Informal Complementarity

As global health has become more deeply integrated into a regime complex straddling multiple issue areas, actors, and logics, new forms of interaction are taking place. There has been a considerable push for formal cooperation, entailing partnerships across sectors and actor-types. This creates policy coherence within many spheres of health governance, but also risks co-opting the agendas of grassroots actors by more powerful organizations promoting consensus ideals in global health. With those controversies in mind, this form of cooperation formally aligns the goals and objectives of disparate actors. This includes but is not limited to the interstate cooperation of membership based multilateral organizations such as the WHO. Beyond this, formal cooperation is also evident in the constellation of activities driven by public-private hybrid organizations such as the Global Fund. The activities are not managed by an overarching global "architecture" but entail alignments in goals and approaches toward public health. Informal complementarity by contrast requires no formal agreements, codification, or central coordination. It occurs in the form of specialization between actors seeking political roles under conditions of decentralized governance. This is this area in which critics of global health governance deride the disparate, disharmonious, and unaligned activities of the regime. Because of this, the international aid community has sought to instill a degree of formality in this disparate activity, initiating agreements—most notably the Paris Declaration—committing aid producers to limit inefficiencies in resource distribution. Yet, amidst these challenges, informal complementarity suggests evidence of an emergent informal division of labor.

An increased number of actors in the global health regime has not meant perfect competition, where a multiplicity of autonomous market entrants produces functionally indistinguishable goods. Rather, relationships between agencies entail high degrees of connectivity, both in terms of personnel and financial resources, in practice sidestepping principles of "creative destruction" under conditions of market competition. Moreover, IOs engaged in the global health regime persistently seek to provide unique inputs. The survival of long-existent organizations is not at stake due to the emergence of new actors (indeed, such actors routinely create, sponsor, or partner with new agencies). The expanded health regime places a great deal of emphasis on partnership rather than creative destruction. Yet the regime complex for global health has meant that agencies also struggle for relevance in a more competitive environment.

Nowhere have competitive pressures been more evident than in the case of the WHO. With the rise of rival agencies and limited resources it has economized its activities into comparative advantages, increasingly sharing some aspects of its role in global health governance. If this suggests a more circumscribed role, it is important to note that the WHO has nevertheless been active in regulating the activities of other actors, as exemplified in the International Health Regulation revisions of 2005, which call for more assertive protocols for global disease monitoring and responses (see chapter 3). For Fidler, this indicates a greater cognizance by the WHO of its participation in a decentralized regime, connecting the discourses of state interests, health, security and trade.[52] Once the primary global public health organization, it must now define its own specialized roles in relation to other actors, and adapt to a regime in which governing actions are increasingly decentralized.

Other institutions have felt similar pressures, and initiated reforms in the direction of specialization. Lacking the deep pockets necessary to function as a major aid distributor, the UNDP has asserted a ground-level coordinating role. It has embedded itself deeply, as with other UN actors, into the system of informal complementarity. The UNDP assists governments in navigating an increasingly dense public health network.[53] Even the World Bank, which has emerged as the largest multilateral financial arm in global health, has been forced to specialize.[54] The Bank's most recent IDA replenishment report, for instance, stresses the reduction of overlap amidst increasing regime density.[55]

Specialization

Specialization occurs when individual actors within the global health regime adopt unique approaches, or address a small number of issue areas, thus meeting a perceived gap in the activity of the global regime. It is one of the most salient issues in the global health regime that has gone under-discussed. Specialization in global public health is a countervailing force against potential macro-inefficiencies due to regime expansion, and thereby serves in part to undercut the narrative of overexpansion. It serves to decrease overlap and, in the case of global health, comes closer to addressing the global burden of disease than either global health critics or the regime complexity school would expect. Specialized patterns are evident in the development assistance trajectories of major aid distributors, many of whom prioritize one or a small handful of issues rather than attempting to address the entire spectrum of the global disease burden. While the United States devotes considerable attention to other health issues, HIV/AIDS received half of all the ODA that the United States distributed toward global health in 2006, and nearly triple the amount of the next largest category. Its pattern of aid distribution is particularly unique, because it specialized for decades in maternal health. Maternal health was the US's leading recipient of health aid in the 1980s and 1990s, despite being relatively neglected by the rest of the world. Today, the United States with its vertical PEPFAR program is the single largest driver of the swift rise in development assistance toward AIDS. In fact, the United States accounted for nearly half of all development assistance to AIDS in the five-year cycle from 2002 to 2006, reaching nearly 55 percent as PEPFAR expanded in 2006.

Though critics have lamented that growth in assistance toward AIDS has outpaced other issues, individual patterns of assistance offer a much different picture. There is a distinct class of bilateral aid producers highly specialized in issues other than AIDS.[56] Japan devotes 78 percent of its health ODA to water sanitation (and 23 percent of the world total in this category).[57] Forty-three percent of Swedish ODA to health goes to health sector development, which its development agency considers a pocket of strength given Sweden's own successful universal system. Similarly Norway devoted 57 percent of its health ODA to general health sector development. Switzerland devoted 96 percent of its health ODA to infrastructure and water sanitation together. These two issue families are common priorities among European actors. Like Switzerland, France devoted a combined 96 percent of health aid to these two issues. Italy devotes 89 percent of its health allocations to infrastructure and water sanitation, roughly the same percentages as Denmark. The Netherlands devotes three-quarters of its aid to these categories. Germany, for its part, devotes nearly 60 percent of its ODA to water sanitation alone.

Outside Europe, Australia is also highly specialized, devoting 62 percent of its aid to general health infrastructure while maintaining relatively low allocations in other categories. Among these actors we see an emphasis beyond the purported myopic focus on HIV/AIDS, which scholars have identified as the central force in driving up overall allocations. Complicating this story is the fact that there are large numbers of DAC bilateral actors that have not taken part in the explosion of AIDS assistance, instead addressing water sanitation or general health development. Canada and the United Kingdom, by contrast, have to some extent joined the United States in the AIDS cause, more closely reflecting the expected pattern. Both have devoted relatively less to other key issues while committing more to HIV/AIDS, obscuring any obvious specialization patterns in comparison with the class of actors mentioned above. Departing from continental European actors, overall aid levels toward water sanitation and health infrastructure declined in both countries while AIDS became central to both programs in the 2000s. Nevertheless general infrastructure remained the top priority for both actors between 2002 and 2006.

Similar distinctions are evident among multilateral aid distributors, which persistently comprise large shares of the overall health picture (see chapter 3). The European Union specializes in water sanitation and health infrastructure and has focused minimally on HIV/AIDS, a pattern similar to the bilateral European cases shown above.[58] The World Bank, for its part, maintained its historic focus on water infrastructure (46 percent of ODA), followed by health infrastructure (27 percent), with increasing funding for AIDS not greatly diminishing those priorities.

The Bank, as we will see below, has been a central purveyor of an economic approach to global health that emphasizes specialization, efficiency, reduced overlap, the utilization of comparative advantages, and cost effective measures that target the global burden of disease. As for regional development banks, the African Development Bank specializes in infrastructure and water sanitation, devoting only small shares to HIV/AIDS. That HIV/AIDS is not a high priority is surprising given the devastation wrought by AIDS in Africa. It is less so when we consider the greatly increased influxes of aid coming from the US, Canada, the World Bank, and other AIDS specialists. The Asian Development Bank by comparison committed 62 percent of its funding to water sanitation, consistent with the Japanese water-centric model.

Role-taking is an equally important qualitative form of specialization, defined by the general approach that actors take to address global health concerns. There have been remarkable role fluctuations in recent years, particularly with multilateral institutions and NGOs. Organizations usurp the positions of others, forcing the marginalized actors to adapt. Capital weak agencies such as UNAIDS, the UNDP, and the WHO seek to exert their influence by assuming coordinating roles. They assist recipient countries in dealing with the influxes of aid, and in navigating the multiple channels for aid that have cropped up as the regime expands—becoming central drivers of the system of informal complementarity. They also use their public legitimacy as political capital, giving them the credibility to impact the world development agenda through advocacy. These organizations have assumed important roles in negotiating down drug prices, pressuring states for aid, and highlighting underfunded diseases. They have also been central to global efforts to enhance efficiency. Meanwhile, organizations with deep pockets dominate aid outlays. The World Bank, for instance, has utilized its significant capitalization to become one of the world's largest purveyors of concessional loans. A similar pattern is becoming more evident among philanthropic foundations as well, with the Bill and Melinda Gates Foundation assuming a major role in global aid distribution and in global governance over development issues generally.

Economism

The growing role of economism in the multilateral health effort has been influenced greatly by the emergence of the World Bank as a central ideational force in the global health arena. As Lee argues, "economic rationalism" has remained a core driver of global health policy.[59] The economization of health provides broader context for the system of specialization that has coalesced around an expanding health regime. The economic approach emphasizes liberal principles of comparative advantage in the allocation of resources. Health's role by this perspective becomes embedded in larger notions of the global economy. The state of the former becomes a precondition for the performance of the latter. Health, according to this view, is a paramount economic issue, both because healthy communities boost productivity, and because high disease burdens undermine it. Diseases perceived as threats to global commerce and travel, such as the so-called "big three" conditions of AIDS, malaria, and tuberculosis, by this logic receive special priority. Health statistics, as we've seen above, are deeply connected to economic productivity, especially in a regime complex in which these imperatives closely overlap.

The international commitment to increase development assistance in the 2000s was coupled with equally forceful narratives concerning efficiency. "Cost-effectiveness" became a standard mantra in the development discourse, emphasized most prominently through major development agreements such as the Paris Declaration and its follow-up, 2008's Accra Agenda for Action.[60] This language clearly informs the global consensus on aid, with the Millennium Declaration and UN Millennium Goals also indicating a broader, more targeted global development project. Not only must the DAC members commit greater volumes of funding, they must produce often quantifiable benchmark results. The World Bank's commitment to economic logic has also fueled an emphasis on user fees in health care (veering from imperatives of universal access), and a circumscribed public sector role in domestic health systems.

During the 1990s the international development community fully acknowledged health as a critical component of economic development in poor countries. Its rise represents changing views by many in the international development community in favor of human development indicators and away from the sole focus on traditional monitors like GDP, exports, and inflation. The World Bank embodied this change by embracing human-centered aspects of development like health and nutrition. In this context, global health ideologies cut across disparate sets of actors. These actors appear to promote the same strategies because they share a discourse of health values that permeates the regime. Global health is central to creating growth. Global health strategies should be viewed in an economic context—i.e., what is the most cost-effective way to reduce the economic burdens of poor health?

These hegemonic ideas create conformity across actors, both in what they say and do. Many approaches espoused by the WHO, for instance, sound similar to actors as varied as the World Bank, the government of Sweden, and the Gates Foundation. The economization movement—articulated most prominently by the Paris Declaration—has called for aid optimization on a grand scale, and has been influenced by an "epistemic community" of development experts.[61]

Consensus and Feedback Effects

There is a large movement that has pushed actors to specialize, and has equated aid effectiveness with reaching goals according to disease burden at the minimum possible cost. Forces of normative convergence are evident in an emergent elite ideological consensus that emphasizes the development of complementarity among actors in public health. It calls for economizing aid according to individual comparative advantages, forging a global division of labor that conforms to the burden of disease. Chapter 4 in particular will explore the formal cooperation that often deeply enlists private action while reframing health as a key factor in economic growth. These overlapping concerns create conformity even when the behaviors of those actors should be fundamentally different. They impose economic logic on public health, itself an enterprise concerned with community well-being rather than economic growth per se. Disparate actors are nevertheless connected by dominant ideas that permeate the regime, creating a surprising degree of ideological conformity.

Conformity with the consensus is publically visible (at times even exaggerated). But interests and lobbying, the proverbial underside of politics, play a role in resource allocation as well as the development of specialization patterns. There are positive feedback effects that are both internal and external to actors in the global health regime that reinforce the practice of specialization. This effect for states is, in a large sense, domestic. While state agencies are typically accountable only to domestic funding sources, and thus less subject to competition, specialization is reinforced by domestic ideas and interests that coalesce around particular issue areas. Japan's heavy construction industry, for instance, is a persistent beneficiary of its specialization policy toward large capital projects in the area of water sanitation. In the US, AIDS policy abroad has been greatly affected by its vibrant community of domestic AIDS activists. The massive US health care industry is itself a powerful lobby with a direct interest in development and foreign aid priorities. Domestic politics has helped push advanced nations into fostering constituencies in narrow areas of development, and to specialize in these issue spheres. This is a component that we might expect from scholars of historical institutionalism that see feedback effects as key factors in perpetuating policies. Ikenberry notes "stickiness" in policies, particularly international organizations, which serve a purpose for member states.[62] Pierson's exploration of welfare states identified similar conditions in which interest group support and sunk costs provide positive feedback effects.[63]

Plan of the Book

This book explores key bilateral, multilateral, and non-state case studies for the purpose of understanding their specialization patterns, and to explore why they chose to prioritize the way they did. Each set of cases receives its own chapter. These chapter headings are idealizations, particularly under conditions of regime complexity, as global health action is increasingly amphibious across actor-types. Readers unfamiliar with the study of international relations may, understandably, find this chapter organization peculiar, as it centers on the "building blocks" of policy action that form the basic elements of international relations analysis. This is particularly important as, under conditions of regime complexity, these actors assume a decentralized, amorphous nature where lines between traditional international relations terminologies—"state" and "non-state," "public" and "private," "governmental" and "NGO"— often blur in practice. Despite these drawbacks, the case studies this book employs at length in the following chapters were selected for their diversity, their central importance to the global health regime, and in several cases both of these reasons. Beyond merely looking at their patterns of specialization, these empirical chapters offer special insight into how these agencies interact with one another, and collectively influence each other's activities in a crowded regime. From an international relations perspective, by dividing the cases into type, we learn key nuances about what idiosyncrasies exist between agencies that are bilateral, multilateral, or non-state; as well as what factors influence behavior across actor-type. From a global health perspective, this approach addresses the all-important question of whether or not these actors can organize to prioritize resources effectively relative to the public health challenges in resource poor settings. In anticipation of a readership from both perspectives, this book takes care to define basic terminologies that may be unfamiliar to those not acquainted with one (or both) of these fields. This approach is for the purpose of any cross disciplinary dialogue this book may foster, hopefully making the risk of overemphasizing basic vocabulary a worthwhile one.

The next chapter explores bilateral cases: the US, Japan, Sweden, and Canada. Positive feedback effects, including domestic interests, are the internal factors most responsible for state specialization patterns. There is also an observed impetus on these states to advance internationally agreed upon development goals, of which global health is prominent. They cite the following factors in their prioritization decisions: technological expertise, geographic knowledge, and domestic experience with particular health issues.

States are the traditional focal point of cooperation in the international relations literature. In a decentralized regime complex, states and state interests remain essential to global health cooperation, although private actors are contributing increasing resources. State interests of security and economy help underpin the rationalized logic of the regime complex for global health. Political imperatives, such as "cost effectiveness" per dollar spent, color debates over global health priorities, particularly as states commit greater resources. We see this constellation of factors at work with PEPFAR, through which the United States came to drive (financially) the global anti-AIDS effort. Additionally, this chapter addresses a class of aid production that is likely to be more important as the global health regime continues to evolve: south-to-south aid transfers. It speculates on how these actors may alter the dominant logics of global health.

Multilateral cases (chapter 3) include the WHO, World Bank, UNDP, and EU. While multilateral financing has held steady as a share of public aid to health, organizations such as the UN have become less of a driving force in health financing, and subject to heightened competition. These cases too represent state led "Westphalian" entities, in which state members and financiers play a role in the direction of the multilateral actors, though increasingly private actors are making their presence felt in so-called intergovernmental institutions.

Chapter 4 engages non-state actors, exploring the Bill and Melinda Gates Foundation and the Carter Foundation, but examines more broadly the roles played by the thousands of private actors in global health. This chapter also looks at the growing hybridization between public and private. Chapter 4 will explore the formal cooperation that often deeply involves a range of private actor types, under the rubric of multi-sectoralism. Implicit in this discourse is the potential erosion of state-centered governance, with non-state actors partially usurping state authority as "building blocks" of global governance. At the domestic level this also means a potential erosion of the public sector in health provisions.

A concluding chapter discusses fully the normative and public policy implications touched upon here. In sum, the rise of global health supports the case that greater aid amounts can be allocated effectively. Indeed, they will have to be allocated effectively, and in sufficient volume, in order to address the world's worst health crises in its poorest places.

∾

A major public policy implication of the arguments presented so far is that the regime complex for global health can sensibly expand. In this period in which all too many government programs in advanced countries are deemed subordinate to the interests of austerity, those which help capitalize the poorest regions of the world face particularly intense scrutiny. Given inevitable inefficiencies, critics suggest, it is not within our capability to engage the complex social challenges surrounding poverty—however immoral it may be to ignore the ongoing plight of a human civilization in which half the world lives on $2.50 per day or less. In their domestic contexts, these arguments have long been used to preclude the formation of welfare states, or historic episodes such as the "war on poverty" in the US. The findings of this book challenge that rhetoric in a global context, suggesting a redistributive "war on poverty" is very much possible worldwide. The case proceeds in the next chapter with the primary elemental unit of global governance, the state.

CHAPTER 2

Specialization Among States

Finding Roles, Narrowing Priorities

If the regime complex for global health has indeed entered a "post-Westphalian" phase, states nevertheless retain immense influence, in some instances expanding their reach.[1] While non-state actors have become a hallmark of global health production, orchestrating their activities in increasing independence, states have markedly increased health financing. They retain corresponding influence in power relations between "donors" in the global north and "recipients" in developing countries. Indeed much of the neoliberal consensus on world health has been ushered in from decidedly Westphalian halls of power in New York, Washington, Paris, London, Geneva, and other traditional global north centers. Bilateral patterns of ODA suggest that regime complex characteristics did not result in disarray, and that states pursued global goals through informal complementarity.

For those unfamiliar with the commonly used categorizations of international relations, "states" refer to governmental actors, more specifically territorial entities controlled by governments. Thus we exclude governing entities that do not identify with a territory or population, reserving this discussion for the following two chapters. Despite this delineation—rooted in the study of international relations, which sees the state as an elemental building block of world diplomacy and policy creation—it is important to note that states very much engage in forms of governance that could be described as transnational or global rather than "international." As we saw in the previous chapter, this is particularly clear under conditions of decentralized "regime complexity." Though existent according to the logic of borders, states play central roles in forging the regime complex. They are also instrumental in fostering the conditions of globalization that have underpinned contemporary understandings of epidemics and public health approaches.[2]

What, then, is the role of bilateral actors in global health governance, and what factors influence their decisions to specialize in some issues over others? This chapter addresses the distinctive approaches of four states: The United States, Japan, Sweden, and Canada, and the roles they have played in governing global health. Variation is evident in their respective specialization patterns. The United States and Canada specialize in HIV/AIDS, Japan specializes in water sanitation, and Sweden in health infrastructure. The ODA patterns of each case have been the focus of extensive study, and scholars have found distinct underlying characteristics in each. The most widely held finding on the United States, currently the world's largest distributor of ODA, is that security considerations heavily impact its development priorities. Japan is said to distribute ODA on the basis of maintaining and enhancing its trade position among Asian countries in the developing world. Canada is predominately thought to utilize its foreign aid to enhance its global influence in lieu of robust military power. Sweden is a quintessential practitioner of the "Scandinavian model" of aid distribution, whose utility function is driven by humanitarian concerns. These distinctions also occur in a global context, informed by an emergent "millennial" consensus emphasizing human development issues (for which health is central).[3]

In this regard, bilateral case studies in foreign aid should be viewed not in isolation, but in the context of the prevailing material and ideational factors influencing their distributional patterns. Specialization among these four cases conforms to the general push in the international donor community to narrow activities and avoid overlapping tasks. These include the international drive to commit to health in a development context, and to maximize resources in health in order to create the conditions for growth in lesser developed economies. In this regard, aid distributors' narrowing focus on fewer issues and regions is consistent with the international effort to produce aid more efficiently and effectively according to largely quantitative standards set by (or imposed on) development agencies. These cases also show domestic interests playing a role in spurring and reinforcing the development of specializations, thereby providing economized inputs to the overall global health picture in a manner consistent with the neoliberal consensus.

Bilateral ODA—that which derives from state governments—is the most voluminous form of aid to health, eclipsing both multilateral and non-state aid. Many of the most important developments in global health have come in the form of new bilateral programs such as PEPFAR, which assumed a central role in an unprecedented global push to fight HIV/ AIDS. This came in the wake of a near universal lamentation of the decline of development assistance from DAC countries. According to Therien and Lloyd, because of factors "including the end of the Cold War, domestic economic difficulties in developed countries and the increased flow of private capital towards the Third World, aid is undergoing a profound crisis."[4] OECD data show that bilateral development assistance declined drastically in the mid-1990s. The overall volume of aid continues to fall short of agreed-upon targets for states. The average DAC member annually disperses roughly 0.3 percent of its GDP in development assistance, according to the OECD. This is well below what many say is necessary to stimulate "convergence" between developing and developed countries, let alone compensate the global south for extractive trade, security, agricultural, and climate "debts" incurred by historic and continuing practices by the global north.[5] In *Foreign Affairs*, Jeffrey Sachs—one in a chorus of critics arguing aid amounts are too small—dismissed US aid levels as "utterly inadequate."[6] ODA to global health nevertheless saw substantial gains during this period, bucking the overall stagnant trend. Bilateral aid to health nearly doubled between 2000 and 2006, to $13.3 billion.[7] Within this broader trend there were distinct variations among bilateral actors, underscored by the strong tendency among aid producers to specialize in a small number of health issues.

Why do individual bilateral patterns of aid seldom reflect the general bilateral ODA pattern? Why have states generally *narrowed* their priorities despite increasing the overall pool of health assistance? In sum, combined specialization patterns suggest the emergence of a global division of labor through which the broader bilateral donor community addresses a set of public health priorities. (Though, as we saw in the previous chapter, this set of priorities persistently under serves neglected tropical diseases as well as many important non-communicable epidemics, which bear less of a global economic threat despite their all-too-real role in causing pain and suffering). This is evident through an emphasis on vertical programming and, less formally, through distinctive but complementary patterns of aid specialization.

This chapter proceeds in two parts. The first section explores the emergence of the new consensus in global health enshrined by the

Millennium Declaration. The second section shows specialization in the context of ideological conformity across each of the four cases, as well as idiosyncratic domestic factors underlying shifts in global health policy and the development of comparative advantages.

The Big Picture: Bilateral Aid and the Emergent Consensus

In this neoliberal age it is important to remember that the world's agreed-upon health targets have a distinctly public imprimatur, and reflect a consensus for which state support is essential. This includes the unanimous vote of 189 states in favor of the Millennium Development Goals (MDGs) in the UN General Assembly. The goals reflect the consensus paradigm, calling for a series of vertical health interventions and for deep cooperation between state and non-state stakeholders. Given the degree of unanimity toward its overarching elements, the centrality of the goals in the policy statements of a broad range of bilateral actors in international development is hardly a surprise. It figures heavily into the policy goals outlined by each bilateral development agency under study here, save for the United States, which has largely adopted its priorities despite its tendency to avoid citing the goals as a catalyst for domestic policy.

The 2000 Millennium Declaration correspondingly enshrined global health as one of, if not *the*, centerpiece issues in global development. Six of the eight Millennium Development Goals address global health. Nine of the Declaration's twenty-one time-bound targets—to be achieved by 2015—directly address global health issues (all shown in table 2.1).[8] The Millennium Declaration addresses several epidemics or risk factors by name: HIV/AIDS, malaria, tuberculosis, malnourishment, child and maternal health, and waterborne communicable disease; leaving room to address "other diseases." The Declaration says much about conditions of global poverty, and speaks little to the more controversial issues of systemic global inequality or power imbalances between rich and poor. The inclusion of private sector actors (including pharmaceutical companies), implies that the global development effort would be at least partially privatized. In short, the Millennium Goals were couched in terms that could be agreed upon by virtually all of the world's nation-states, including the all-important members of the Development Assistance Committee that would fuel forthcoming increases in global aid for development.

Table 2.1. Health Related Millennium Development Goals and Targets

Goals	Targets
1: Eradicated extreme poverty and hunger	1C: Halved, between 1990 and 2015, the proportion of people who suffer from hunger
4: Reduce child mortality	4A: Reduce by two-thirds, between 1990 and 2015, the under-five mortality rate
5: Improve maternal health	5A: Reduce by three-quarters the maternal mortality ratio
	5B: Achieve universal access to reproductive health
6: Combat HIV/AIDS, malaria, and other diseases	6A: Have halted by 2015 and begun to reverse the spread of HIV/AIDS
	6B: Achieve, by 2010, universal access to treatment for HIV/AIDS for all those who need it
	6C: Have halted by 2015 and begun to reverse the incidence of malaria and other major diseases
7: Ensure environmental sustainability	7C: Halved, by 2015, the proportion of the population without sustainable access to safe drinking water and basic sanitation
8: Develop a global partnership for development	8E: In cooperation with pharmaceutical companies, provide access to affordable essential drugs in developing countries

The Goals resultantly invite criticism from a variety of perspectives. Their emphasis on private sector involvement signaled that much of the development effort could be beyond public control. Most importantly from the vantage point of regime critics, the goals single out a handful of specific diseases rather than the broader aim of general health sector development. This raised the possibility that the international response to health would be all too narrow. The goals appeared to foreshadow a vertical approach to health rather than the more holistic effort many critics call for. Moreover, while the Declaration called for more development assistance, it did not mark a return to previous "primary care"-based understandings of health. The latter had not only called for more holistic, community based approaches to care, but indicted the system of global capitalism itself for fostering inequalities in health (as we will see in chapter 3). The goals nevertheless foreshadowed gradual increases in global foreign aid budgets, and solidified the centrality of human development goals over one-dimensional economic growth imperatives. This arguably represented a departure from the "Washington Consensus" discourse that had dominated development policy in the 1980s.

The emphasis on aid demonstrated DAC participation in the goals, making it harder for the world's wealthiest countries to ignore foreign aid programs (a likely reason for persistent US friction). Either way, the 2000s marked a new era for development assistance after a long period of decline following the Cold War. However it is worth remembering from chapter 1 that aid to health continued to rise even as the overall aid picture looked bleak. In that sense the goals gave official imprimatur to activities already underway. Additionally, it is important to note that as of 2010 only five countries (including Sweden) met the UN target of aid commitments of at least 0.7 percent of GNI for DAC members.[9] Figure 2.1 illustrates historic trends in overall development assistance. This illustration—popularized by the UNDP's extraordinary 2005 *Human Development Report* on the twin issues of poverty and inequality—shows that, despite the renaissance in international aid, development assistance had not increased as fast as wealth in the DAC countries.

The emergent consensus as articulated in the Paris and Accra declarations also calls for aid producers to maximize the efficiency of increased resources by specializing. This is happening, though causation is difficult to determine. States develop technical expertise and experience in key priority areas of global health, choosing a small number in which to devote large shares of their resources. However, domestic processes of resource allocation by states are so intensely political that it is difficult to distinguish the impact of emergent international norms from the wrangling of domestic politics. Another component of specialization among actors is geographic. Donor states establish expertise in specific areas, with development agencies ostensibly becoming particularly adept

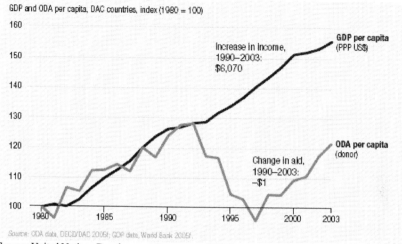

Source: United Nations Development Programme (2005).

Figure 2.1. Development Assistance and GDP Per Capita Among DAC Members

at understanding the burden of diseases in focus countries. States initiate long range programs among a select number of focus countries, and in the process expand relationships with local governments. Japan's development programs, for example—aided by Japan's long-standing regional relationships—make Asia their central region of focus. As a result, the disease burden there has impacted aid flows. Sweden, in a similar fashion, has sought to expand development programs in nearby Eastern Europe. Again we see idiosyncratic domestic factors, as north-south power politics plays a role in establishing these relationships.

We also see another important trend: the paring down of geographic specialties. Even as their volume of ODA expands, Canada and Sweden, for example, have sought to minimize the number of aid targets to a handful of "focus countries." From the perspective of bilateral development agencies, forging extended partnerships with a smaller number of countries ostensibly helps build on their knowledge of focus areas, both in terms of their developmental needs and of their domestic political and cultural environments. Enhancing this knowledge through partnerships, development agencies contend, allows them to develop more effective development assistance programs.

Overall, figure 2.2 shows bilateral commitments to global health far outweighing those of multilateral development agencies, consistently comprising roughly two-thirds of aid to health since the 1970s. It is important to note that this gap is most likely overstated in the OECD data, which have traditionally undercounted multilateral agencies in comparison with states. Data on multilateral agencies also tend not to date as far back as that for the DAC members, so this data should be considered an incomplete approximation of relative aid volumes. While this is certainly a limitation due to insufficient historic data collection, it is also important to note the inordinate influence states have over allocation decisions made by multilateral organizations. At any rate, states are widely regarded as the largest set of actors in global health causes.[10]

Hence the data show bilateral aid patterns driving global patterns observed in the previous chapter. Consistent with the overall global picture, aid to health from bilateral agencies rose markedly in the 1990s and 2000s. In 1974, bilateral aid to health totaled $1.2 billion. By 2006 it exceeded $13 billion. This is roughly consistent with the tenfold inflation adjusted increase we observe in the global figures for aid to health (again, recalling that the OECD data underestimate other forms of assistance). As table 2.2 shows, estimates of bilateral aid to health approached $50 billion during the five-year period between 2002 and 2006. As scholars of realism and many neoliberal institutionalists in the international relations discipline would predict, there is a state-driven element to global health priorities.

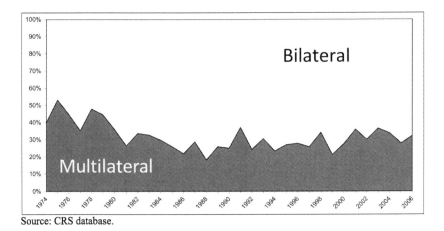

Source: CRS database.

Figure 2.2. Bilateral Aid's Share of Total World Health ODA

Table 2.2. Growth in Bilateral Aid to Health by Five-Year Intervals

Year	Bilateral Health ODA
1977–1981	$8.4 billion
1982–1986	$14.3b
1987–1991	$17.5b
1992–1996	$24b
1997–2001	$31b
2002–2006	$48.7b

    Water sanitation is estimated to be the largest recipient of bilateral development assistance to health, followed by general health infrastructure and HIV/AIDS (see figure 2.3). The latter sees the swiftest increases during the 2000s, which emerges *after* AIDS had worsened into a global pandemic, intensifying especially dangerously in East Africa. As we will see below, this is largely brought about by the United States's considerable efforts to contribute funds to global AIDS, though the US aid program in this area was preceded by important multilateral actors such as the Global Fund. Similarly, Japan is the largest purveyor of aid to water projects by a significant margin, and both in essence skew the overall

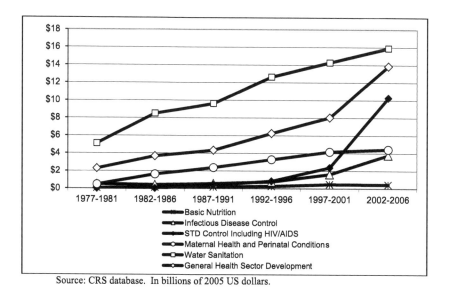

Source: CRS database. In billions of 2005 US dollars.

Figure 2.3. Bilateral ODA to Major Issue Areas

bilateral pattern. This is especially the case with the United States and AIDS, which make the global AIDS effort appear more broad-based than it is. In reality, the United States is the major driver behind this effort, accounting for over half of AIDS funding annually. In this light, specialization patterns put into sharper relief key nuances in global health priorities. This is especially important when considering the outsized role of the United States in the global health regime.

The United States

While the United States has distanced itself from the Millennium Goals, its proclamations and initiatives nevertheless reflect their emphasis on human development issues such as global health. It has tied these concerns closely to security in the wake of the September 11, 2001, attacks, while utilizing the logic of economism. *Foreign Aid in the National Interest*, a landmark blueprint for US foreign aid policy released in 2002, framed improving global health across a myriad of indicators as "important for raising productivity, reducing poverty and sustaining economic growth."[11] HIV/AIDS, USAID noted in a 2004 report to Congress, threatens to "erase decades of development progress."[12] Global infectious disease, the report notes, "affects the health and wealth of individuals and nations alike and is a major constraint to economic development."[13] This evinces the acceptance of the consensus that global health is essential to stimulating economic growth. This is a significant reversal from the US-led Washington Consensus which held that improved human development follows growth through markets. The new consensus instead contends that the relationship between economic growth and public health is reciprocal, with one promoting or holding back the other.

The US government is the largest distributor of aid to health in absolute terms, including all public and non-state actors. This is consistent with its position as the world's largest overall provider of aid since 2001 (table 2.3 compares US aid levels to all DAC member states). The sheer size of its global health outlay also makes it the world's most broad-based aid distributor across issue areas, providing significant funding to all major health categories. However, it is still highly specialized, devoting more than half of its global health funding to the single issue of HIV/AIDS by the mid-2000s. Figure 2.4 dramatically illustrates the stark pattern of specialization in the United States, with HIV/AIDS funding exceeding $7 billion while no other major issue reaches half

Table 2.3. DAC Members Ranked by Aid Volume in 2010

United States	$30.15 billion
United Kingdom	13.76
France	12.92
Germany	12.72
Japan	11.05
Netherlands	6.35
Spain	5.92
Canada	5.13
Norway	4.58
Sweden	4.53
Australia	3.85
Italy	3.11
Belgium	3.0
Denmark	2.87
Switzerland	2.3
Finland	1.34
Austria	1.2
South Korea	1.17
Ireland	0.9
Portugal	0.65
Greece	0.5
Luxembourg	0.4
New Zealand	0.35
DAC Bilateral Total	128.8

Source: CRS Database. In 2010 dollars.

this figure. US aid for HIV/AIDS constituted more than 76 percent of all such funding among DAC countries. Counting multilateral aid, more than half of all AIDS funding around the world was distributed by the United States that year. Regionally, it pours considerable resources into Sub-Saharan Africa. In absolute terms, all major categories save maternal health and nutrition financing have seen gains in funding between 2002 and 2006, though none has risen as steeply as HIV/AIDS. In relative terms, shown in figure 2.5, HIV/AIDS and other communicable diseases see increases, reflecting a sharp prioritization toward communicable disease in Africa during this period. General health sector development sees modest relative increases. This change in priorities by the United States qualifies as one of the most significant developments in global public health over the past decade.

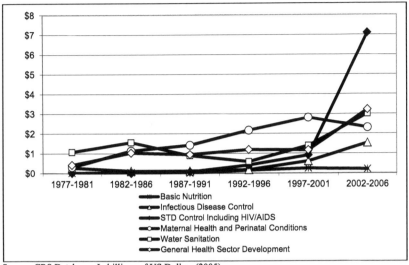

Source: CRS Database. In billions of US Dollars (2005).

Figure 2.4. US Health ODA to Major Issue Areas

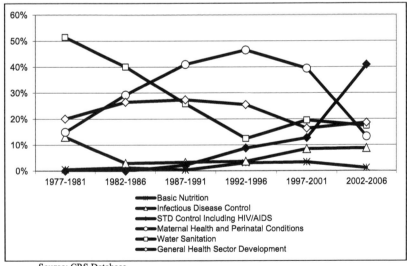

Source: CRS Database.

Figure 2.5. US Health ODA to Major Issue Areas by Percentage Share

Overall US funding for global public health causes has steadily increased since 1974. That year, the United States contributed an estimated $191 million to global health. By 1990 the figure had increased to more than $850 million in constant dollars but was jeopardized by the end of the Cold War, which marked a general downward transition in US aid to health. By 1996, estimates for aid to health declined significantly, to $715 million from more than a billion dollars the previous year. While the US foreign assistance program declined, surpassed by both Japan and France, global health in most regions had improved. The exception was Sub-Saharan Africa (particularly along its southeastern tier), where the global AIDS epidemic reached disastrous proportions, becoming the leading cause of disease burden in Africa by 2001. By 1996, as the US global health program shrank, there were 22 million HIV/AIDS cases worldwide, concentrated mainly in Sub-Saharan African countries. Yet only $292 million worldwide had been raised that year to combat the epidemic.[14] During that year UNAIDS became operational with the promise of leading a coordinated multilateral response to the epidemic, along with renewed efforts by the WHO and other international institutions within the UN family. This multilateral expansion culminated in 2002 with the creation of the Global Fund, one year prior to the United States launching of a major HIV/AIDS oriented agency of its own, the President's Emergency Program for AIDS Relief.

The push to confront HIV/AIDS, and to ramp up global health support more generally, also came from within the United States during this period. The Institute of Medicine, a nonprofit chartered by Congress, issued a crucial report entitled *America's Vital Interest in Global Health*, which charged the United States with failing to use its immense wealth and scientific expertise to improve international health. *The Lancet*, one of the most influential journals in global public health, editorialized on the "great danger that Congress will ignore" the IOM's appeal.[15] Domestic interests were also vocal about pressing the government to provide funding for HIV/AIDS programs both domestically and abroad.[16] The epidemic's emergent presence there resulted in the formation of what was effectively an AIDS bureaucracy working across existing institutions such as Health and Human Services, the Center for Disease Control, the National Institutes of Health, and USAID. The activists who would eventually lead internal lobbying efforts for the global pandemic emerged from existing and newly created offices within these agencies.

Similarly, activist groups such as ACT UP and others that originated in response to the domestic epidemic helped foment pressure on the government to act abroad. In sum, the United States was under tremendous domestic and international pressure to expand its global health apparatus, and to address the AIDS crisis in particular. Within a short period of time the United States did just that, increasing aid to health to more than $1.3 billion by 2000 and more than $4.8 billion by 2006. The initiatives which channeled funding in this direction are the 1998 Infectious Disease Initiative and PEPFAR.

The most prominent policy statement to emerge for public consumption during this time was *Foreign Aid in the National Interest*, which USAID drafted just as the United States began to scale up its anti-AIDS initiatives. The document, one of the first official policy statements on foreign aid after the September 11th attacks, offered a blueprint for the next several years of ODA allocations. It places foreign aid in the context of the so-called war on terrorism. Consistent with the George W. Bush administration's post-September 11th rhetoric, it posits that foreign aid can facilitate the emergence of (presumably less threatening) free-market democracies. This is reflected directly in the creation of the Millennium Challenge Account, which ostensibly privileges states that show evidence of verging toward free market systems. HIV/AIDS figures heavily into US policy, and is blamed for reversing development gains in affected regions. It is also cited for its potential to "wreak havoc" in populous countries including China and India—a prediction that has yet to come to fruition.[17]

Foreign Aid elucidates what USAID deems a changed strategy for the twenty-first century. "What is striking," the report notes, "is the progress that has been made, albeit with continued serious lags in the least developed countries."[18] While the report subsequently calls for addressing the changing disease burden (toward non-communicable diseases) in the developing world, it places a greater emphasis on the "serious lags" in the least developed regions. It was after this period that AIDS and other communicable diseases became a clear priority. What led to this shift in priorities was the move toward specialization based on region and disease type. Despite its sheer size—the annual US aid allocation remains robust—the United States has winnowed down target states and issue areas.

The United States had been the leading purveyor of its namesake, the Washington Consensus (with the notable cooperation of other global north countries and interlocutors in the global south). In the post-Washington Consensus era it forges a syncretism between economic growth, free trade, and human development goals such as those elucidated in the Millennium Declaration. In essence, the rise of global health in the United States must be viewed in the context of US-led globalization, the emergence of the "war on terrorism," and persistent hegemonic competition in places such as Sub-Saharan Africa. Increased US engagement with African development coincided with increased military engagement in the region as well, evidenced by the initiation of AFRICOM in 2007, the Central Command in the region. According to its mission statement, "U.S. Africa Command protects and defends the national security interests of the United States by strengthening the defense capabilities of African states and regional organizations and, when directed, conducts military operations, in order to deter and defeat transnational threats and to provide a security environment conducive to good governance and development."[19] Viewed in its totality, US engagement in Africa suggests a securitized utilitarian logic surrounding its public health initiatives.

Despite obvious differences between the foreign policies of presidents George W. Bush and Barack Obama, US unilateralism is embedded in the creation of the centerpiece in the US global health enterprise, PEPFAR, making drastic change unlikely. PEPFAR itself was an attempt to "go it alone," creating a whole new program instead of committing resources to existing programs (despite the US role in creating the Global Fund). The existence of PEPFAR alongside the Global Fund and the World Bank's Multi-Country AIDS Program for Africa (MAP), means the task duplication that is the bane of global harmonization efforts.[20]

The Infectious Disease Initiative, launched in 1998 to combat communicable disease, exemplifies the utilitarian approach, basing USAID's strategy on "the recognition that maximum impact will be achieved by focusing on a few diseases which are sources of significant mortality."[21] This approach directed the agency's attention toward tuberculosis and malaria, two of the "big three" diseases considered threats to the global economic system. These two diseases have consequently seen large absolute and relative gains in aid since 2000.[22] USAID cites long-standing partnerships with NGOs and universities, both with experience in combating communicable disease, as comparative advantages. More significantly, it cites the "preeminence" of the US research community, which can be "put to use in developing long range solutions" toward slowing communicable disease epidemics. The United States cites the research and development component of foreign assistance programs as central to its overall global health program. It advances "research and innovation" in selected health issues impacting the developing world, and the transfer of "new technologies" to the field.[23] In testimony to Congress during the AIDS epidemic's early years, USAID cited a strong capacity to convert experiences in maternal health and family planning toward effective anti-AIDS policy.[24]

PEPFAR, the world's largest single-issue public health program, reflects the general trend of geographic specialization in global health. It began with 15 high risk focus countries in Sub-Saharan Africa, including heavily impacted Botswana, South Africa, and Uganda. It now operates in 30 countries. The program additionally seeks to harness US expertise in biotech research, in areas such as vaccination development, distribution mechanisms for antiretroviral drugs, as well as clinic and laboratory design. The program has disseminated $18.8 billion to date. It was reauthorized in 2008 with $39 billion in new funding.[25] These considerable new funds, accompanied by a ten-year goal to support three million people on ARV drugs, assure that HIV/AIDS will remain the central priority of the United States for the foreseeable future. Additionally, it solidifies the US position as the leading specialist in HIV/AIDS. While PEPFAR was welcome by many activists for its extensive commitments to the epidemic, its approaches have not come without controversy. It is a vertical program that critics argue only partially addresses the disease burdens facing Africa. It has also been criticized for placing too great an emphasis on geographic specialization, addressing too few AIDS impacted regions. Moreover, it has at times sparked international controversy for its morality based spending restrictions, refusing partnerships with local groups that fail to renounce prostitution, making cutbacks in condom distribution, and for a broader US policy denying funding to groups that condone safe abortion as part of overall family planning. The nuances of PEPFAR illustrate how global health programming can operate at cross-purposes. For instance, PEPFAR's "anti-prostitution pledge" required of non-US groups that receive PEPFAR funding has been the source of considerable controversy. This is prompting some groups to forego funding rather than curtail support services for sex workers—undermining the consensus notion of partnership.[26] Needle exchange programs, which PEPFAR originally pledged not to support, were included in its program to reach drug users since 2010, which creates space for harm reduction strategies.[27] Furthermore, PEPFARs requirement that 55 percent of its funds go toward treatment, 20 percent on prevention (emphasizing abstinence), 15 percent on care, and 10 percent on orphans and children invites potential conflict with the agendas of local partner countries.[28] Requirements that PEPFAR funds purchase only FDA-approved drugs can ultimately undermine the stated aim of cost-effectiveness by creating barriers to using some generic drugs.[29]

The move toward specialization in the United States has meant that other major issues have seen relative declines. Larger interventions in a few key areas cause funding in other areas to be crowded out. Geographically, the system of regional prioritization adopted by USAID reflects the general pattern in donor specialization. At the top of its three-tiered system of global health priorities, "Joint Programming Countries," are those with the highest potential worldwide health impact—i.e., high disease burdens that can be cost effectively addressed.[30] Geographic specialization also means increasing or decreasing funding based on changing conditions in recipient countries' disease burdens. Together geographic and issue-based specialization can lead to budget cuts. The most dramatic of these decreases is in financing for maternal health, an issue where the United States had been a world leader. This occurred, USAID argues, because maternal mortality is on the decline in several US assisted countries, where other diseases like tuberculosis had worsened.[31] Thus the focus country system can affect prioritization as aid distributors respond to changing conditions among selected recipients. Instead of expanding into regions where maternal health is of greater concern, it has focused instead on addressing what it sees as the most pressing challenges in existing priority countries.

PEPFAR has significant activist support despite the aforementioned controversies that have colored its history. Given the prolonged economic downturn, high levels of development assistance will be difficult to maintain in a US congress often hostile to global development initiatives. Perhaps because of this, there is tremendous pressure for aid programs to operate efficiently. This is reflected in the Global Health Initiative, initiated under Barack Obama in 2009 as a way of improving internal coordination among US global health programs.[32] This includes the promise of unified public health budgeting (traditionally divided between the major agencies that allocate for global health: USAID, the State Department, and the Centers for Disease Control and Prevention). Geographic specialization is part of this policy formula. Characteristically, the GHI includes a tiered focus-country system. While the GHI is intended to encompass the gamut of health issues, 73 percent of US global health funding now goes toward HIV/AIDS programs. This makes the United States more specialized than at any time in recent history. It is also worth noting that, despite the potential for austerity measures to roll back increases in global health funding, numerous domestic interests in the United States are likely to lobby for its persistence. Domestic AIDS activists in the United States have a strong track record in spearheading efforts to gain and sustain funding for programs such as PEPFAR.

US businesses, contractors, government agencies, and academic institutions also have a stake in maintaining robust global health programs, and may well be effective in future fights—to borrow political scientist Harold Lasswell's famous phrase—over "who gets what, when, how." Public health financing may also benefit from the reality that much of it is long-term and recurring—such as PEPFAR's vast AIDS treatment programs—and thus less vulnerable to sudden cuts. Interestingly, global health enjoys unique levels of popular support. Where majorities of Americans say the United States spends too much on foreign aid, 76 percent say that it spends too little or the right amount on aid to health, according to the Kaiser Foundation.[33]

What has been referred to as a "health-industrial complex" in the United States, a health sector that now encompasses 17 percent of US GDP, also generates a complex constellation of stakeholders in global public health policy.[34] These stakeholders include, but are by no means limited to, government agencies, research institutions, pharmaceutical manufacturers, medical personnel, academia, philanthropic foundations, biotech industries, and so on. Where applicable all such groups leave their imprimatur on US approaches to global public health. Pharmaceutical firms, for instance, have been key participants in global health initiatives (in the United States and beyond), but have also deeply impacted access to treatment by lobbying for excessive international patent protections. Profit motive is embedded in the design of US foreign policy toward development and health, and its approach to market globalization. Resultantly the US role in shaping free trade rules leaves a dearth of affordable drugs for health conditions impacting the developing world, and aid that is "tied" to domestic rather than foreign producers.

Japan

Japan's official development assistance charter, revised in 2003, sees improved health as central to global poverty reduction.[35] Junichiro Koizumi (at the time of this writing the last prime minister to serve an extended term) called this "human-centered development."[36] The threat of infectious disease, Japan's development agency contends, "will have a significant impact on society by taking a toll not only on [national economies], but also on household finances."[37] In response to these challenges, Japan's former foreign minister, Masahiko Koumura, cited increasing awareness of the need for international action on infectious diseases, which was catalyzed by the 2000 Millennium Summit.[38] Japan officially ascribes the Millennium Goals a central place in poverty reduction, which it asserts will lower the burden of health care costs among working families, enlarge the workforce and provide enhanced educational opportunities. The result if the goals are achieved, according to Japan's development agency, will be dramatic socioeconomic advancements.[39]

Japan, once the largest purveyor of development assistance in the world, relinquished its position to the United States in 2001, corresponding with its relative economic decline. It now ranks fifth. It is also highly specialized by both region and issue area. Its region of specialization is Asia, which receives 90 percent of Japanese aid.[40] The academic consensus is that Japanese aid serves to increase its influence among its regional neighbors, ostensibly to expand its export market and secure its access to natural resources.[41] As Taro Aso (then foreign minister) noted, Japanese aid "is essentially about having other countries first use precious money of the Japanese people for the benefit of the Japanese people later on."[42] In part for these reasons, Japan is known—like the United States—for its use of "tied" aid that ultimately benefits domestic rent seekers, bypassing the use of labor and production in target countries. Japan resultantly tends to rate low on the Center for Global Development's annual Commitment to Development Index, ranking second to last in 2011. Nevertheless, Japan has (at least officially) institutionalized humanitarian and social development components into its ODA program. Its development assistance charter was revised in 2003 to better reflect these values, framing international development as a human rights issue. The revision, the first since the charter's ratification in 1992, also calls on Japan to utilize its comparative advantage in prioritizing development assistance. This includes, according to the charter, "its advanced technologies, expertise, human resources, and institutions."[43] The charter, in short, officially calls on Japan to specialize.

Japan credits its foreign aid programs for recent development successes in Southeast Asia, and has begun to export what it calls the "Asian model" to Africa.[44] Despite the decline in Japanese ODA, aid to health has remained steady, totaling an estimated $1.6 billion in 2006. Figures 2.6 and 2.7—which show Japanese aid in absolute terms and by share respectively—illustrate the highly specialized nature of Japanese aid. Japan's approach to global health, in short, has been to specialize in water sanitation projects. Seventy-eight percent of all Japanese development assistance went toward water sanitation projects between 2002 and 2006. During that period Japan committed nearly a quarter of all

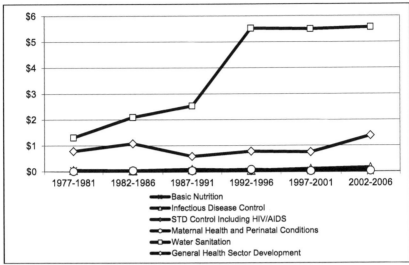

Source: CRS Database. In billions of US Dollars (2005).

Figure 2.6. Japanese Health ODA to Major Health Issues

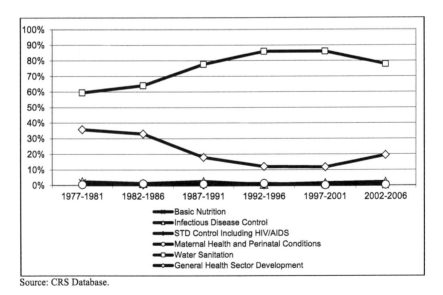

Source: CRS Database.

Figure 2.7. Japanese Health ODA to Major Issues Areas by Percentage Share

development assistance in this area, and 35 percent of all water-related aid committed by DAC members. Substantial funding also goes toward basic health infrastructure. These priorities reflect Japan's traditional focus on large, capital intensive projects in its international development program. Given Japan's approach to ODA, it is not surprising that urban water sanitation is an area of specialization. In addition to taking advantage of its wealth of experience in such projects domestically, Japan has occasionally held up these large projects as examples of its own model of state-led intervention as an alternative to the Washington Consensus.[45] Infrastructural projects typically consume about 40 percent of Japan's total ODA budget, an unusually high figure.[46]

Japan's high degree of specialization is due in part to budget limitations imposed on its aid programs after its deep recession. The Japan International Cooperation Agency (JICA), the agency chiefly responsible for international development and ODA distribution, called for "more effective" use of its aid amidst budget cuts. Its plan, outlined in 2003, prioritized "country-specific and issue-specific activities" that offer cost-effective solutions and take advantage of what Japan sees as its comparative advantages.[47] For Japan, this has meant a continued focus on its traditional priority of water sanitation, where overall funding levels over the past decade held steady despite budget cuts in other areas (see figure 2.6). This has made Japan the world's largest donor in this area. This policy, Japan argues, fulfills a specialized role toward the Millennium Goal of halving the proportion of the world population without safe drinking water by 2015.[48] Although it has tried to increase its focus on "soft" interventions, water sanitation remains its primary area of specialization. Indeed, Japan is a prime example of single issue specialization. Why does it specialize in this particular area?

The primary reasons for Japan's specialization in water sanitation can be boiled down to related factors: domestic experience in this area, major industrial interests surrounding it, and a corresponding wealth in expertise. It is, in short, a product of its advanced capability in water sanitation projects, which figured heavily into its own rapid post-war development. Japan also argues, ex post facto, that there is a great global need for such technologies, which is articulated in the Millennium Goals. It cites the global fresh water shortage (only 0.01 percent of all water on earth is potable) in the face of increased consumption, making dehydration and waterborne illness leading factors in the global burden of disease. More than a billion people lack safe drinking water and, Japan's development agency contends, 80 percent of communicable disease in the developing world are contracted through polluted water. Despite the obvious domestic factors leading to this allocation, this places Japan centrally within the goals, which calls for halving the number of people without access to basic sanitation by 2015. This specialization, Japan contends, also indirectly contributes to other goals such as the reduction of child mortality. As advocates of the foreign policy model would point out, Japan's focus on enhancing the clean water supply is also reflective of its own sensitivity to water shortages. As a net importer of water resources, Japan sees addressing the global fresh water shortage as central to its own interests.

With equal importance, domestic politics greatly influences decision-making at the state level, with interest groups vying over the use of tied aid. These feedback effects make certain specializations self-reinforcing, and also inspire criticisms over the politicization of development assistance that more greatly affects states than multilateral organizations. Yet Japan's water sanitation policy is driven primarily by domestic interests that emerged during its own rapid development in the postwar era. The Japanese government cites its own experiences dealing with water shortages as a comparative advantage. Water sanitation infrastructure was a central issue during Japan's rise from a developing economy to an advanced industrial leader in the Post-War era. Rapid urbanization, modern industrial agriculture, and the concurrent depletion of rivers and lakes—challenges similar to those facing the developing world—led to massive domestic initiatives in clean water infrastructure. As Marie Soderberg argues, "Infrastructure is an area where Japan is strong. They have considerable know-how, a number of well-trained engineers and many construction companies."[49] The Japanese government sees this knowledge as transferable to recipient states. But, as Soderberg points out, its prowess in this area is also the result of extensive domestic industries prepared to offer readymade solutions to the global health crisis.

Japan's official reports essentially make this case, but they unsurprisingly leave out the connection between domestic interests and its aid policy—the "who gets what" component of specialization that development agencies are reluctant to discuss. Japan's prowess in large scale water sanitation is cited as a historic "comparative advantage," not a politically powerful component of Japan's industrial economy. An influential 2003 JICA report notes that "Japan, which has accumulated experience in the water sector through rapid modernization after World

War II, has a prominent role to play in development assistance in this sector."[50] Similar to the US case regarding HIV/AIDS, Japan sees itself as having a unique ability to provide transfers of technology to the developing world in specific areas of expertise. In reality, these areas of global health concern have large domestic constituencies in their respective countries. Japanese policy planners seek to export the bureaucratic structure that underlies the rapid development of clean water and sanitation facilities that occurred during its own period of expansion. It cites basic water sanitation as an area of specialization in the global division of labor, owing to "methods established from Japan's experience," resulting in "high quality assistance based on Japan's comparative advantage."[51]

Even though Japan has voiced support for an expanded emphasis on non-infrastructural aid, water sanitation is poised to remain the centerpiece for Japanese global health policy. Its traditional approach was reiterated in the Initiative for Sustainable Development in the 21st Century. This is Japan's comprehensive approach to water supply and sanitation, and its largest global health initiative.[52] At the 2003 World Water Forum, Japan announced the Initiative for Japan ODA on Water. The program called for utilizing Japan's technical expertise in improving the building and finance capacities for water sanitation in recipient countries.[53] It specifically focused on large-scale programs in urban areas. Japan's continued domestic investments in infrastructure (spurred by a construction spree during its early recession) and rapid urbanization in the developing world are likely to keep the focus on large-scale projects like water sanitation. The current recession makes it likely that the government will continue to utilize foreign aid to finance domestic construction sectors. Moreover, its position as the world's leading donor in this area gives it a unique distinction in a global health regime that is increasingly crowded. As the regime grows denser, Japanese policymakers maintain a unique niche in water sanitation.

As the world's leading donor in this area, Japan is a central presence in international venues such as the World Water Forum, which calls for improved water management. It contends that "the water crisis is deepening and increasing in complexity due to rapid socioeconomic changes, which were caused by population growth, urbanization, industrialization and excessive agricultural development on a global scale."[54] JICA is also in the process of expanding this area of development assistance to Africa and Latin America in addition to its traditional recipient, Asia.[55] Japan has also used its expertise in this area in partnerships with other countries, culminating in the collaborative Water and Sanitation

Broad Partnership Initiative. This initiative is designed to bolster coop-eration with multilateral institutions and other bilateral actors. It has since announced a partnership with the United States. Direct Japanese ODA toward all other major health issues remains relatively small. While JICA recognizes the need to diversify in order to address changes in the global burden of disease, it has chosen—in part because of a shrinking budget—to focus on a handful of countries and issues. By specializing in a few target issues, JICA contends that it can make better use of its limited funds.[56] It can also avoid overlap with other actors, another component of the approach advocated in *Investing in Health*, and in the Paris Declaration on ODA effectiveness.

Direct support for HIV/AIDS has been minimal relative to other major actors. This is likely because the HIV/AIDS epidemic did not hit Japan on the scale that it did the United States and Canada, ensuring that it did not develop the domestic constituencies around the AIDS issue that those countries have. Nevertheless, JICA has framed HIV/AIDS as a development issue that "hinders development, affects national health, national welfare and labor supplies in developing countries."[57] As with all of our cases in this chapter, its language is highly reflective of the consensus. But its own activities toward AIDS have been lim-ited in scope, focusing on technical improvements for testing and the distribution of contraceptives in traditional recipient countries such as Vietnam.[58] Additionally, JICA has expanded these activities into Afri-ca. The bulk of its support for HIV/AIDS, however, has come through multilateral channels, which it should be noted do not register in the CRS bilateral data recorded in the charts above. The most significant of these contributions was a 2005 commitment under Junichiro Koizumi to contribute $500 million to the Global Fund (which Japan played a key role in developing).[59] Its deference to international institutions suggests Japan prefers to specialize in water sanitation directly, while deferring to multilateral institutions on issues outside its purview.

Sweden

Sweden's official position holds that addressing global disease entails looking beyond strictly epidemiological issues to socioeconomic factors in disease transmission. The stated overarching goal of the Swedish International Development Agency (SIDA) is poverty reduction, toward which it sees eliminating global disease as central. Sweden views itself as part of a growing international effort to place global health at the center of the development agenda:

> In recent years, there has been a shift in the global response to the remaining and widening gaps in world health and the unfinished agenda of the health of the poor. Health is no longer seen as a technical issue solely under the responsibility of health ministries but as part of social and economic development, with major implications for poverty reduction.[60]

Improvements in global health are as much contributors to economic development as outcomes of it, a consensus which Sweden sees as enshrined in the Millennium Declaration.

Sweden is the largest Scandinavian donor in the area of public health and is considered by scholars to adhere to the Scandinavian model of development assistance. This so-called "good" model (whose reputed purveyors include the Netherlands) contends that these actors place global development interests over foreign policy expediency. It exceeds the 2002 Monterrey Conference goal of allocating at least 0.7 percent of GNI to development assistance (see table 2.4). Sweden currently commits nearly 1 percent of GNI to international aid, making it consistently among the world's largest distributors of aid as a percentage of national income, ranking third in the world by this standard. Sweden also commits substantial levels of aid in absolute terms. Despite its relatively small size, Sweden is in the top ten of all DAC members in terms of absolute volume (see table 2.3).

The Center for Global Development rated Sweden first overall in its 2011 Commitment to Development index, which measures wealthy countries' overall commitment to aid across a broad spectrum of metrics including the quality of development assistance, trade policy, foreign investments, and environmental policy.[61] This is in stark contrast to Japan, which tends to rank low in such studies in large part because of its reputation for placing foreign policy interests ahead of global development, and its use of tied aid (see table 2.5). Where Japan locates the majority of its aid in regions where it has a strong economic interest, and is known for tying aid to domestic industries, Swedish ODA focuses on Africa where it has fewer direct ties.[62] Indexes such as the CGD's development rankings lend quantitative weight to the scholarly

Table 2.4. DAC Members Ranked by Aid Levels as a Share of
GNI in 2010

Norway	1.10
Luxembourg	1.09
Sweden	0.97
Denmark	0.90
Netherlands	0.81
Belgium	0.64
United Kingdom	0.56
Finland	0.55
Ireland	0.53
France	0.50
Spain	0.43
Switzerland	0.41
Germany	0.38
Canada	0.33
Austria	0.32
Australia	0.32
Portugal	0.29
New Zealand	0.26
United States	0.21
Japan	0.20
Greece	0.17
Italy	0.15
South Korea	0.12
DAC Total	0.32

Source: CRS Database. In 2010 dollars.

consensus on the "Scandinavian model." In sum, Sweden's aid program is broadly thought to maintain persistently large volumes of high quality development assistance.

It is important to note that the Scandinavian model is not beyond reproach despite its persistently strong reputation in academic and policy circles. In the wake of criticisms over its efficiency—culminating in a corruption scandal involving aid to Zambia and the subsequent firing of SIDA director general Anders Nordstrom in 2010—Sweden announced a restructuring of its development assistance program. It has spent recent years pushing toward specialization in all areas, including public health. Gunilla Carlsson, the current Minister for International Development, puts the overarching goal of the restructuring succinctly

Table 2.5. CGD's 2011 "Commitment to Development" Index

DAC Member	Overall Score
Sweden	7.7
Norway	7.0
Denmark	6.9
Netherlands	6.7
United States	6.4
Finland	6.1
New Zealand	6.0
Austria	6.0
Portugal	5.5
Ireland	5.5
Australia	5.5
United Kingdom	5.4
Canada	5.4
Spain	5.3
Germany	5.3
Belgium	5.2
France	5.2
Switzerland	5.1
Greece	4.9
Italy	4.8
Japan	3.7
South Korea	3.1

in a way that reflects two components of the global consensus: more aid and better efficiency. "Sweden is a leading country when it comes to the volume of development assistance," she notes, "It is my goal that Sweden also become a leading country in terms of quality and efficiency."[63] The new "results-based" focus is consistent with the trends among other aid producers, involving an increased emphasis on more specialized aid. Sweden's general focus when it comes to development assistance is geographic, officially concentrating on "the places where Sweden's assistance is most useful and where Sweden's long-term involvement is best justified."[64] SIDA contends that this approach will bring much needed clarity of purpose to Swedish aid, and ensure that its functions do not overlap with that of other actors. This has meant a department-wide scaling back in the number of recipient states, to places where Swedish aid, SIDA argues, can be used most effectively. As Carlsson boasted in a speech, "one of the first measures I undertook [when taking office] was to limit the number of Swedish partner countries: increased country focus. I have also been very strict in ensuring that Swedish aid will be provided in a maximum of three sectors in each partner country."[65] In its move toward geographic specialization SIDA has called for a particular focus on two regions: Eastern Europe and Sub-Saharan Africa. The former because of its proximity and relative importance to Sweden, and the latter because of its urgent development needs. Sweden's official policy is to select specific focus countries within these regions, and to phase out recipient regions where other aid producers have more prevalent ties.

So far Sweden's scaled down approach has not meant a decline in the overall size of its ODA outlays, which continue to constitute a high percentage of GNI. In the area of global health, its allocations have also remained large—which promises to persist as Sweden weathers the global economic downturn with relative success. As with most other aid producers, its total allocations to global health have increased significantly in the past decade, which is on pace to become its largest ever. Between 2002 and 2006, Swedish development assistance for health approached an estimated $1.4 billion, nearly double what Sweden committed over the previous five year period. Its primary issue of specialization is general health sector development, though HIV/AIDS has received significant attention in this decade, owing to Sweden's renewed focus on Africa. Health sector development is Sweden's traditional focus, comprising between 30 and 50 percent of Swedish ODA to health for each five-year time period shown in figure 2.8.

SIDA places health in the context of international development and sees it as instrumental in achieving its overarching goal of poverty reduction. As with the other bilateral cases explored in this chapter, Sweden's reorientation of its program coincided with the Millennium Declaration. Its health program seeks to maximize its resources toward the realization of the declaration by 2015. Along with the consensus that places health at the center of international development, Sweden sees health as "one of the keys to both economic and social development, and thereby to poverty reduction and elimination."[66] As Sweden's Ministry of Foreign Affairs recently noted, its new policy of "focused bilateral" cooperation was designed to accomplish "reduced poverty and achievement of the Millennium Development Goals."[67] This means geographic specialization. Sweden's aid reorientation calls for paring down the number of recipient countries to thirty. Once again we see stated

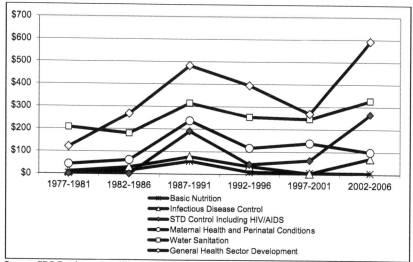

Source: CRS Database. In millions of US Dollars (2005).

Figure 2.8. Swedish Health ODA to Major Issue Areas

ideas that conform to the consensus, and official policies that move in that direction.

SIDA has two stated criteria for the selection of focus countries (in addition to safeguards such as the rule of law and respect for human rights). First, it officially seeks to place resources in places where the need is greatest. Its assessments calculate local incomes as well as human development indicators such as infant mortality. The second factor is the degree of value-added by Swedish development assistance over other actors—an increasingly important factor in a crowded field of participants. This includes consideration of Sweden's linkages to potential recipients, which theoretically enhance its knowledge of the local system. Additionally, SIDA considers "demand for Swedish expertise (from the business sector, government agencies or organizations) as well as Swedish comparative advantages and Swedish know-how in relation to other donors."[68] This policy ultimately entailed a renewed focus on Africa, where the development needs are greatest, and Eastern Europe, where Sweden maintains close ties. Of the twelve focus countries toward which Sweden pledges "long-term development cooperation," nine are in Africa, while just three are in Asia and one is in Latin America.[69]

An influential policy document issued by SIDA, *Health is Wealth*, outlined Sweden's newly specialized global health policy in the context of its larger reorientation. The report identifies specific areas where Sweden has a comparative advantage. They are oriented toward establishing Sweden's role in a division of labor, and toward achieving the Millennium Development Goals. SIDA sees its role as utilizing "Swedish know-how and resource base and to contribute to technical and policy development."[70] Here again we see domestic factors playing a large role in foreign aid prioritization. It incorporates this into its primary specialization of strengthening local health systems. This category of aid is seen as a form of soft power which is exportable. Sweden's position as a world leader in publicly financed, single-payer health care gives it a unique ability to facilitate the development and governance of complex new systems abroad. As *Health Is Wealth* implores, Sweden's "guiding principle" in the area of public health is "to work towards a publicly financed health system through general taxation or social insurance."[71] This is in contrast to the World Bank's long-standing calls for out-of-pocket individualized health financing.

Sweden sees its domestic approach to health as a purveyor of public goods. Correspondingly its development agency seeks to replicate this in the developing world. Public goods, which it defines as utilitarian activities which are undersupplied by the market and thus require public investment, are particularly important for the developing world, whose health issues are widely ignored by global research and development efforts. As a result, SIDA has made research and development in communicable disease a central priority (a category which falls under "general health sector development" in figures 2.8 and 2.9). This includes an extensive program to establish domestic research facilities in recipient countries, which are more likely to prioritize local disease burdens than Western-centric research laboratories. Money devoted to this area has increased significantly in recent years, from virtually nothing at the beginning of the decade to more than $50 million between 2002 and 2006. Its health education program (another subcategory within general health sector development) has also grown considerably, with annual allocations in the 2000s exceeding $100 million, up from just a fraction of this total in the 1990s. It seeks to prioritize "information and communication" initiatives, especially in the area of communicable disease in Africa, where such programs have not been instituted.[72]

The second major priority during Sweden's reorientation is HIV/AIDS. Though its overall allocation is small, totaling less than eight

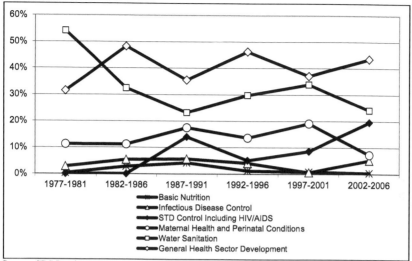

Source: CRS Database.

Figure 2.9. Swedish Health ODA to Major Issue Areas by Percentage Share

percent of Swedish ODA to health in 2006, its level of support in this decade has been historically high. It was the fastest rising issue area, behind health sector development, in the five-year period between 2002 and 2006, owing largely to a geographic specialization in Africa. Consistent with the consensus, it sees anti-AIDS programs as necessary ingredients toward achieving SIDA's overarching goal of poverty reduction. Central to its logic is the reciprocal relationship between disease and poverty. High levels of disease burden cause poverty by reducing the productive potential of working age individuals, while high levels of poverty reduce a society's ability to combat disease due to insufficiently funded health infrastructure. As a result, the Swedish government announced a shift from "mainly a health approach, to a multi-sectoral strategy for dealing with HIV and AIDS."[73]

Sweden even voices support for a far more cooperative division of labor in which aid distributors directly coordinate in ways that they do not today. "The aim," according to SIDA's central HIV/AIDS policy paper, *Investing for Future Generations*, "will be to achieve a synergy between Sweden's efforts and other kinds of input," creating a "strategic combination" that makes better use of available resources.[74] One intangible area where Sweden advances a similar progressivism is in international advocacy. Utilizing its reputation as one of the world's most generous and effective providers of global development assistance, Sweden sees itself as having the moral standing to push other wealthy actors toward a greater response. Like several of the multilateral and NGO cases, Sweden, as a smaller state, has sought to advance its moral standing and play a part in advocacy. This was announced as a central component of its AIDS program in 1999.[75] This approach includes, specifically, a greater recognition of the disease as a development issue by global policymakers.

Its program includes the creation of AIDS specific public agencies, the early development of antibody tests and especially what Sweden calls its "long tradition of sex education for young people."[76] The latter component, sex education, has been central to Sweden's anti-AIDS approach, just as health education has to its health sector development program. As a result of these domestic factors, Sweden runs an anti-AIDS program that it asserts has a progressive quality that can enhance its global impact. SIDA seeks to be ahead of the curve in emphasizing and advocating for the political and social dimensions of the disease, in addition to its traditional commitments to prevention and care. In comparison with the United States and Japan, Sweden has been out front as an advocate for the emergent consensus in global public health. Its official discourse explicitly reflects the prevalent view of health as a human right, the centrality of health in international development, and the need to optimize aid through a division of labor—and its policies have generally moved in these directions as well.

Canada

As a middle power Canada compares more closely with Sweden than with our great power cases. However, compared with the other three cases explored here, scholars are less sanguine about the central motivations behind Canada's ODA patterns. The debate thus far has centered around whether Canada allocates ODA based on humanitarian, commercial, or political considerations.[77] Its foreign assistance programs were heavily rooted in Cold War security concerns, with early Canadian aid following US leadership during this period of liberal internationalism.[78] However, as the Cold War ended, Canada focused more closely on economic logics without the burden of Cold War expediency, a trend we see among other state actors. Membership in the Commonwealth and La Francophonie impacted aid, reflecting an important form of geographic specialization.[79]

The Canadian ODA program is relatively small, dropping to 0.33 percent of GNI by 2010. This is considerably below the Monterrey target of 0.7 percent for OECD countries, and well below the 0.5 percent level reached by Canada in the mid-1980s under Prime Minister Brian Mulroney. (Ironically it was Lester Pearson, then a recently departed Canadian prime minister, who headed the expert commission at the UN that first established the necessity of the 0.7 percent threshold in 1969). This is a large distinction between Canada and the progressive Scandinavian aid producers toward which it is often compared. Nevertheless, it is the OECD's eighth largest donor in absolute terms, and a major contributor to public health.[80] Canadian ODA to health, while remaining relatively stable throughout the 70s, 80s, and 90s, increased markedly in the 2000s. In the five-year period from 1997 to 2001, Canada committed an estimated $519 million to global health. Between 2002 and 2006 this figure nearly trebled to $1.5 billion. This is by far greater than at any time dating back to 1974. Once a specialist in water sanitation, Canada has become relatively less specialized (by issue area) over time, in stark contrast to our other cases (evident in figure 2.10). Yet a still-significant specialized role

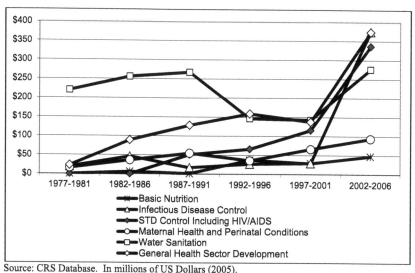

Source: CRS Database. In millions of US Dollars (2005).

Figure 2.10. Canadian Health ODA to Major Issue Areas

in communicable illness emerged alongside the overall increase in funds. Nearly one-quarter of Canadian aid to health went to HIV/AIDS between 2002 and 2006. Infectious disease control was another area that saw steep gains, also constituting a quarter of Canadian aid to health during this time. This joins general health infrastructure in the top three Canadian commitments, followed by increases in water sanitation. Despite a push to specialize geographically, Canada maintains broad commitments across a variety of issue areas. Still, as we will see below, Canada has pressed to develop other forms of specialization and value-added approaches to health, even as its aid portfolio defies global trends.

Nevertheless aid has been the focal point of cuts in Canada's efforts to reduce the national deficit under Prime Minister Stephen Harper.[81] In April 2012, after an extended budget freeze, Harper announced three years of cuts to foreign aid.[82] The end of the Cold War, an important cornerstone of Canadian foreign policy, meant the decline of foreign aid, largely under Prime Minister Jean Chrétien, whose tenure coincided with broader global aid declines in the 1990s. Harper's tenure, argues Colleen O'Manique, has meant a continued shift away from human security toward an emphasis on security and business interests.[83]

As with the other cases explored in this study, the Millennium Declaration figures centrally in Canadian statements and policies. The Canadian government officially argues that there is "a new international consensus on the need to take concerted action to address the most pressing challenges faced by developing countries" in the wake of the precipitous drop in ODA during the 1990s. *Canada in the World*, the Canadian Bureau of Foreign Affairs and International Trade's central policy statement, places global health in the context of development and poverty reduction, with an emphasis on the global burden of disease. More specifically, this major policy statement outlines a blueprint for the maximization of Canadian resources in this area. In achieving the Millennium Goals, Canada's official policy is to specialize in areas that "match our strengths to developing country needs."[84]

Geographic specialization has become more important to Canadian strategy. As with other cases, this means limiting its scope to a relatively small number of focus countries. There are three stated criteria for focus country selection, which mirror those developed by Sweden. First, it selects focus countries based on need, seeking to devote resources to places where the development gap is great. Second, it assesses geopolitical importance. This has meant a specific focus on Eastern Europe, which Canada sees as central to global security. Third, Canada seeks recipient states that are most likely to benefit from Canada's areas of specialization.

For Canada's development agency this means ensuring that "Canadian know-how is put to work for the benefit of developing countries in activities where Canada has a clear comparative advantage."[85]

Like Sweden, it has assumed the role of normative advocate for the HIV/AIDS cause. CIDA takes advantage of Canada's "history of internationalism," and its unique history as a wealthy Western country that did not have a colonial empire. This gives it a moral platform for AIDS advocacy that can be effective in the realms of both the global north and south. While lacking in sheer size, Canada seeks to expand its soft power by building on its moral standing. Where the global North is concerned, Canada sees its special partnership with the United States as a unique lobbying position for more AIDS resources. In the global south, it utilizes its special connections with developing Francophone and Anglophone countries.[86] As a result, calls for greater material support are central to its global HIV/AIDS strategy. As Beaudry-Somcynsky put it, "Through its links with the Commonwealth and the Francophone countries, and its role as an honest broker in numerous circumstances, Canada had increasingly been requested to play a role on the international cooperation scene that went way beyond its ODA budget."[87] Thus Harper's call for cuts in the foreign aid budget prompted public debate about Canada's role in the world.

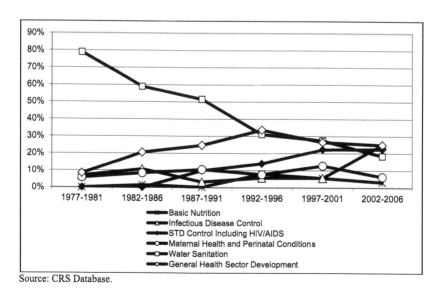

Source: CRS Database.

Figure 2.11. Canadian Health ODA to Major Issue Areas by Percentage Share

Domestic factors in Canada also invite comparison with the United States. Like the United States, Canada has had considerable experience coping with the HIV/AIDS epidemic domestically. Canada was a major Western epicenter for the disease in the 1980s. There were 56,000 Canadians living with the disease in 2002.[88] The Canadian government sees the approaches it has taken as worthy of export through its development agency, a process it describes as sharing best practices. Its own experience with AIDS, it contends, has forced it to grapple with the main challenges confronting the development of AIDS prevention and treatment. These include social stigma among the affected, and inequality among vulnerable populations. In CIDA's view, Canada's experience in dealing with marginalized groups within its own population (including sex workers, needle users, the LGBTQ community, and people living with HIV/AIDS) enables it to take a leadership role in addressing these challenges in recipient countries. More importantly, these marginalized groups are important constituencies in Canada, both inside and outside of government. As with the US case, AIDS activism did not disappear when governments finally moved to address the disease domestically. Instead it took on an international dimension, and existent AIDS fighting bureaucracies in Canada began to merge domestic AIDS fighting plans with a larger global agenda.

Correspondingly, Canada claims a specialized role in the dissemination of information to marginalized groups, which, as in Canada, requires overcoming social barriers. This includes an emphasis on programs that adapt to local cultures, ranging from aboriginal societies to LGBTQ communities. This knowledge and approach was developed domestically, through years of instituting AIDS relief programs among the LGBTQ, First Nation, and recent immigrant communities in Canada, as well as with experience monitoring the epidemic among these communities. Canada's approach also includes programs aimed at injection drug users, including harm reducing measures like needle exchanges, substitution therapy (like methadone) and safe injection sites.[89] This gives Canada a niche in global AIDS relief not filled by the US, where such measures are banned both domestically and abroad—despite conservative resistance to domestic public health efforts such as safe injection sites.[90]

The second central component to Canada's anti-AIDS program is research and development. This area is also a significant strength identified by CIDA, since Canada was among the first wealthy countries faced with developing and disseminating ARV programs. CIDA contends that it is particularly well-suited to exporting its expertise in this area, including methods to track and monitor the disease, develop better medications, and streamline research programs.[91] Not surprisingly, AIDS figures centrally to Canada's 2005 International Policy Statement, which was a set of three public directives to improve worldwide health outcomes. It pledges, first, to address the global burden of disease, putting a central focus on specialization in HIV/AIDS. The second directive calls for strengthening health system capacities in lesser developed countries. The third directive provides research and funding toward the development of an AIDS vaccine, particularly addressed because of Canada's expertise in this area.[92]

General health system development, especially in Africa, is the second prominent role that Canada has taken in the global division of labor. Like Sweden, Canada's program utilizes the focus-country system. Canada has winnowed down its commitments to a handful of countries in an effort to enhance its knowledge and expertise in these regions, as well as to concentrate limited resources. This includes what CIDA calls a process of developing a thorough knowledge of local conditions by "drawing on lessons learned, in order to inform policies and ongoing programming."[93] The Canadian government's primary response to the Millennium Declaration is the Catalytic Initiative to Save a Million Lives. The initiative is billed as Canada's best possible avenue toward progress on the health-related Millennium Goals. The program focuses on lending Canadian expertise toward building domestic health systems in Africa and Asia. Its primary focus is on training community workers to deliver basic health services, such as malarial nets, inoculations, and vitamin A. The program—which aims to train 40,000 frontline health workers within its focus countries—concentrates on Africa.

This initiative has since been buttressed by the African Health Systems Initiative, which, as its name implies, seeks to expand health systems in support of achieving the Millennium Goals in Sub-Saharan Africa. As with the Catalytic Initiative, the African Health Systems Initiative seeks to address gaps in local health systems utilizing Canadian expertise. These programs are geared toward maximizing resources for the burden of disease and finding a niche in the global regime. Canada's pilot program in Tanzania utilizes this logic, with CIDA contending that it is premised on the belief that "people's health can be improved not only by spending more money, but also by spending money more wisely where the needs are greatest."[94] This CIDA contends, means targeting the burden of disease, utilizing to the largest extent possible Canada's domestic expertise and capability—a stated policy position that is wholly reflective of the emergent global health consensus.

South-to-South Aid Expansion

In all likelihood the global public health regime will grow in size and become increasingly complex. This is especially likely given that its center of gravity could move southward as the newest "nontraditional" actors assert themselves. Emerging powers including India, China, and Brazil—which themselves contain a large portion of the world's poor—have become more active distributors of aid. With varying degrees of help from the outside world these countries have aggressively tackled public health problems among their own deeply impoverished slums and rural country sides. Despite still being recipients of aid, these countries have the potential to become major aid producers due to their rapid economic growth. China is the leader among developing world aid distributors, especially in Africa where it promises to expend billions in new funds. If that trend grows, we can expect more competitive pressures to be placed on the existing regimes, even for traditional state actors.

The overarching normative changes that have occurred over the past two decades have significant influences over the practices of states, multilateral institutions, and NGOs. As this book argues, we see evidence that the forces of convergence are deeply ingrained among these actors. There is increasing agreement over development strategies and patterns of activity in global health. Yet there is one distinction worth making when we refer to "states." The states under study above were all DAC members, regularly referred to in development circles as "traditional" or "established" providers of development assistance. These countries today deliver the vast majority of international aid. However, if current trajectories are an indication, we are likely to see non-OECD aid producers comprise much larger shares in the future. There is a growing volume of south-to-south transfers of aid. This emerging category of actors includes cash rich oil producers such as the Persian Gulf states and Venezuela, and emergent world powers like China, India, and Brazil. This development has been met with trepidation by Western observers, particularly as these countries make rapid advances in economic growth and spending power relative to the leading northern states. As Western and Japanese economies declined after the financial crisis, now showing only tentative evidence of recovery, Venezuela, China, India and Brazil continued their remarkable growth patterns.[95]

These countries, particularly China, have become more assertive in the realm of international development. While China provided aid throughout the Cold War, it now has the ability as the World's second largest economy to transfer wealth in greater volumes, and it is doing so. In November of 2009 China announced $10 billion in aid to Africa over three years, twice its 2006 commitment.[96] In a startling 2007 opinion piece in the *New York Times*, international affairs commentator Moisés Naim argued that nontraditional state actors were undermining traditional norms of aid distribution. "In recent years, wealthy non-democratic regimes have begun to undermine development policy through their own activist aid programs," argued Naim. "Call it rogue aid. It is development assistance that is non-democratic in origin and nontransparent in practice, and its effect is typically to stifle real progress while hurting ordinary citizens."[97] Chinese aid, he said, was driven by "money, international politics and access to raw materials." He also cites Venezuela's efforts to utilize its oil-derived wealth to recruit allies in the Western Hemisphere. Naim likens these foreign aid policies to those which prevailed during the Cold War, with both the United States and Soviet Union eagerly willing to lavish funds on dictatorial regimes in the global south without much expectation for results.

The emergence of these actors raises interesting questions. How well will emergent states assimilate to the global public health regime's accepted norms and standards? Will they adhere to traditional norms associating global health with individual human rights? Or, equally interesting, will they alter, modify, or completely overturn accepted understandings of international aid? Much of the emergent norms of international development at the state-level explored here are arguably rooted in northern interests and values that might be less germane to southern powers. How the emergence of nontraditional state actors affects the larger regime will be a fascinating avenue for research in the near future. This book offers some conjectures: Greater regime density, we have seen, encourages specialization among existing actors. It would not be surprising if the presence of new actors pressured today's leading figures to further define specialized roles and increase their value-added. Additionally, we may expect emerging aid distributors, especially China, India, Brazil, and Venezuela, to export their myriad domestic innovations in poverty relief. These countries, after all, remain mired in many of the same challenges facing Africa and South Asia, and by themselves contain a substantial portion of the world's poor. It is likely that they will see their own methods of delivering health-related services under these conditions as transferable.

South-to-south cooperation does not eliminate paternalistic power relations. Yet, if this is worrisome, so are the persistently exploitive relationships western powers forge in the global south. It is important not to evaluate the "goodness" of emergent aid distributors through nationalistic lenses. Aid is a tool capable of productive use or misuse, of real social change through redistribution, or of deepening power imbalances. These quandaries should be applied to nontraditional actors no less than the former colonial powers that make up the bulk of the DAC. But nontraditional actors should not be described as singularly unique in their willingness to jettison norms of self-determination or good governance in small, poor countries. International relations scholarship is beginning to address this issue. Ngaire Woods offers a more nuanced picture of what has been dubbed "toxic aid" by Naim:

> The world of development assistance is being shaken by the power shift occurring across the global economy. Emerging economies are quietly beginning to change the rules of the game. China, the United Arab Emirates, Saudi Arabia, Korea, Venezuela, India, Kuwait and Brazil, among others, have been increasing their aid to poorer countries. They are giving aid on terms of their choosing.[98]

Woods contends that "the available evidence does not fully bear out these anxieties."[99] There are positive developments in Africa associated with closer relations between it and China, including strong economic growth, an improved public sector and increased trading. The apparent proclivities of nontraditional actors for low-grade aid with little conditionality do in fact present challenges. However it is deficiencies with the traditional aid regime that makes new aid distributors more attractive for developing countries seeking partnerships. OECD states have not kept up pledges to produce dramatically increased aid with less conditionality. Unsurprisingly governments across the developing world are looking for new partners.

Another point Naim and other critics of emergent aid distributors would do well to raise: The record for western aid producers—most particularly the United States, World Bank, and IMF—is fiercely criticized in the global south for the counterproductive effects of imposed conditionality.[100] Conversely, BRIC countries have been instrumental in fostering "access to health" norms, with Brazil and India particularly active in pressuring the north to lower the draconian patent restrictions on medicines.[101] It is once again not surprising given this historical context that low income countries may seek alternatives to traditional avenues of development assistance. This gives small, poor countries a degree of lever-age—the ability to "forum shop," in the language of the regime complex literature—for better terms of aid and borrowing. In sum, as more actors enter the arena of development assistance, the regime further takes on the characteristics of a regime complex. The rise of nontraditional aid producers means that recipient states will have an increasing multitude of forums through which to seek better terms. With growing regime density in terms of the number of competing aid channels, traditional actors will have to more favorably position themselves relative to emerging great powers (at least on cases where coercion does not work). This could make unfair aid conditionality more difficult to impose in the future, and—if we may indulge in some optimism—place a greater degree of autonomy in the hands of local governments. This potential is lamented by Naim and other critics who worry about the decline in aid conditionality, though it may well empower decision-makers in developing countries, seeking to utilize development assistance on their own terms.

Meanwhile innovative partnerships promise to provide new formal channels for aid coordination between states. One of the most notable is UNITAID, which was founded by states in both the north and south to finance and coordinate activities promoting access to treatment for HIV/AIDS, malaria, and tuberculosis. The partnership has since expanded to include non-state actors as well as a more inclusive roster of states, with Africa particularly well represented.[102] A number of its state members have committed to a small airline tax which contributes more than half of the organization's funds while Norway commits money through a carbon tax.[103] Though voluntary and on a relatively small scale, this approach suggests the possibility for redistributive mechanisms that operate glob-ally, addressing the increasingly denationalized nature of global poverty. This recalls the conclusion of the so-called Brandt Commission, headed by West German chancellor Willy Brandt, which proposed a global sys-tem of transnational redistribution—albeit larger scale and more rooted in Keynesian economics than anything under consideration today.[104] More immediately, the UNITAID model marshals new resources while creating a node of cooperation between myriad state actors, poor countries included.

~

Despite their idiosyncrasies, the four bilateral actors share key common-alities that manifest themselves in a global consensus. For all the hard economic power these actors wield—particularly Japan and the United

States—these cases underscore the importance of prevailing ideas. They also reveal the logical, often interest-based ways policymakers address world health challenges. A discussion of state priorities does not fully capture how the global consensus took shape, or how key ideas about health arose while others were pushed aside. Addressing those questions merits exploration of the organizations at the center of global health cooperation: intergovernmental organizations, to which we turn in the next chapter.

CHAPTER 3

Multilateral Specialization

Institutional Roles amidst Emergent Regime Density

What is the role of multilateral actors in public health? How do multilateral actors differ from state actors? What major factors inform their decisions to prioritize certain issues over others? Has the proliferation of new agencies hindered these actors' abilities to function? This chapter explores multilateral agencies' efforts to address the inefficiencies that regime complex theory predicts. It illustrates the formal cooperation and informal complementarity among agencies, involving relationships that are competitive but entail surprising degrees of partnership and shared financing. As with bilateral agencies, specialized roles offset the damaging effects of overlapping tasks. However, multilateral agencies are fundamentally unique since they are dependent on states for material support and have difficulty shaping their own agendas in deference to states. As they are partially removed from domestic political processes, these agencies are thought to provide so-called good aid unencumbered from political interests.[1] By "multilateral actors," we are specifically referring to intergovernmental actors whose memberships are comprised of states. Yet as we have already seen, greater incorporation among non-state actors, as well as (to a degree) autonomous action among multilateral actors themselves has made this description something of an idealization—though an analytically useful one. Under conditions of regime complexity, multilateral organizations face distinct challenges and have had to adapt.

Nowhere has this been clearer than with this chapter's first case study, the WHO, which has narrowed the scope of its activities due to resource constraint. This is because of intense pressure from member states over the so-called politicization of global health, the WHO's own shortcomings (at least in comparison to the immensity of its institutional goals), and also because of the International Development Association's (IDA) position as a large concessional lender. The World Bank emerged as a preeminent financial power over health, giving it influence over health reform implementation that the WHO lacks. The pressure from increased competition—including perilous member-state divestments in the 80s and 90s—has forced the WHO to reform, establishing increasingly specialized roles in global health that belie its expansive primary care driven mission of "health for all." Under former Director General Gro Harlem Brundtland the WHO reformed in ways that directly reflect the consensus. This has led many to predict the WHO's decline, yet it has actually enhanced its role as a forum for international regulations. It has brokered considerable international consensus in economic development, social health, and drug access, among other areas. The network of multilateral institutions includes the creation of new public health agencies and the entry of development institutions into global health policy (see table 1.2 in the first chapter). Among existing development agencies, the expanded list of involvement in global health includes the World Bank and UNDP. These institutions have become increasingly powerful in shaping the global health agenda. The World Bank itself has increasingly specialized amidst regime density. Through its reforms it has helped define an economically oriented global consensus on health and development. The UNDP, lacking the World Bank's financial advantages, has taken on a coordination and advocacy role, becoming itself a major purveyor of the millennial consensus. The European Union has specialized in water sanitation and infrastructure development, notably straying from the US-led prioritization of HIV/AIDS.

The newest multilateral global health activity is characterized by its focus on just a handful of issues, and in some cases singular issues. This verticalization of global health is controversial within the development community. In part because of this reason, critics cite the new multilateral architecture as inefficient. There is potential, they say, for a few well-supported disease initiatives to crowd out funding for other pressing health matters. They contend that this marks a departure from the holistic, horizontal approach previously advocated within the WHO. The World Health Assembly, by comparison, had in 1978 sought the broader goal of "health for all" by the year 2000. While primary care doctrine met resistance from the beginning, and has been sidestepped by key actors such as the World Bank, it is an idea that has been revisited by a reformed WHO.

The increasingly complex institutional arrangement of the global public health regime has also generated frustration in recipient countries which must work with a vast array of external assistance programs. Having so many partners, they say, costs developing states valuable resources and makes coordination difficult. Development agencies have been forced to address the issue. As funds and bureaucracy from aid programs have become more difficult to manage, there has been a movement among OECD countries to promote specialization, resource harmonization, and the reduction of overlapping tasks. Reform within these multilateral institutions over time has also entailed significant turf battles between organizations to decide who gets authority over new resources and emergent agencies. The WHO, for instance, had arguably been marginalized by the early 1990s, having been forced to accept a narrower mandate amidst newly emergent actors and traditional UN rivals. The World Bank has correspondingly gained normative influence, embodying and shaping consensus principles. Recall that the global health consensus promoted by multilateral institutions is predicated on the following dominant contentions. Public health's centrality to human development demands more aid. There must be strong measures to reduce overlap. Low-cost, disease-specific interventions are the most efficient ways of improving public health. Globalization and an integrated world trading system have brought greater attention to world epidemics, but those perceived to impact this system most directly gain the greatest attention. This consensus provides the intellectual context under which multilaterals have increasingly specialized. While states possess much of the hard power through which important changes in the international system occur, much of the prevailing ideas within health were developed within multilateral forums.

These cases have important similarities with the bilateral cases explored in the previous chapter. Both sets of cases show high degrees of specialization, and both sets show narrowing priorities even when overall resources increase. Moreover global aid patterns between bilateral and multilateral actors, in aggregate, show markedly similar priorities. What the cases in this chapter also show is that multilateral organizations, like states, are subject to intense political pressures. However, as discussed in the previous chapter, domestic political processes largely affect what states choose to specialize in. Multilateral organizations feel greater competitive pressure than states. Lacking their own tax bases, they must compete for international funds toward health, and they often do so by finding unique roles in the regime.

This chapter proceeds in two parts. The first section briefly looks at the relative importance of multilateral aid. This follows with an examination of each case, beginning with the evolution of the WHO. While these cases differ widely in many respects, important threads connect them. Each case has struggled to carve out specialized roles amidst increasingly dense regime architecture. Each reflects the global consensus, and each has conformed to it while actively purveying it.

The Multilateral Presence

Multilateral channels have long been a major component of aid distribution in global health. Like bilateral aid, multilateral aid has increased significantly. In 1974 multilateral organizations distributed an estimated $765 million to global health. Thirty years later, annual multilateral aid distribution was $6.2 billion, roughly an eightfold increase.[2] Multilateral aid more than doubled over the past decade, though it is important to reiterate that development assistance data recorded by the OECD are less comprehensive than that for states. That caveat in mind, the percentage of health ODA distributed by multilateral organizations has generally held steady at roughly a third since the 1980s (see figure 2.2 in the previous chapter).[3] Figure 3.1 shows overall multilateral priorities. Realist theory would predict that multilateral priorities would closely reflect those of states, and this appears to be mostly the case. As with the bilateral allocations explored in chapter two, water sanitation was the leading recipient of multilateral health assistance in the most recent five-year frame.

As figure 3.2 shows, this issue has seen a relative decline (as it has in bilateral assistance) since the 1970s. HIV/AIDS is increasing rapidly as a priority, actually surpassing general health sector development in the period between 2002 and 2006. For its part, health sector development has remained a steady priority. Fitting with the broader picture, overall aid patterns diversified in the 2000s, touching a wider array of issues. Yet basic nutrition remains underfunded. Also, as we have seen, the sheer number of organizations involved in global health has risen, and more development institutions like the World Bank entered the fray. In addition to their importance as aid channels, international organizations

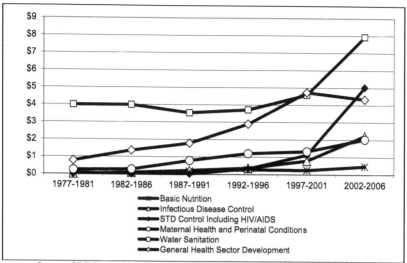

Source: CRS database. In billions of 2005 US dollars.

Figure 3.1. Multilateral Health ODA to Major Issue Areas

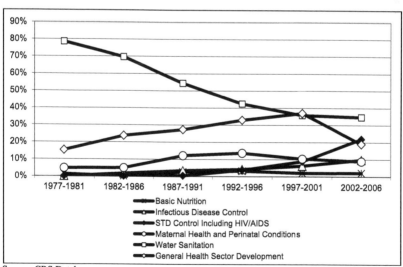

Source: CRS Database.

Figure 3.2. Multilateral Health ODA to Major Issue Areas by Percentage Share

have specialized expertise in global health that afford them leadership positions with considerable agenda setting and coordination powers. These organizations must craftily utilize both advantages in their efforts to find their niches in an increasingly crowded global health regime.

Helen Milner argues that delegation to multilateral agencies is puzzling, given inevitable principle-agent problems and hence diminished ability for states to exert direct influence over the funds. While multilateral aid might be more needs based, she asserts, it provides less political utility for states' domestic interests.[4] What is surprising, given these differences, is that bilateral and multilateral aid tends to prioritize the same issues. This holds true despite the characteristic differences between bilateral and multilateral agencies that Milner and others point out. Both bilateral and multilateral aid patterns follow global health's general trends. Health infrastructure and water sanitation are top priorities, while AIDS and other communicable diseases see sharp increases in aid. The similarities in priorities suggest that multilateral organizations are simply carrying out the agendas of their member states. This is indeed an important truth in how international organizations work. Yet this underestimates the influence that multilateral organizations have to impact their strategic environments, rather than simply the other way around. These agencies have high levels of expertise and experience with issues, and may be better positioned to carry out the goals of states with fewer overhead costs. States regularly defer to multilateral agencies specializing in certain areas rather than develop new programs themselves. A notable example of this is Japan, which has made large contributions to the Global Fund, but has not developed extensive in-house HIV/AIDS programs of its own. With equal importance—as we will see below—multilateral institutions played a profound role in forging the development consensus that led to the rise of global health.

This is evident in the efforts of multilateral agencies to follow up on broad calls for efficiency articulated in the 2005 Paris Agenda for Aid Effectiveness and other key agreements. In January 2004, representatives from a number of bilateral and multilateral global health agencies and initiatives met in Geneva for the first High Level Forum on the Health Millennium Development Goals. They determined that progress had been too slow on the health-related goals.[5] Its efforts reflected the broader established consensus for expanded resources and greater material efficiency. One of the outcomes of this effort to harmonize global resources was the creation of the Health Metrics Network under the auspices of the WHO, which seeks to bolster health information systems in order to better position resources.[6] As key global declarations on aid harmonization took form in the mid-2000s, coordination became the order of the day, with a series of corresponding partnerships among various agencies. These efforts brought together eight "leading" global health agencies—the Bill and Melinda Gates Foundation, UNAIDS, the GAVI Alliance, the Global Fund, the UN Population Fund, the WHO, UNICEF, and the World Bank—to form the Health 8.[7] The H8, formally established in 2007, is intended to galvanize resources for public health in poor countries, as well as coordinate interagency efforts. Its formation constitutes one of the most significant developments linked to the principles established with the Paris agenda, and a key manifestation of the global consensus.

The WHO: Controversy, Decline, and Reform

The WHO began in 1948 as the centerpiece for the global public health regime. While there had been regional and international health organizations, including one within the League of Nations, none had the mandate and powers of the WHO. Shortly after the WHO's creation, Charles E. Allen argued that jurisdictional problems and the need for expanded powers "made it necessary to bring all international health work under the aegis of a single worldwide organization."[8] This centrality is hardly the case today as the global health regime has become larger and more fragmented. Yet out of all the institutions under study here, its mandate is the broadest and most directly related to public health. Article I of its constitution states that its main objective is "the attainment of all peoples of the highest possible level of health." It defines health as "a state of complete physical, mental and social well-being and not merely the absence of disease or infirmity."[9] This definition reflects the intention of its founders to broaden the WHO's approach beyond a mere biomedical mandate, toward a more holistic political, social, and humanitarian one. This dichotomy has remained contentious within the organization. Should the WHO take this broader approach, or maintain a narrower biomedical focus? The pendulum has swung both ways. Brock Chisholm, the organization's charismatic first director general, favored the broader approach, which views the spread of disease and risk factors in a social context, while later reformers such as Gro Harlem Brundtland have taken arguably narrower approaches.

There remains significant tension over the scope of issues the WHO should address. Should the organization stick to the broader mandate of attaining the "highest possible level of health," or should it channel its limited resources into halting a small number of major diseases? Should it address inequities in the global economic system so long as they underpin patterns of disease? This debate contentiously surrounds the WHO because of what is arguably its moral obligation to take a holistic, human rights-oriented approach to public health and advocate for general health as a public good. Throughout its history it has engaged in both horizontal holistic approaches to health and vertical single issue campaigns.[10] In the mid-1970s it appeared as if the broader approach would win out. At the 1978 Alma Ata conference on primary health care held in (then) Soviet Kazakhstan, the World Health Assembly adopted the ambitious goal of "health for all by the year 2000."[11] In addition to universal access to basic health provisions, the declaration also called for addressing the broader political, social, and economic factors affecting health—ultimately indicting the status quo of global capitalism.

This movement which viewed health care in a social context was advocated by former director general Halfdan Mahler, who advocated a humanitarian approach to public health led by the global south. As Kelley Lee notes, Alma Ata represented a rejection of the "top-down, high-tech and vertical (disease-focused) approaches in favor of accessible, integrated care that recognized the key role of local communities, affordable and appropriate technologies, and the need to address the underlying political, social and economic causes of poor health."[12] External pressures made this movement difficult to carry out. States accused the WHO, along with other UN agencies, including UNICEF (which had helped articulate the primary care agenda), of "politicization" by unduly addressing the broader social determinates of health. The WHO would be hit especially hard as leading industrialized countries imposed constraints on budgets across the United Nations.

This is the most prominent manifestation of a long schism in public health between selective economic approaches and more robust needs-based understandings of aid allocation. The latter approach emphasizes humanitarian logic, alongside the language of social change absent from the discourse of today's Gates Foundation or World Bank. This movement, an expression of rebellion against the economization of health and its emphasis on neoliberalism, is conveyed most clearly in the Alma Ata declaration.[13] The declaration is also the most significant manifesto of the Primary Health Care (PHC) movement which called for a more holistic, community-based approach to care. That movement eschewed industrial-scale health interventions, instead emphasizing the broader goals of fundamental economic reform. PHC has its origins in developing country domestic movements, predicated on the idea of creating positive health outcomes for the poor, giving emphasis to social justice. Rooted in the politics of the Cold War non-aligned movement, PHC criticized so-called modernization paradigms, intentionally challenging a status quo that emphasized Western cultural superiority, cataclysmic infusions of development capital, and a "boot straps" approach to poverty. PHC represented an intense dissatisfaction with the big-ticket, infrastructure-driven aid projects of the time which, the movement argued, ignored local input, invited corruption, and inhumanely transfigured village life. The PHC movement also focused on the gross inequality inherent in the global economy, where the contemporary language of mainstream development tends to focus instead on the less controversial metrics of poverty alone.[14]

The PHC movement gained official currency with the landmark 1975 co-publication by the WHO and UNICEF, *Alternative Approaches to Meeting Basic Health Needs in Developing Countries*, an indispensable expression of primary care foreshadowing Alma Ata.[15] The resultant Alma Ata declaration proved to be the most progressive official document in global health's modern history, and this reality led to a significant pushback from the global north. "The existing gross inequality in the health status of the people . . . ," stated Article II, "is politically, socially, and economically unacceptable."[16] This passage revisits the emphasis on inequality rather than simply poverty or ill-health, establishing a connection between status-quo privilege and concurrent mass depravation in the global south. Moreover, asserts Article III, "Economic and social development, based on a *New International Economic Order*, is of basic importance to the fullest attainment of health for all"[17] (emphasis mine). The declaration placed public health in the context of distributional economics, a wholly different economic logic than the individualist market centrism of present day economism. Improving public health outcomes was framed as part of a broader effort to reorder fundamental structures of concentrated political and economic power. Directly to the point of public health interventions, Article IV of the declaration calls upon governments to guarantee, at a minimum, the following: health education, proper nutrition, safe water and sanitation, maternal and child care, immunization, disease prevention, and essential medicines.[18]

This apparently ascendant approach to public health met with swift resistance, particularly from key OECD member states, and major private nonprofits. In the wake of Alma Ata, the Rockefeller Foundation proposed a less ambitious "interim solution," ushering in the "Selective Primary Health Care" countermovement. SPHC responded to PHC on two essential grounds. First it deemphasized politics in global health. Concurrently, UNICEF and the WHO faced criticisms of "politicization," particularly from within wealthy governments. This helped usher in a UN-wide defunding that was particularly harsh on the WHO, whose regular budget stagnated throughout the 1980s and 90s.[19] The resultant change of course at the UN prompted David Werner—whose seminal work, *Where There is no Doctor*, helped influence the PHC movement—to criticize its agencies for changing course toward a minimalist approach.[20] SPHC by contrast retreated from a discourse of inequality, instead focusing on the less controversial discourse of poverty. Second, the SPHC movement, underscoring the insufficient resources to take such a broad-based approach to health, focused on resource maximization. This meant taking on targets of opportunity rather than the gamut of health issues facing the poor. True to its name, public health interventions would have to be selective. SPHC gave emphasis to single issue, "vertical" programs rather than the broad-based approaches called for by PHC.[21]

Encapsulated in this exchange is the ongoing tension of health regime expansion. Should the regime apply a broad-based approach to health, perhaps even encouraging social change in terms of the distribution of wealth? Or should it adopt a narrower approach underpinned by the economization of resources, circumventing deeper ethical questions. The major UN agencies—particularly the WHO—reformed in the latter direction, and Alma Ata arguably represents the high-water mark for the PHC movement. Nevertheless, similar rejections of economism remain. *Global Health Watch* and *Global Health Watch 2*, self-described alternative world health reports, both place health in a broader political-economic context. Partners in Health (PIH), a global NGO based most prominently in Haiti, has successfully forged a model that emphasized holistic community-based care over vertical approaches, prioritizing funds on the basis of need rather than cost-effectiveness. Paul Farmer, one of its cofounders, argues forcefully that the ends of cost-effectiveness and replicability threaten to undermine health interventions by allowing conditions such as multi-drug-resistant tuberculosis to worsen, resulting in greater long-term costs and, more importantly, the loss of human life.[22] For this school of thought, adverse health outcomes result directly from social inequality.

There would be additional pressures on the WHO by the 1980s. The AIDS pandemic was a further harbinger of decline for the WHO.[23]

It figured heavily into the global crisis of confidence in the agency. It was not until 1986 that the WHO's first dedicated unit emerged to address the epidemic globally. The WHO's Global Programme on AIDS (GPA) became the central AIDS unit within the UN system.[24] The program worked primarily to build up and fund anti-AIDS programs in developing countries. The new agency was initially constrained by a lack of resources and a small staff, though consistent advocacy and persuasion led by Jonathan Mann, the GPA's charismatic director, fostered increases in resources and a considerable turnaround in the urgency with which the WHO addressed the crisis. The disease, in Mann's view, preyed upon "les exlus," marginalized members of society who are less able or likely to seek out information about the disease.[25] For Mann, AIDS agencies could tap what he saw as "a new globalism" centered on an international humanitarian concern for widespread global problems.[26]

Through Mann's constant advocacy, eventually well received by Mahler, the program expanded. However the succession of Mahler by Hiroshi Nakajima as director general swung the pendulum back toward a biomedical approach and away from the multi-sectoral AIDS advocacy that marked Mann's leadership. Growth at the GPA slowed, and Nakajima sought to lower the profile of Mann's normative advocacy. Amidst the inevitable tensions, Mann resigned. As the leadership's emphasis on AIDS declined, the organization became the subject of fierce criticism and simultaneously saw its role in the AIDS pandemic (which would soon to become a primary driver of health resources) in steep decline. AIDS advocates within the US government led by Health and Human Services secretary Donna Shalala pressured the WHO to keep Nakajima from running for a second term as director general.[27] UNDP leadership led calls within the UN for a multi-sector, human rights-oriented approach.[28]

The vacuum created by the WHO and growing demand for a multi-sector approach to AIDS led to increased network density. There were new participant actors and subsequently damaging turf battles over who should lead the response (and benefit from new funds). A multi-sector approach emerged but with little coordination. Other specialized agencies within the UN addressed the epidemic on their own. For example, the UN Population Fund included AIDS education as part of its family planning program. UNICEF and the UN Educational, Scientific and Cultural Organization (UNESCO) sponsored children's education programs on AIDS.[29] The Economic and Social Council (ECOSOC) created UNAIDS in 1994 both to lead an expanded response and to coordinate these disparate activities within the UN system and beyond. During this process the WHO's stature declined from a central position on AIDS (with the GPA) to merely one of six original UNAIDS cosponsors. While UNAIDS consisted mainly of former GPA staff, the new central AIDS program in the UN was moved out of the WHO and into the UN secretariat as a standalone agency. This happened despite the WHO's efforts to maintain some authority over the new program in its proposal stages.[30] This was due to widespread dissatisfaction by member states over the WHO's handling of the GPA under Nakajima, particularly his hostility toward the multi-sector, development-centered approach that reflected the global health consensus.[31]

The WHO that had begun, as Allen noted, as the organization that would bring together "all international health work" saw its role vastly diminished toward the world's fastest growing global health concern. This was exacerbated by the simultaneous budgetary pressure placed on the WHO (as with the rest of the UN), which had frozen its regular budget and forced it to rely on less predictable extra budgetary funds over which it had less autonomy. During the mid-90s critics in public health wondered aloud about what the WHO's role should be, given its usurpation by other agencies. Gill Walt noted that "doubts have been cast on the effectiveness of some of its operational activities. This discontent cannot be ignored if the organization is to retain the esteem in which it is generally held."[32] A controversial series of articles by Fiona Godlee in *The British Medical Journal* claimed that the WHO had "sunk into a policy vacuum and is in danger of losing the initiative on international health issues."[33] The organization, she said, had lost ground to other agencies such as the UNDP and World Bank, which were independently taking the lead in global health with the WHO in a supporting role. As Brown, Cueto and Fee summarized, the WHO "moved from being the unquestioned leader of international health to searching for its place in the contested world of global health."[34]

Nakajima had narrowed the WHO's role to a biomedical one, and in large part because of the WHO's handling of the AIDS crisis, the international community had largely lost faith in the organization to take the lead in global public health matters. This feeling was most dramatically expressed with the creation of UNAIDS, which, as we have seen, pulled the central multilateral responsibility for AIDS out of the WHO. The World Bank started taking the lead in some public health discussions. The Bank's advantage over the WHO was stark: the World Bank Group had an enormous lending portfolio and was devoting it increasingly to public health. The WHO, by contrast, focuses on policy collaboration, global health regulation, international standards, and coordination over direct lending. Resultantly, it can only advance its priorities indirectly through its influence on other actors. The Bank's large budget and willingness to lend concessionally in public health through the IDA (which distributes its development assistance) put it in a strong position to exert its influence.

These realities pressed internal questioning within the agency: What, then, should be the WHO's role? What issues should it prioritize, and why? In particular, what are the WHO's comparative advantages and how could they be more effectively utilized? These central questions guided Nakajima's reformist successor, Gro Harlem Brundtland, who took pains to identify the organization's role and priorities. Under Brundtland the organization developed a narrower focus based on cost-effectiveness and the WHO's comparative advantages. She began her term with the announcement of a "new WHO" and what she called the "100 days of structural change."[35] The program emphasized producing greater results per dollar spent, intervening against diseases with higher burdens, and a general focus on health in the context of economic development. This entailed a major emphasis on the "big three" diseases of malaria, tuberculosis, and AIDS. The WHO assumed the lead role in both Stop TB and Roll Back Malaria, two vertical programs aimed at advocating for and coordinating the responses to their respective diseases of focus. There was also renewed activity toward HIV/AIDS, most prominently through the "3 by 5" initiative, the UN's target for coverage of 3 million people on AIDS medication by 2005.[36] The WHO's increasingly central role in this area suggests that it had, to a degree, seen a return in international confidence.

Brundtland's reconfiguration of the WHO also reflected the general consensus of global health as a development issue. Brundtland said in 2000 that the public health community was "now learning about the true economic impact of disease [and] the potential economic benefits of better health."[37] By this time economism was having a major influence on public health thinking, and affected the WHO's strategy significantly. The prominent liberal economist Jeffrey Sachs chaired the Commission for Macroeconomics and Health, which sought economists' perspectives on health in the context of international development. The committee explored issues including the impact of public health on economic growth, the health impact of trade policies, and ways to improve development assistance. The central conclusion of its report reflected the emerging global health consensus: that there was a reciprocal relationship between health and economic development, and that public health should be central to the development strategy of poor countries.[38] This was a recurrent theme for Brundtland as well. Early in her tenure as director general she argued that the "WHO has to be the vocal force to drive home the message that poverty remains the biggest source of ill-health—and that ill-health in turn breeds poverty." Investing in health, she said, "means investing in a strong economy."[39] In a 2000 address she stressed that "good health can fuel the engine of development and add significant momentum to the forces of economic development and poverty reduction."[40]

Yet restructuring the WHO in the 1990s also meant limiting the focus of its activities. As the global health regime expanded, the priorities of its central organization paradoxically shrank. Even the most broadly mandated of all the agencies involved in public health narrowed its priorities.[41] This passage from Brundtland, from a speech to the executive board, was indicative of the WHO's new direction:

> What is our comparative advantage? Given our mandate and our human and financial resources, what are the functions that WHO is best placed to carry out more effectively than others? How can we shift the balance of our work to focus even more forcefully in areas where our comparative advantage lies? And most importantly, how can we increase the impact of our contribution by engaging a variety of partners who can supplement and complement that contribution?[42]

This reflects the WHO's position in an increasingly dense regime. Where it was previously the undisputed primary global public health forum, it must now define its position (and bureaucratic turf) in relation to other actors. Note also how significantly this narrower approach differed from the WHO's previous articulations of the primary care movement—which had emphasized an expansive, community-oriented approach to health. PHC had challenged the economic status quo, while the reformed WHO acted in deference to it.

Reform at the WHO, in short, meant the adoption of a leaner, more specialized approach to global health. Brundtland initiated a sharp reduction in high-level appointments, and a streamlining of WHO bureaucracy. Fifty programs were reduced to 35, and grouped into nine "clusters."[43] According to the WHO's eleventh work plan—the public document which outlines the agency's long term priorities—the WHO identifies itself as having a unique level of legitimacy in public health. It also has a high degree of ministerial access due to its presence in 150 countries. It runs country offices in close contact with public officials in the developing world. This allows it to be directly involved in national policymaking, giving it a large role in the early stages of policy development.[44] Mainly, the WHO has a biomedical staff and strong technical expertise that make it essential to the operations of other organizations. Its information gathering, policy research, and disease monitoring remain essential to public health operations globally. It has the monitoring capacity that other organizations frequently rely on. The WHO argues that these advantages put it in a strong position to function as a global policy coordinator, to establish partnerships with emergent agencies like UNAIDS and the Global Fund, and to address issues of harmonization.[45] The WHO also has, more than any other organization, the credibility to devise international health guidelines and standards for other actors in global public health to follow.[46]

Stemming from its biomedical credibility, the WHO is also a central public health advocate. Among multilateral institutions, the WHO has played the most prominent role in global advocacy, both for general public health and for specific diseases. The drive to reassert this role—which figured prominently during the tenure of charismatic directors general including Brock Chisholm and Halfdan Mahler—helped spur the election of Brundtland. She had considerable political experience, having previously been prime minister of Norway. Under her tenure the WHO reasserted its position as an advocate for the political and social dimensions of global health, going beyond a biomedical approach. The WHO has since been a central advocate for placing public health on the multilateral agenda.

The WHO's reforms during this period came about amidst unprecedented external pressure. This pressure highlights a perhaps insurmountable conundrum facing agencies across the UN system: how to square virtually unlimited spheres of responsibility with inadequate levels of funding. Expectations on these agencies are drastically expansive, but their funding streams are chronically unreliable. Reform at the WHO reflects this harsh reality. The agency is doing what it can. This agenda threatens to exclude the task of fully taking on the state and corporate forces whose authority shapes the world economic system, and thus the patterns of inequality that underpin global health conditions.

These adaptations to the institutional environment in a regime complex underpin the narrowed set of priorities taken by the WHO during the critical years of the 1980s and 90s. WHO reform during this time correspondingly augurs the dangers confronting international organizations under conditions of regime complexity. Greater competition and constant adjustments underscore the potential for institutional dysfunction. Conditions of regime complexity have nevertheless also created opportunities. Perhaps the most significant WHO undertaking in recent years has been the revisions of the International Health Regulations (IHRs) in 2005, implementing standardized global protocols for reporting potentially transnational epidemics.[47] The decentralization of global health amidst globalization had paradoxically necessitated a stronger regime for global health intervention. The WHO was the primary forum for these negotiations, and it plays a central role in the implementation of the adapted regulations. As an increasingly borderless economy elevates the threat of transnational outbreaks, the WHO thereby retains elevated importance. The reformed IHRs are far reaching, and constitute binding international law. WHO member states (barring those that choose not to take part) are required to report potentially threatening disease outbreaks to the WHO, as well as maintain minimum global standards for surveillance and response capacities. These requirements are broad based but emphasize sinews of globalization such as shipping ports and airports.[48]

As Harman puts it, "the WHO uses international law as a function of global health governance," noting the importance of the 2003 Framework Convention on Tobacco Control (FCTC) as the first binding international law on states negotiated within the WHO.[49] Despite the WHO's lack of hard power and the global influence of tobacco producing multinationals, the FCTC impacted regulations at the state level. These include introducing global standards for advertising (including specific provisions for children), warning labels, product descriptions, taxation, education aimed at reducing consumption, and standards for reducing the exposure of non-tobacco users.[50] (Though as Harman and others have pointed out, there is inevitable variance in state compliance).[51] This introduced a degree of global standardization, and addressed growing global risk factors associated with tobacco use. Again, despite attendant challenges, we see the potential opportunities presented under conditions of decentralized regime complexity. Issues such as tobacco became increasingly embedded in transnational commercial activity, prompting renewed global attention and thereby creating political space for a more active WHO. The growing emphasis on public health in a globalizing world created overlapping spheres of governance, but also created space for a (then struggling) WHO to correspondingly expand its presence in an increasingly dense global legal structure.

The WHO's 2007 *World Health Report*, issued the year the reformed IHRs came into effect, emphasized the need for a revised international regulatory regime to address the challenges of globalization. It contends that, in the twenty-first century, "borders alone" cannot halt the spread of disease.[52] Reflective of the global health imperative embodied in the consensus, the 2007 report sounded the theme of security amidst unprecedented globalization, justifying the IHRs on this basis. "In recent decades," the report argues, "diseases have spread faster than ever before, aided by high-speed travel and trade in goods and services between countries and continents, often during the incubation period before the signs and symptoms of disease are visible."[53] In this context, the WHO argues that the reformed IHRs offer the requisite flexibility for international surveillance and response, requiring states to report even single cases of any disease with the potential to spread globally. Moreover, the IHRs empower the WHO to circumvent official sources, relying when appropriate on non-state actors for information.[54]

As Fidler has argued (see chapter 1), the IHRs constitute recognition of a decentralized, non-hierarchical regime, as well as the attendant importance of globalization as the context for governance. While the WHO has taken a central role in global governance, it nevertheless retains significant constraints, and at times struggles to retain its centrality in a dense regime. Key factors such as the global recession have put significant budgetary pressure on the organization. The WHO's proposed budget for the 2012–2013 cycle is well below that of the previous two budget cycles.[55] Nor has the WHO resolved its continuing reliance on episodic, voluntary contributions, undermining budget coherence. Actual member state assessments for this cycle are projected to cover only 24 percent of the WHO's budget. The remainder will be funded through voluntary contributions, which are subject to the terms and conditions of the contributors, and arguably undermine long-term agenda setting.[56]

The emphasis on globalization also calls attention to the importance of security and economism within the consensus underpinning the rise of global health. While the WHO effectively sounds these themes in conformity with broader trends, it is also a central forum for underrepresented ideas in the larger regime. Under the directorship of Margaret Chan, it has revisited the overarching issues of political, social, and economic inequality which receive less attention given the millennial emphasis on poverty alone. The Commission on the Social Determinants of Health (commissioned under Lee Jong Wook before his passing in 2006) emphasized "closing the gap" in health disparities within a generation. Echoing previous, more expansive discourses on public health, its final report iterates the relevance of economic liberalization's adverse impacts on public health outcomes. One report produced for the commission linked trade liberalization to "specific risks associated with increased economic insecurity, trade in products leading to increased health risks, and loss of tariff revenues that are important for reducing disparities in access to [social determinates of health] in many developing countries."[57] These risks include limitations to health care access, clean water, sanitation, and nutrition among other deleterious effects.[58] While no longer asserting the need for a "new international economic order," the WHO revisited calls for primary care in its 2008 annual report, *Primary Health Care: Now More Than Ever*. The report argues the possibility of achieving universal care in resource poor settings.[59]

The WHO has also expanded its role in global governance to include drug access—a quintessential example of regime overlap, spanning intellectual property, trade, health, and other spheres of transnational activity. Medical products under patent monopoly are broadly inaccessible to resource-poor areas. Profit imperatives also skew research and development toward so-called "Type I" diseases, those which greatly impact the global north, while under serving conditions primarily found in the global south.[60] The WHO's Commission on Public Health, Innovation, and Intellectual Property Rights took up this array of concerns (the ordering of the themes in its title is indicative of its priorities). As the following chapter shows, global activists outside the UN system played a central role in forcing down global pricing for drugs such as antiretrovirals (ARVs) used to treat HIV/AIDS. In this context, the WHO also played a key role in asserting intellectual property and scientific innovation as issues for global health as well as for trade and commerce. The Uruguay trade round, which concluded in 1994 with the creation of the World Trade Organization (WTO) and the Agreement on Trade Related Aspects of Intellectual Property Rights (TRIPS), controversially undercut access to medical production in much of the global south.[61] As had many public health proponents, the commission took a critical stance toward TRIPS. Its report asserted that the effort to create global standards for intellectual property had not served its self-professed function to stimulate innovation in medicine.[62] Indeed it had stifled it. Developing countries such as India, the report noted, had been able to develop robust pharmaceutical manufacturing prior to the new regime's implementation. TRIPS would ultimately require India to end its decades-long tradition of not allowing patents for finished pharmaceutical products, though India was able to take advantage of an extended implementation deadline.[63] Prior to 2005 (which included a transition period after India joined the WTO in 1995), India allowed only patents on process, enabling its own emergent industries to effectively reverse engineer-essential medicines. The emphasis on medicines for diseases affecting developing countries may have declined in the years following WTO entry, favoring instead more profitable research investments in areas affecting affluent populations.[64] Though patent logic has long held that the promise of monopoly rights incentivizes innovation, extensive study under the auspices of the WHO commission found this to be inaccurate in practice. The implementation of TRIPS has generally slowed technological advances in the global south, limited technological diffusion, and further oriented research and development away from diseases affecting the poor.[65]

In sum, the creation of the WTO as the central forum for global trade and intellectual property law was broadly considered a victory for the global north, and a setback for developing countries.[66] It is also worth mentioning that this resulted in the relative decline of the World Intellectual Property Organization, a more democratic forum where southern countries have greater influence—a consequential forum shift.[67] These changes were met with varying degrees of criticism from global activists in the north and south, public health advocates such as the WHO, and developing countries. It was the latter that have pressed loudest to address the problems of TRIPS under the auspices of WTO ministerial meetings. This resulted in the Doha Declaration of 2001, which clarified the circumstances under which developing countries may circumvent patents.[68]

The WHO, for its part, has sought to integrate public health logics into the overlapping regimes of public health and global trade. This includes most prominently its efforts to seek alternatives to excessive patenting, summarized most prominently by the findings in the final report of the WHO Commission on Public Health, Innovation, and Intellectual Property Rights. These proposals include mobilizing international research for neglected diseases through "open source" approaches that enable information sharing rather than closing off collaboration between scientists through competitive patenting.[69] In general, the commission found, governments should take steps to encourage such "networks" and make public investments that finance (or incentivize) technological diffusion to the global south.[70] This initiative culminated with a far reaching World Health Assembly resolution in 2008 calling for a reorientation of pharmaceutical development from excessive patents to one focused on the needs of developing countries. This "global strategy" gives heavy emphasis to technology transfers to the global south. It particularly addresses the need to reach Type II and Type III diseases, those most likely to impact poor areas in isolation, thus facing neglect in drug development.[71] Civil society organizations also played key roles in challenging the patent regime, which we will explore further in the next chapter.

The World Bank and Public Health

The World Bank steadily acquired influence in global health as its lending portfolio in this arena grew. The Bank's influence is tied to its corresponding spending power. The Bank also has a notable place as a Bretton Woods institution closely tied to the United States, which retains significant authority over its direction. The Bank's expanded presence in global health was a major event in the emergence of the regime complex.[72] Its health-related lending portfolio regularly exceeds the WHO's entire budget. Its annual outlays to Health, Nutrition, and Population vary, peaking at $4.2 billion in 2010 and generally increasing over time in the 2000s.[73] While the Bank possesses neither the WHO's biomedical expertise, nor its credibility as a regulatory authority and forum for negotiating global policy standards, the Bank's influence over the broader scheme of development is considerable. Its protocols for promoting economic growth in the world's poorest enclaves impact epidemiological patterns, arguably worsening inequality in health.[74] It has played a central role in promoting austerity, open markets, and privatization in developing countries, prompting specialist Ngaire Woods to deem it a "globalizing" institution.[75]

For these reasons, the World Bank's position as a prominent multilateral actor in public health is surprising for many and filled with tension. For years the organization was seen as hostile to government's role in public health. Harsh austerity measures imposed by the Bank on debtor countries entailed cuts in public health systems, unequal privatization, and increased user fees in poor countries. Indeed this was one of the main reasons for widespread global protest against Bank policies and the Washington Consensus. In this context, public health advocates and experts view the Bank's increased role in public health with skepticism, despite the Bank's role in providing otherwise welcome new resources for health after years of underinvestment.[76] However it too sees its relative prominence in doubt amidst growing regime density. The Bank is resultantly narrowing its focus and becoming more specialized.

The World Bank's involvement in the global public health regime changed the professional makeup of global health. The centrality of the WHO in public health meant that normative trends in this area originated mainly from those with medical backgrounds. The World Bank's rapid entry into the global public health regime meant a greater influence from other disciplines, particularly economics.[77] This was a major factor in the rise of economism in global health, and for the central placement of global public health in international development in the 2000s. Global public health is no longer the domain of medical personnel, as it was during the WHO ascendancy.[78] It is today a much more multifaceted environment, with economists, medical personnel, and social scientists influencing policy. This body of experts forms what Haas calls an epistemic community, whose expertise has a large influence on public policy.[79] As the regime has expanded, so has the range of experts that comprise its personnel. The regime's focus on economism reflects the heightened voice of economists.

The watershed document that signified the Bank's centrality to public health was its 1993 development report, *Investing in Health*. The document relied heavily on recent innovations calculating the global burden of disease in order to identify cost-effective interventions.[80] Poor countries, the Bank argued, should focus on low-cost interventions measured in terms of dollars per life saved. The document called for more funding for public health, but also called for narrowing the scope of interventions toward those that are most cost effective and are directed at the poorest populations. "Public money," the report argued, "is spent on health interventions of low cost-effectiveness, such as surgery for most cancers, at the same time that critical and highly cost-effective interventions, such as treatment of tuberculosis and sexually transmitted diseases (STDs), remain underfunded."[81] The ethical danger is that this focus on cost-effectiveness obviates key health interventions that may be medically necessary, however expensive. The report nevertheless called for trimming down priorities to a narrow focus on issues that meet these criteria. "Only by reducing or eliminating spending on clinical services that are outside the nationally defined essential package," the Bank argued, "can governments concentrate on ensuring essential clinical care for the poor."[82] This precludes public universal health care, because such a system effectively subsidizes middle and upper income groups who could pay for their own services.[83] In any event, the report argued, "government run health systems in many developing countries are overextended and need to be scaled back."[84] The report calls for drastic increases in funding to health, and cost effective reprioritization. There is particular emphasis on resource effectiveness, which can be improved through "increased investment in basic public health measures," while spending for costly measures such as the specialization of medical personnel and tertiary care hospitals should be "reduced or eliminated."[85]

Investing in Health prefigures many of the main components of the public health consensus of the 2000s. Consistent with the emergent consensus, it establishes public health and economic growth as codependent.[86] This represents a break from the Bank's previous ideology which saw economic growth as a precondition for other development goals such as health. The report also argues that funding for global health did not come close to what was needed to address pressing needs, including the HIV/AIDS crisis which expanded rapidly during this period.[87] Yet even as it called for an expanded response, it also called for a narrowed approach to public health in which governments limit their focus to a reduced number of priority issues.

The report offers tepid assent to the World Health Assembly's Alma Ata declaration of "health for all" by 2000.[88] Yet it clearly marked a shift away from the primary health care movement. The Alma Ata declaration had called for a broader based, horizontal approach to public health, and established access to primary health care as a basic human right. While partially addressing these values, *Investing in Health* put a greater emphasis on economism and cost-effective prioritization. The report also reflects the growing influence of economists in the formulation of public health approaches. While the WHO had partnered with the World Bank in producing *Investing in Health*, the report is a departure from its old primary care ideas in favor of the Bank's economics-based approach.

The influence of *Investing in Health* should not be understated. For instance, the document appears to have directly inspired Bill Gates to emphasize health during the formative years of the Bill and Melinda Gates Foundation. Particularly appealing for Gates were the report's themes of cost-effective, technology driven innovations that could produce quantifiable results.[89] More broadly, the document signified the changes that had occurred in the elite thinking on global health, and serves as a manifesto for the consensus tenet of economism. That economism, with its predications on the sheer rational efficiency of resources, would come to dominate the global public health regime is hardly surprising given the prevailing world economic system emphasizing neoliberalism. In the neoliberal context, economism offers a high degree of mainstream compatibility given its underlying motive of making markets work by improving the health of the productive population. The leading institutions that have most forcefully pushed for economic approaches to global health—particularly the World Bank and Bill and Melinda Gates Foundation—have also promoted and profited from neoliberal policies. The main characteristics of economism are generally consistent with the global economy's dominant market-based logics.

Additionally, in line with *Investing in Health*, "cost-effectiveness" has been a standard mantra emphasized most forcefully by the World Bank since the 1980s, wending its way through major development agreements such as 2005's Paris Declaration and its follow-up, 2008's Accra Agenda for Action.[90] Not only must the global actors commit greater volumes of funding (a consensus at least until the global recession cast a pall over agreed-upon targets), they must produce benchmark results intended to prove these funds are applied effectively. With equally great significance, public health resources must address development challenges, taking steps to increase productivity while lessening economic burdens on growth brought on by epidemics. The economic logic fostered the emergence of the World Bank's burden of disease studies, including the landmark DALY measure for identifying geographic need, thus providing a state-of-the-art quantitative measure for the allocation of aid to health. But the DALY system also drew criticism for assigning greater values to healthy life years lost during the most fiscally productive working-age adult years in the human lifecycle.[91] In this way, the World Bank and WHO resultantly face criticism for subordinating the interests of health to those of economic growth.

The Bank, for its part, has had to respond to criticism surrounding its structural adjustment focus. This is particularly the case in areas hard hit by epidemics, but which nevertheless pursued austerity in accordance with World Bank recommendations.[92] In 1995, two years after the publication of *Investing in Health*, James Wolfensohn assumed his ten-year presidency of the World Bank. It was a watershed presidency that marked tectonic shifts away from the era of structural adjustment and a softening of previous stances, while retaining persistent criticisms for its continued neoliberal emphasis. Key figures during this time included Richard

Feachem, who as Director for Health, Nutrition and Population backed away from the structural adjustment theme in favor of sustainable development.[93] Chief economist Joseph Stiglitz had during this time directly criticized the central tenets of the Washington Consensus approach. For Stiglitz, poverty reduction included, when necessary, capital controls, social safety nets, political empowerment for the poor, as well as their input in development matters. Austerity and market integration alone could not reduce poverty, and even invited harmful effects.[94] While the Bank has never fully adopted the largely Keynesian perspective of Stiglitz, it did effectively shift away from the structural adjustment era during this time, in pursuit of a "post-Washington Consensus." It shed the language of structural adjustment for the much less controversial one of poverty reduction. Sophie Harman identifies a "soft politics" of intervention in a reformed bank, promoting "sector-wide" strategies that eschew vertical intervention for more holistic approaches, while integrating community and state input.[95] This approach is incorporated into the country level Poverty Reduction Strategy Papers (PRSPs). The PRSPs, initiated in 1999, are ostensibly intended to develop country-wide development strategies with local input while improving resource coordination. They also give Bank programming a collaborative veneer. This is intended to address a key problem with the Bank's approach: initiating policy by way of debt conditionality with little democratic input. But it is not without its critics. For Harman, the Bank continues to retain inordinate power over developing countries, with the Bank as "benevolent leader" alongside communities and client states. The latter must internalize the principles of liberal economism—or face blame in an environment nominally based on partnership.[96]

Despite its influence, the World Bank has not been immune to the pressures of emergent network density. The increasing complexity of the regime has forced it to define its own domains within global public health. These pressures, the overarching drive to reduce overlap, and the Bank's own economic approach to public health, have combined to influence how its development assistance is channeled. The World Bank Group distributes development assistance through the IDA, its concessional lending fund, which is replenished every three years.[97] The IDA's disbursements are large and thus potentially diverse. However, as figure 3.3 shows, it remains specialized. Historically, the Bank has prioritized mainly water sanitation and health infrastructure, reflecting its specialization in the big-ticket infrastructural projects that it is known for (and which are often criticized for their industrial-scale, top-down implemen-

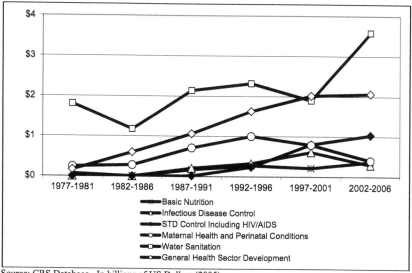

Source: CRS Database. In billions of US Dollars (2005).

Figure 3.3. World Bank Health ODA to Major Issue Areas

tation). HIV/AIDS shows notable increases in the 2000s. However, with the US and multilateral agencies such as the Global Fund addressing this issue, the Bank's traditional areas of focus have persisted. Funding for water sanitation projects grew faster than did HIV/AIDS during this period. Despite US dominance within the Bank, the United States did not recreate its domestic priorities in IDA disbursements. Instead, the Bank appears to be continuing with its own unique specializations. This has been coupled with noticeable decreases in funds for maternal health, during the period from 2002 to 2006. Infectious disease control also saw steady declines during this period, while nutritional assistance remained low.

While the World Bank enjoys a leading position, it too has had to adapt to growing competition, and deal with the issues of harmonization and overlap. The question of emerging regime density has been the focus of official discussion at the Bank. A 2007 report on Health, Nutrition and Population priorities lamented that "[t]en years ago, the Bank was the main financier of HNP. Today, in addition to the Bank, new multilateral organizations, initiatives, and foundations have assumed a prominent role in financing HNP, among them the Global Fund, GAVI, GAIN, and the Bill and Melinda Gates Foundation."[98] The report noted that the number of vertical bilateral programs had also increased greatly, threatening to crowd out other issues such as nutrition. As is typical in these times of regime expansion, this report reflects pressure on the Bank to produce ground level results. This means better coordination and the reduction of overlap.

Consistent with the consensus on aid prioritization, it has sought to address these concerns through specialization. Reflecting the agendas of other actors, the Bank has called for a "selective and disciplined framework" in aid prioritization.[99] Where the WHO provides medical expertise, the World Bank has sought to utilize its capacity in economics and financing. In the Bank's view, its presence in developing countries gives it an intimate knowledge of local economies and systems.[100] The Bank planned to serve these economic functions in health systems development while other organizations such as the WHO address the biomedical aspects of development. Also, amidst the rapid verticalization of the regime, the World Bank has sought to sustain its position by providing general health systems financing. Expanding and improving the quality of local health sectors, the Bank argues, will enhance local capacities to handle the influx of new vertical funds.[101] The Bank sees its longstanding work in health systems design and development (articulated most famously in *Investing in Health*) as its area of technical expertise through which it contributes to the global division of labor.

The Bank's most recent IDA replenishment report (these reports are intended to outline the fund's priorities over three year periods) stresses the reduction of overlap amidst increasing regime density. The report contended that, given the influx of vertical aid, "the IDA can support the integration of horizontal and vertical aid by providing a 'horizontal platform' upon which the vertical funds . . . can operate effectively and mitigate the risks associated with vertical aid."[102] IDA 13 (which signified the thirteenth cycle of replenishment, in 2002) was significant because it called for a consolidation of the IDA's activities in a manner consistent with the emerging consensus. The report, which reflects the debates and agreements among creditor members, contended that the "IDA needs to identify more precisely what it can (and cannot) commit to do, based on countries' needs and absorptive capacity and on IDA's comparative advantage."[103] During this period the IDA narrowed its mandate more closely around its areas of expertise in development capacity and infrastructure building. IDA 13 also utilizes the Millennium Development Goals for measuring the results of the IDA's activity, underscoring the importance of the goals since their adoption in 2000.

Much of the philosophy outlined in *Investing in Health* persists. The Bank's approach reflects the consensus belief in the interconnectedness between economic development and health. The Bank was also instrumental in reprioritizing public health in terms of low cost interventions intended to increase productivity and spur development. It is also important to note that the Bank's expanded contributions to public health have come not in the name of public health itself, but under the rubric of poverty reduction. Previously the Bank saw health as something that follows robust growth. Public health now prefigures growth because of its ability to spur economic expansion through increased productivity. This is the Bank's contemporary philosophy as well as a central part of the public health consensus.

Another key factor in the Bank's approach has been its efforts to cope with growing competition. Virtually all three-year replenishments have come during a denser environment than the last. They stress reducing transaction costs, enhancing harmonization, and producing more narrowly focused (albeit consecutively larger) budget plans. The IDA

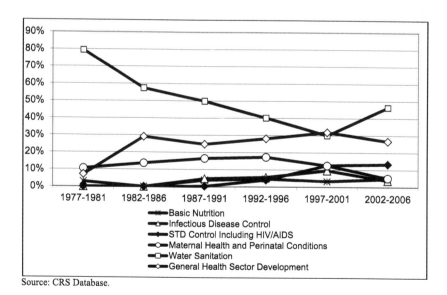

Source: CRS Database.

Figure 3.4. World Bank Health ODA to Major Issue Areas by Percentage Share

has even voiced support for taking on secondary roles in areas that are not in their sphere of expertise. These measures suggest the recognition of a relative decline in the Bank's position, not to any single agency but to a growing, decentralizing regime that increasingly lacks a center. The World Bank contributed to increased regime density by entering into the global health fray. It too is feeling competition's effects. In short, the major trends identified in this book are prevalent in this case, including the Bank's general support for the global health consensus, pressure from multilateral competitors, increased overall aid, and narrowing specialization. With equal importance, the World Bank greatly influenced the ideological blueprint for development consensus.

The UNDP's Supporting and Conflicting Role

The UNDP has at times found itself at odds with the WHO, particularly during the onset of the HIV/AIDS crisis. It has also had to triangulate its position between the WHO and World Bank in public health, establishing a unique role that separates it from the other two agencies. The UNDP underwent of period of financial strain after the Cold War, a period in which the UN system struggled to redefine itself. The UNDP does not have the sizeable resources of the Bank, and so has had to settle for a secondary role in the provision of direct assistance. Its influence is therefore dramatically different from that of the Bank, despite their overlapping issue spheres. Where the Bank has leveraged its financial resources to shape public health strategies at the national level, the UNDP has been influential in the realm of ideas. The ideational shift toward human development, for example, was largely articulated under its auspices, and it is currently influential in measuring human progress in its ongoing development index. Additionally it remains instrumental in monitoring progress on the Millennium Development Goals. In this regard it has taken on roles that arguably would have been the WHO's had that agency not diminished in stature during the 1990s. This was the case regarding HIV/AIDS, when the two organizations came into direct conflict. UNDP personnel were critical of what they saw as the WHO's biomedical approach to the disease. The WHO leadership by contrast was resentful over the UNDP's encroachments on its bureaucratic turf in the area of diseases.

The UNDP has nevertheless struggled to define its role while contending with limited funding. Even so, it has gradually made public health a central component of its development agenda. Within the context of overlapping governance areas in a regime complex, the UNDP's emphasis on human development has made it an influential forum. It functions as a central advocate for world poverty relief. It is also a major purveyor of health as a development issue—particularly as it took the lead in shaping the Millennium Goals. In defining its role, the UNDP has had to address two central questions posed by the consensus: What can this organization do more effectively than others? What gap can it fill in the global division of labor? As a central presence in the global south (and one more likely to be trusted there than the Bank) the UNDP has also played a central role in efforts to streamline the channeling of ODA. Its activities also emphasize more efficient spending and cost-effective measures. This movement characterized the reorganization period under its reformist administrator Mark Malloch Brown.

The HIV/AIDS debate in the early 1990s exposed significant differences within the UN system over what approach these organizations should take. The WHO by this time had retreated from the multisectoral, human rights-oriented response practiced during Mann's tenure as head of the GPA. There was vocal criticism from other actors in the UN system who lamented the WHO's narrower, biomedical approach to AIDS. The UNDP began addressing the issue independently of the GPA. It criticized the WHO for not pushing for a broader response that emphasized the disease's political, social and developmental components. The UNDP, for its part, was visceral in its critiques of the GPA and WHO. In particular, Elizabeth Reid, the formidable founder of the UNDP's HIV and Development Program, was critical of the GPA for its narrow approach to AIDS. At times during this period, officials within these organizations were reportedly not on direct speaking terms, forced instead to rely on intermediaries.[104]

The UNDP was well-positioned to take a central role on AIDS as the UN system came to embrace human rights oriented, multi-sectoral measures. Its position relative to HIV/AIDS was also strengthened by its political legitimacy in the developing world. This legitimacy has been aided by its often independent positions, which included skepticism of the World Bank's structural adjustment policies. It is also helped by its deep connections with developing states and NGOs. As Craig N. Murphy, a leading UNDP scholar (and the organization's official historian) argues, this was an area in which "UNDP could do something that others really could not do."[105] For Murphy, the centrality of HIV/AIDS to development afforded the UNDP the opportunity to fund an important niche in the global division of labor. "The UNDP," he contends, "does not have the medical expertise of the WHO or the knowledge of reproductive health issues of the UN Population Fund, but it has the *combination* of connections with policymakers, nationally and regionally, and with potentially concerned NGOs that some other relevant members of the UN family do not have"[106] (emphasis his). This, Murphy argues, enables the UNDP to specialize in capacity building, enabling governments to address disease, and to engage in normative advocacy in the context of poverty relief.

During the 1990s the UNDP subsumed global health activities that might have been done by the WHO, and partnered with the WHO on others. The organization gained turf in global health within the UN system, but nonetheless faced significant pressures. After the Cold War, funding for the UNDP stagnated, and it found itself in decline relative to the World Bank. The Bank, by virtue of its large resources and lending portfolio, overshadowed the troubled UN system. In short, as Murphy phrased it, there was a "shrinking development assistance pie," and the UNDP received "a shrinking proportion of it."[107] The UNDP has had to carve out a role that is complementary to the major engines of development assistance like the United States and the World Bank. It bases its prioritization on its agenda setting power rather than spending power. The UNDP has had to make do with notoriously squeezed budgets, with success measured by how creatively it can maximize institutional legitimacy, giving it a kind of soft power. This power is nevertheless significant. The UNDP, for instance, was able to carve out a central role for itself in shaping the Millennium Declaration. More than any other document the Declaration defines how the international community measures economic progress.

Mark Malloch Brown assumed the administrator position during the UN's post-Cold War period of uncertainty and took on the role of reformer. As with the WHO's Gro Harlem Brundtland, Malloch Brown had to reassert his organization's relevance amidst potentially unyielding financial weakness. It is worth pointing out the similarities between his approach and Brundtland's (in fact, Brown consulted Brundtland). Brown's approach focused on maximizing resources. This entailed shrinking the UNDP bureaucracy and narrowing the agency's central functions. Malloch Brown's UNDP, like Brundtland's WHO, stressed a corporate atmosphere. Malloch Brown's plan called for a 25 percent staff reduction and a 15 percent cut in field office budgets.[108] It placed greater emphasis on producing ground-level results, retraining staff for field work, reducing favoritism, limiting job security, and increasing transparency within the agency.

The UNDP is still a major figure in international development even with its financial strain. It has influence over aid allocations because of its presence in developing countries and its role in devising local development strategies. It also has influence at a macro level. Despite hostility from then-US ambassador John Bolton, it was Malloch Brown who accepted official responsibility for reporting progress on the Millennium Goals, strengthening the agency's position. Today they figure heavily into the UNDP's annual human development reports. An innovation of the ground breaking economist Mahbub ul Haq beginning in 1990, these reports are informed by the concept of human development as opposed to structural adjustment (see chapter 5).[109] For ul Haq and his collaborators, they represented a departure from the market efficiencies of neoliberalism toward values of personal empowerment. Nevertheless it may be argued that the UNDP's activities have come to include key components of economic rationalism despite its traditionally holistic approach to development. The UNDP increasingly favors an expanded response to confronting disease based on low cost interventions and harmonization. This in practice means leading the movement to reduce overlap in aid programs, in addition to continued advocacy for greater aid volumes. In addition to pressing for more aid, contemporary advocacy has shifted toward the axiom of making aid work, including meeting quantifiable benchmarks set by the global north.

Increasing regime density is of great concern to experts within the UNDP for practical reasons: the agency surmises that with a drastic proliferation in aid channels comes major inefficiencies. First, aid in a dense regime is difficult to coordinate, resulting in overlap. Second, the proliferation of aid channels creates even greater problems for recipient states. These governments must devote an enormous amount of time and resources to the bureaucratic processes of each respective channel. There is the fear that the global public health regime will grow more inefficient as it grows larger. Increasing density also raises political concerns, because the organization itself has to define its own role amidst institutional crowding. While the UNDP has spent decades courting creditor states and multilateral institutions to become more involved in global development, the fact that many have done so has partially subsumed it. "What do you do," asked Malloch Brown, "when you have done such a good job of persuading others that you have the right ideas that they are doing them as well now, and on a much bigger scale with a lot more resources?"[110]

Lacking the deep pockets of the World Bank, the UNDP cannot assert its influence through development assistance and hope to have a valued, distinguished role as a miniature version of the big aid distributors. Instead it has sought to play an advisory role in developing countries. The UNDP takes advantage of its close relationships with global south governments. It also has a historic willingness (especially relative to the Bank) to take into account the ideas and interests of actors in the global south. This also makes the UNDP a central figure in the aid harmonization movement. The UNDP assists governments in navigating an increasingly dense public health network. As the central UN agency for international development, the UNDP is heavily responsible for coordinating UN work.[111] The UNDP sees an advantage in this area because its role in development is the most multifaceted among UN agencies involved in public health. The UNDP has the most extensive background in addressing the political, social, and multi-sectoral aspects of development. By comparison the World Bank focuses on the economic and financial components of public health, and the WHO emphasizes its biomedical components.[112]

The UNDP provides services to local governments that are designed to make progress on the Millennium Goals but are also tailored to in-country needs. The agency has deliberately sought to present its policies as client friendly. This way it distinguishes itself from the Bank's unpopular "one size fits all" policies. Normative advocacy is the second part of its approach. The UNDP has sought to foster a normative consensus in which improved standards of living and democratization are basic human rights. It has actively sought to institutionalize this notion within the UN's development apparatus. This is apparent with its role as the central advocate for the Millennium Declaration. It is also worth reiterating that the Declaration heavily reflects the consensus with its emphasis on vertical, low cost interventions, and the reciprocal relationship between health and wealth.

Among our cases it appears that the UNDP has much in common with the World Bank. Like the Bank, the UNDP is focused on poverty alleviation, albeit with a more political, social, and human rights-oriented approach. If we look at the recent history of the Bank we can see a transformation in the UNDP's direction. The Bank has become more attuned to issues other than growth, taking the more holistic approach that has been a hallmark of the UNDP. The Bank appears to have come to the realization that lifting countries out of poverty requires direct injections of ODA rather than a pure reliance on systemic reform and market forces. There is the implicit understanding, at long last, that decades of Washington Consensus policies predicated on reducing the public sector did not produce the promised results, that poverty is a market failure rather than a failure of the state, or of the poor themselves. This odd convergence has made these two organizations superficially more alike. With equal importance, the discourse of the UNDP began to look more like that of the Bank, putting greater emphasis on economism. The UNDP is now calling for more cost-effective approaches to development as the Bank had long ago advocated. According to the 2003 *Human Development Report*, there should be an emphasis on select "priority countries."[113] The report also argues that a failure to invest in global health will cause "economic growth to eventually peter out because of an insufficient number of healthy, skilled workers."[114] The report, reflecting the influence of guest editor Jeffrey Sachs, contends that investments in health are needed to spur countries out of "poverty traps." Such traps happen when regions are too poor to invest in human development, while a lack of human development inhibits growth. The report ultimately contends that only growth can sustain rapid gains in health.[115]

It is historically unusual for these two organizations to advance such convergent messages. The World Bank has traditionally emphasized growth and free markets over and above human development issues. The UNDP, by contrast, has traditionally represented a more global south-friendly set of ideas. This reflects their natural constituencies. The governance structure of the World Bank is dominated by the interests of wealthy aid distributors, particularly the United States.[116] The UNDP (in addition to the same pressures from wealthy countries) is answerable to developing state governments that it partners with in ways that the Bank is not.[117] This has traditionally meant stark differences between the two organizations when it comes to global health. The Bank had pushed for cuts in many clients' health programs while AIDS grew worse. The UNDP by contrast, led by Elizabeth Reid, pressured the international community (and the WHO) for a multi-sectoral, humanitarian response.

In this ideational sense the organizations appear to have grown closer, but in other respects they differ greatly. The World Bank provides large sums of development assistance. The UNDP functions as a facilitator, pushing for aid harmonization. It is also a central figure in the role of ideas, advancing global health in the context of social development and human rights. In this respect, the role played by the UNDP bears more similarity to that of the WHO. It seeks to influence the behavior of other actors through coordination and advocacy. To do so it utilizes its technical and moral authority. The UNDP possesses technical authority by virtue of its large and specialized bureaucracies of experts, and moral authority based on its perceived legitimacy relative to large global north powers whose credibility is often suspect in the developing world. In this way its strengths are comparable to the WHO's. This closeness explains why the UNDP and WHO have at times found themselves in direct competition over resources, as they were when major creditors scaled up the HIV/AIDS response. It also revives the chronic conundrum of high expectations in UN agencies, despite relatively few resources and massive constraints imposed by powerful states.

The European Union: Specialization and Conformity

The European Union is the world's largest overall distributor of development assistance when counting bilateral channels from member states. The multilateral organization itself has become a cooperative interface through which member states advance their aid preferences, just as it has advanced European interests in other spheres. Multilateral funding from the European Union by itself accounted for 10 percent of world aid in 2000, making it the world's fourth largest aid distributor.[118] In the area of global health, the European Union takes a highly specialized approach, both geographically and in terms of issue prioritization. Its overall allocation to health has increased significantly, rising from $864 million in 2000 to nearly $1.3 billion in 2006. Patterns of aid distribution shown in figures 3.5 and 3.6 clearly reflect what can be called a distinctly European pattern of aid to health among advanced countries. As with most large creditors in the European Union, the largest categories of aid are in water sanitation and health infrastructure. All other categories receive relatively modest attention. Clearly the European Union has taken an alternative path to the North American DAC members—most prominently the United States—which alternatively emerged as the major specializers in HIV/AIDS. Much has been made, as we saw in chapter 1, of the dramatic rise of HIV/AIDS as a priority in global health. But as a closer inspection of the data shows, these dramatic increases were led by the United States, not the European Union. Direct contributions to HIV/AIDS remained small throughout the 2000s. HIV/AIDS saw moder-

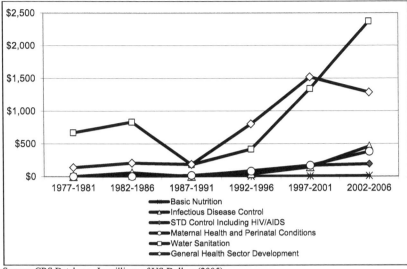

Source: CRS Database. In millions of US Dollars (2005).

Figure 3.5. European Union Health ODA to Major Issue Areas

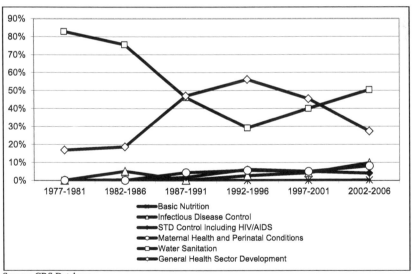

Source: CRS Database.

Figure 3.6. European Union Health ODA to Major Issue Areas by Percentage Share

ate increases in European Union aid from the period between 2002 and 2006, as did maternal health funding and infectious disease control. In all, though, these categories combined for less than $500 million during a period in which water sanitation funding alone approached $2.5 billion. EU members, through both bilateral and multilateral channels, have assumed roles distinct from that of the United States.

The European Union is also geographically specialized to an unusual degree that reflects its strong member state influence. Major powers including the UK, France, and Germany exert a large influence over its funding, and in general maintain strong influences over the multilateral organization's priorities. Where scholars generally see multilaterals as "good" distributors of development assistance, and their bilateral counterparts as self-interested, discussion is mixed on the European Union. "The EU, as a major multilateral donor, is perhaps less partisan than major bilateral donors (the USA and France, for example)," Frederick Nixson contends, "but the geographical distribution of its aid nevertheless reflects its perceptions of regional and global interests."[119]

Much of this line of criticism stems from its geographic specialization, which focuses on former colonies. This was enshrined in the Cotonou agreement, which reaffirmed development and trade cooperation between the European Union and the former colonies that comprise the Africa, Pacific and Caribbean (ACP) group of states. This arrangement arguably conflicts with a clear poverty focus, emphasizing established relationships between the European powers and their former colonies instead of international development needs. As Stephen Dearden points out, the agreement excludes deeply impoverished Bangladesh, for instance.[120] These geographic specializations can also be viewed in a post-colonial context, arguing that foreign aid patterns represent a broader effort to retain influence and dependency over subordinate former colonial states. It has been argued, conversely, that EU member states' knowledge of these countries gives them a geographic comparative advantage among ACP partners, as former colonial powers often claim. This gives rise to an attendant controversy in the global aid program generally: to what extent does the supposed generosity of international "donors" perpetuate rather than resolve longstanding north-south power imbalances? The European Union, after all, is a global economic power that strives to advance its member states' interests, which clearly do not conform to those of the south on trade matters. In trade negotiations it has significant advantages over many of the European nations' former colonies in the south, including the ability to leverage its vast economic markets through well financed and organized delegations to key forums such as the WTO. Like the United States, the European Union is the site of a large pharmaceutical industry that influences its perspectives within trading arenas. It has resultantly taken a traditionally expansive view of intellectual property rights. In the official language of the EU Commission in 1998, "No priority should be given to health over intellectual property rights," a position that brought with it persistent international pressure to conform to emergent right to health norms.[121]

EU trading preferences toward developing countries are embedded in the language of the Cotonou Agreement. The agreement heavily emphasizes development and human rights, although its deepest implications arguably involve competitive free trade. Breaking precedent from previous agreements between the ACP and European powers, the agreement institutes increasingly "reciprocal" trade principles. This rolls back preferential trading norms favoring developing countries, enabling the European Union to export goods duty free to some ACP countries.[122] The overall contribution to development promises to be ambiguous at best. For example, while the agreement emphasizes strategies to assist farmers in developing countries, it does not curb crippling EU farm subsidies known to displace rural smallholders.[123] The program similarly promises to help scale up HIV/AIDS treatment, but without removing persistent patent restrictions on the latest medicines. In fact the agreement reaffirms the TRIPS patent protection regime which severely limits technology transfers to the global south.[124] As poor working conditions threaten health, the agreement also places restrictions on labor standards thought to be used "for protectionist purposes."[125] This is consistent with the EU's role in global trade negotiations generally, using its formidable power within the WTO to influence outcomes on patent protections, labor standards and other key trade issues that are potentially harmful to health outcomes in the global south.

It is important to understand the EU's developmental role in this context. At the same time the European Union has vocally supported and at times led the development consensus. In 2005 the European Union issued a policy statement called the "European Consensus" that was reflective of the broader global agenda in key ways. The document makes global health central to Europe's development agenda, using the Millennium Goals as benchmarks. It sets a timetable for achieving the Monterrey targets, pledging aid amounts totaling 0.56 percent of GNI by

2010 (for which most large European countries fell short). It also calls for prioritizing the poorest countries. The European consensus devotes considerable attention to promoting aid effectiveness through specialization. Adopting much of the language of the Paris Declaration, the document calls for reducing transaction costs in aid and improving aid harmonization. Aid coming from the Commission itself, the document pledges, must be done in a way that complements other actors (particularly EU member states) based on technical expertise and institutional value-added. It also offers thinly veiled concern over the proliferation of vertical agencies, calling for greater institutionalization of these organizations within the national budgets of recipient states.[126]

There have been forceful calls for conformity with the Paris Declaration on Aid Effectiveness, and its follow-up, the Accra agenda. Indeed, this by itself is a relative advantage of EU multilateral aid as the global public health network grows denser. Dearden offers speculation on the ability of the European Union to streamline the aid distribution process:

> As a multilateral aid mechanism, the EU should be able to offer a number of significant advantages in achieving global poverty reduction over bilateral programs. It should be able to avoid unnecessary duplication of assistance, including the administrative burden on recipient governments and it should yield economies of scale in administration and the benefits of untied aid.[127]

In theory, then, multilateral EU aid should cut down on the inefficiency problems facing the global public health regime. The EU's aid policies, however, suggest a more complicated picture. It has positioned itself as a potential answer to the streamlining challenges raised by the global health consensus. It has also prioritized based on technological and geographic knowledge that is unique to Europe.

Correspondingly the European Union is deeply embedded in broader global standards for effectiveness. Its reports in these areas use the goals outlined in the Paris Declaration as benchmarks. The commission contends that too many EU states are "still present in too many countries, with too many projects with limited impact."[128] It is active in promoting a global division of labor among its member states. Even as aid increases, there is a movement among member states and the European Union itself to target this aid more narrowly. The European

Union is narrowing its number of recipients (usually those with ties to Europe) as well as the number of issues it addresses. This has been at the forefront of EU thinking on development assistance in this decade. The EU's Code of Conduct of Complementarity and Division of Labor codifies these consensus principles among European states.[129] "Division of labor," the European Commission's development administration argues, "may mean countries and aid sectors have to be abandoned in the name of aid efficiency."[130] Thus far the priorities of the European Union and its member states have been pared down significantly. The European Union reports that most of its member states concentrate in three or fewer sectors, largely corroborated in the disaggregated data presented in this book.[131] Larger shares of European aid are going to priority countries, and major member states are reducing the quantity of priority states. Germany, the European Union's largest bilateral actor, has reduced its number of priority states from 118 at the beginning of the decade, to 57.[132]

A primary role for the commission in this decade has been to promote specialization within its own member states. European Union policy includes compulsory assessments of comparative advantages on the part of member states. Europe's strategy for aid calls for taking into account "the significant differences between EU donors."[133] It envisions a "tool kit" approach to aid that reflects a division of labor based on comparative advantages.[134] The commission encourages a twofold approach to establishing specialties. Specialization, it contends, should derive from a state's own domestic experience and expertise. Second, specialization should also be geographic, based on knowledge of recipient state systems. This is key from the vantage point of the European Union, because of the post-colonial relationships maintained between European states and their former colonies. This would support the contention that Europe seeks to maintain influence over former colonies, and has correspondingly taken great interest in these countries' development trajectories.

With its role as a major promoter of aid harmonization, the European Union has also been outwardly critical of verticalization and has called for slowing the increase of regime density. It is currently working on guidelines to assess the added value of new vertical programs and to slow the increased costs (through issues such as additional overhead and recipient state burden) associated with these programs.[135] The European Union states its position concisely on the matter of the regime's verticalization: "[T]hey need to be fully integrated into the Paris agenda and into the discussions on division of labor."[136] For its part, the Commission sees its ability to streamline aid as a comparative advantage in itself. It also has the ability to draw upon the technical expertise of a diverse array of technologically advanced member states.

~

While the consensus calls for ever increasing funding for global health, it also marks a departure from the Alma Ata declaration of "health for all," calling instead for narrowly focused health interventions designed to spur development, and for global north rather than global south leadership. With the consensus, the sphere of debate has narrowed, and systemic reform is off limits, even in a time of global economic crisis. Prevailing market ideology informs this emergent consensus. As we will see in the next chapter, the age of neoliberalism serves as the context for another significant change: the privatization of the global health effort through NGOs, philanthropic foundations, and public-private partnerships—a development that gives rise to a complex series of challenges and opportunities.

CHAPTER 4

Non-State Actors

Community Engagement and Privatized Specialization

Non-state actors are playing increasingly important roles in the global health regime. Though figures vary, sheer numbers illustrate this change. By one count, there are 60,000 NGOs committed to the AIDS epidemic alone, with even more committed to global health generally.[1] Public health also attracts a great deal of attention among private philanthropic foundations. The Foundation Center cites health as the leading overall recipient category for US foundations, accounting for nearly $6.9 billion in 2011, out of a total philanthropic largess approximating $24.6 billion. This makes health the leading category of philanthropic donations domestically in the United States.[2] A wide range of non-state actors are rapidly gaining in scale and enmeshment in the regime complex for global health. Globalization under these conditions has correspondingly reshaped their own traditional activities. The term "non-state" itself is expansive, therein containing an array of differentiated actor-types and logics of action, alongside an equally vast series of real-world conflicts and challenges. Yet, tellingly, they are increasingly called upon to assume a degree of complementarity in the arena of global health, at minimum avoiding harmful activities. More ambitiously, they are enlisted in formal cooperation through "public-private partnerships" and other forms of direct engagement. While it is not the ambition of this chapter to provide a comprehensive typology for non-state actors, it does explore three key areas: civil society organizations (CSOs) engaged in community activism, large private foundations, and public-private partnerships (PPP). This chapter is particularly concerned with how these actors

117

interact within the chessboard of a regime complex. By extension this chapter seeks to articulate the problems and prospects of a global health regime whose public spheres are increasingly impacted by private, independent decision making.

The very complexity of this constellation of actors challenges our powers of description. Given the community orientation and public accountability inherent in many civil society organizations, it is difficult to universally deploy the term "private" to describe them. Indeed many non-state actors emerge from what their memberships would deem participatory public action in the political processes shaping health policy. Even guarded philanthropic foundations have to a great extent entered public policy spheres. However, they do so with clearly different standards of transparency and accountability, and little appetite for opening up their activities to any form of public control. Much of the expansion of non-state activity coincides with the broader movement to "privatize" governance in a post-Keynesian era of anti-statism. On the other side of the spectrum, for-profit multinational corporations have impacted global health in myriad ways, including but not limited to access to medicines, labor conditions, and environmental footprints. They also play direct and formal roles in global governance, often in partnership with nonprofit sectors.

In sum, non-state actors are a major part of what makes global health a regime complex in the first place. Fidler sees them as central to the "unstructured plurality" that has replaced a regime centered on state actors and their traditional multilateral forums for global governance. He contends that governing spheres in health are increasingly accessible to actors lacking the imprimatur of the state.[3] This has contributed greatly to the decentralization of the regime, spawning powerful, independent actors with prerogatives beyond state control. By this logic any notion of centralized global priority-setting is a thing of the past in modern global governance. As Fidler candidly asserts, "The Gates Foundation will no more march to the tune of the WHO than the United States will to the cadence of the UN."[4] This makes the harmonization of global activities in any formal way unlikely despite, as we have seen, so many commitments among actors to do so. However there is important evidence of informal complementarity in the activities of private foundations.

In this light, perhaps one of most unprecedented developments in global health has been the scaling up of large private foundations. This has given them the designation of so-called non-traditional aid distributors, assuming equivalency with major state-based actors in key ways. It has also made them a recognized force in global health governance, which can hardly be ignored by state and multilateral organizations. Private trusts endowed by billionaires such as Bill Gates, Warren Buffet, and George Soros have fueled this trend. The Bill and Melinda Gates Foundation, by far the world's largest private distributor of development assistance to health, now has an aid outflow that is larger than that of most OECD states. The Gates Foundation, furthermore, has made global health its leading priority, an emphasis that is reflective of the millennial development consensus. Despite their vast dispersal, there is significant evidence that they too are moving in the direction of specialization. They also reflect the same forces that operate across all actors in the regime. The health-conscious approach to economic growth has pervaded non-governmental as well as governmental thinking.

What the rise of non-state actors also reveals is a regime increasingly reliant on privatized governance, predicated on notions of private sector efficiency. Much of the surge in their growth came in the 1980s and early 1990s, during the simultaneous emergence of anti-statist ideology in the global economy.[5] Private effort, according to the anti-statist argument, could address development tasks with greater efficiency. As financing for multilateral institutions like the WHO and UNDP declined, non-state actors and public-private partnerships proliferated, filling gaps left by diminishing development assistance as the Cold War ended. These trends invite controversy. Northern-funded NGOs often subsume the responsibilities of southern governments, creating a paternal power structure with little transparency or accountability to the citizens of recipient countries. Priorities in these cases often reflect the interests and knowledge of foreign entities. Critics charge that NGOs' efforts to distribute services themselves, rather than building state capacity to do so, undermines the sustainability of aid. The proliferation of NGOs, they charge, circumvents the traditional social contract in favor of the private provision of services called for by the era's ascendant neoliberalism.

This has led to great controversy over coordination and the managerial burdens placed on recipient governments. "In fact," argues Laurie Garrett, "ministers of health in poor countries now express frustration over their inability to track the operations of foreign organizations operating on their soil, ensure that those organizations are delivering services in sync with government policies and priorities, and avoid duplication in resource-scarce areas."[6] This is a far more Sisyphean task than monitoring the activities of the multitudes of governmental aid producers. Moreover, the massive presence of non-state actors from the power centers of the global north raises questions over who sets priorities for whom. The agenda of the so-called "white savior industrial complex" as one voice bluntly termed this vast philanthropic network, may not mirror that of the societies these organizations intend to help, and may ignore or marginalize local efforts to improve their own conditions.[7]

At the same time, civil society organizations have increasingly been engaged by powerful actors in global development as part of a post-Washington Consensus intended to include input from global south communities. Robert Zoellick, as head of the World Bank, optimistically noted in 2011, "Now it may be time to invest in the private, not-for-profit sector—civil society—to help strengthen the capacity of organizations working on transparency, accountability, and service delivery."[8] Many of these civil society organizations are based in the global south with intimate knowledge of the communities they serve. Despite—or at times because of—their enlarged presences as insiders, civil society organizations have become important catalysts for social change, and have impacted the priorities of state actors. Yet controversy remains over persistent power imbalances between northern and southern actors, the potential cooptation of global activist groups, and their ability to serve a watchdog function.

Civic Engagement in a Global Community

The World Bank defines "civil society organizations" broadly as "the wide array of non-governmental and not-for-profit organizations that have a presence in public life, expressing the interests and values of their members or others, based on ethical, political, scientific, or philanthropic considerations."[9] The WHO, for its part, defines "civil society" as "a social sphere separate from both the state and the market," connected by being non-state, nonprofit, and voluntary.[10] Both organizations have formally recognized their roles in global health governance while actively encouraging their participation and even leadership within parameters. These waters become considerably murkier when considering variation across this set of actors. Large foundations have assumed an authority in governance all their own. Recalling Fidler's metaphor, they will march to their own beat irrespective of state authority. They are pursuing specializations, certainly, but largely through informal complementarity according to their own leadership prerogatives. Massive endowments, in these cases, are a form of power. Non-state actors broadly labeled "CSOs" differ greatly between such foundations and those that pursue advocacy roles. These sets of activities too have been divided along north-south lines, as actors in the global south have hardly been passive agents in the evolution of global governance structures.[11] Arenas such as the World Social Forum bring large numbers of civil society organizations together, often to oppose powerful foundations and multinational corporations.[12] They also reveal fundamental points of contention between civil society organizations engaged in pro-poor advocacy.

These organizations embody innumerable corners of civil society. They reflect the heterogeneity of an increasingly globally conscious world community prepared to engage in health governance. Across this borderless community are litanies of class, geographic, and ideological perspectives that inspire difference as often as connection. These include activist networks comprised around localities in the global south, intent on democratizing the aid process and putting forth local priorities. They also include progressive-minded activists in the global north concerned with the harmful impacts of government and corporate behavior in vulnerable areas. Labor organizations emphasize the connections between working conditions and health. Umbrella groups such as the People's Health Movement seek to link the activities of such actors. Where possible the PHM forges north-south ties and seeks to influence powerful actors such as the WHO.[13] The globalization of civil society has also meant members of the global community ranging from venture capitalists, to celebrities, to their attendant consumers, participate in global health governance in ways hitherto unimagined. One business venture, (Red), relays the profits from various consumer items to the Global Fund—thereby altering the relationship between capitalist forms of consumption and global social movements.[14] The ubiquitous bright red product labeling merges consumer aesthetics with global political action.

This panoply of figures emerging from civil society to impact global health underscores an uneasy, potentially conflicting mixture of voices. Greater elite engagement toward health portends increased funding and a more motivated global aid regime—and, optimistically, improved north-south understanding. But it may well conflict with the aims of community organization in the global south seeking a greater voice in these political processes. There also remains the danger that global health priorities may become publicity driven, overlooking lower profile campaigns to promote mental health, non-communicable epidemics, neglected tropical diseases, and personal injuries.

The rise of non-governmental activity in the global health regime is part of a broader trend in global governance that entailed dramatic increases in the number of international NGOs from the 1970s and into the globalization era. According to the Union of International Associations, the estimated number of international NGOs rose from 13,000 in 1981 to more than 47,000 by 2001. Yet, despite increased civil society involvement in global health, research on these organizations shows that NGOs with global reach are located overwhelmingly in the global north, reminding us of the power differentials inherent in many NGO interactions.[15] Non-state actors were also integral to the rise of global health. The inclusion of non-state actors is itself consistent with the predominate thinking on global development. As we saw in the previous chapter, *Investing in Health* argued forcefully for the inclusion of non-state actors as well as market forces in the allocation of global health resources. Seven years later, another watershed in the history of global health, the Millennium Declaration, explicitly called for the inclusion of non-state actors. It also implicitly placed a degree of responsibility on for-profit pharmaceutical companies for the provision of essential medicines.

It was clear by that time that private actors would play an integral role in the expansion of health in the global development effort. We see this for several reasons. Key agencies across the UN saw their budgets frozen in the 1980s and 90s, making private financing and outsourcing essential to continuing their activities under conditions of state divestment (though reliance on voluntary private support ultimately helps shape many UN priorities in the modern era). WHO executive director David Nabarro's comments, made in the midst of Gro Harlem Brundtland's reforms, are indicative of this trend: "We certainly need private financing. For the past decade governments' financial contributions have dwindled. The main sources of funding are the private sector and the financial markets. And since the American economy is the world's richest, we must make the WHO attractive to the United States and the financial markets."[16] We also see budget cuts in developing countries during this period, brought on by austerity measures influenced by the menu of neoliberal reforms pressed by powerful actors such as the United States, World Bank, and IMF. This often included rolling back state financing for public health activities in resource scarce environments, leaving wide breaches to be filled by NGO service providers.

The same actors that encouraged state divestment in health during the Washington Consensus period also espoused private sector efficiency. Poverty, these economists argued, was a widespread shortcoming of public sectors in developing regions, not a market failure. This view changed during the waning years of the Washington Consensus, brought on by the failures of austerity-oriented policies to reduce poverty, and fears even among Washington Consensus-holders that this approach had actually worsened conditions while subordinating human development priorities. Yet the non-governmental role in health continued expanding. A heightened awareness of global development issues in the 2000s spurred widespread global engagement among private organizations, from grassroots activists to philanthropists. Private sector involvement appealed across the political spectrum. Activist groups called upon the global elite to commit greater resources to health, and supported interventionism to address what was increasingly viewed as a failure of global markets rather than a "boot straps" problem for which the poor bear sole responsibility.[17] This was particularly the case as the AIDS crisis reached an unprecedented scale, by itself undermining development in the worst impacted regions. From a progressive perspective, non-governmental actors carried unique legitimacy. These groups by and large were unencumbered by interest-based governmental politics largely thought to undermine aid effectiveness. Not unrelated, civil society organizations could serve as watchdogs vis-à-vis the broader development effort. Additionally, localized civil society organizations democratized the process by including input from the very citizens who may be affected by global development financing. Among elites—and many reformed Washington Consensus holders—non-state inclusion remedied perceived government inefficiencies. The deployment of non-governmental entities in traditional state roles, by this view, obviates the need for redistributive or statist approaches to development, focusing the development discourse on the much less controversial issue of poverty rather than distributive equality.[18] Even new government affiliated initiatives would greatly involve non-state participation, and elements of market competition.

The increasing privatization of the global health regime provided answers to the challenges posed by economism. The World Bank's seminal 1993 development report consistently argued that more private sector involvement increases efficiency. Moreover, inputs from ground-level civil society groups can provide valuable information to Geneva-, Washington- and New York-based institutions that seek knowledge about local disease burdens and their sociocultural contexts. CSOs, at least in theory, have strong ground-level knowledge of these conditions, particularly those CSOs that originated in the global south.

As a result of this confluence of discourses, an impressive international non-state presence is at work within the global public health regime. While data on NGOs can be inexact due to their sheer volume, and thus estimates vary, there are reportedly approximately 3,000 inter-national NGOs in the area of global health. There are also 80 global public-private partnership organizations. While largely operating outside of state aegis, they have increasingly functioned in tandem with state policy.[19] The WHO alone has official relations with 189 non-governmen-tal groups and maintains cooperative relationships with 284 such actors. PEPFAR, for its part, channels roughly a quarter of its funds through 248 faith-based organizations.[20]

This phenomenon has raised concerns within the development literature. Swidler's iconoclastic essay in *International Affairs* suggests incompatibilities between power structures within the global public health regime and those of African governance. The global health gover-nance structure, she contends, has pushed increasing funds into African governments, particularly those with strong states (such as Botswana). Having such large private governance structures operating outside these states' purviews has paradoxically undermined them. There is a power differential between African states and the massive NGO complexes embedded in local politics. Thus drastically expanded private health operations threaten to offset political balance in Africa, undermining effective state systems. "Indeed," she argues, "the West has been trying to reshape Africa along the lines it thought appropriate for centuries, and only some of those efforts at institutional transformation have taken root, often in ways far removed from what their authors imagined."[21]

Malhotra sees a similar power dynamic between northern NGOs and local communities in the global south. He sees the growing close-ness between northern NGOs and states as a potential strain on local relations. Writing at a time of rapidly diminishing northern aid in the post-Cold War era, he argues that this diminished aid (which had been increasingly channeled through NGOs) was a good thing in the sense that northern NGOs would regain some independence. Without the financial influence of wealthy governments, these organizations could foster improved relationships with local communities that are more in line with domestic government structures.[22] Of course since the time of that writing, both the volume of aid and CSOs' roles in distributing it have increased, leaving many of these philosophical debates to continue.

Civil Society Organizations

There is an elite consensus that non-governmental actors are a perma-nent and essential cornerstone of the global public health regime. Their involvement is not new. CSOs were the driving force, for instance, in demanding urban cleanups in dreadfully filthy cities such as New York in the mid-nineteenth century, presaging modern public health.[23] A significant body of literature within the IR discipline stresses the role of CSOs as issue advocates, seeking to shape norms in the international system. Pushing beyond the state-centric approach advanced by Cold War era realists, neoliberal institutionalists and constructivists have long argued that multilateral institutions impact state behavior and international practices. Keck and Sikkink's contemporary classic *Activists Beyond Borders* contends that non-governmental actors also play a significant role in impacting international politics. Though their "transnational advocacy networks" (TANS) are not entirely limited to civil society, including sympathetic actors within states and IGOs, TANS rely heavily on advocacy and grassroots action.

The activity of CSOs in global health is varied, including advocacy, the dissemination of governmental services, and independent service provision. For example, Medecins Sans Frontiers (MSF) actively lobbies, provides direct medical services and receives state funding. Of these, advocacy is the most high profile (and most adversarial) civil society role. This is the most normatively driven component of CSO public health activity, and one that constructivists in international relations theory have theorized to a great extent. CSOs are arguably the most vociferous and radical promoters of global health. They are also most active in the watchdog function toward other actors, pushing to ensure that other groups increase or honor their commitments. In this capacity civil society initiatives spring up around broader international or state action. The Bretton Woods Project, for instance, monitors the activities of the IMF and World Bank.[24] Kenyan CSO Aidspan emerged to provide accountability to the Global Fund, working solely on matters relating to the Fund.[25] Southern CSOs have forged impressive global knowledge networks helping define problems, provide intellectual and empirical support, and coordinate worldwide action. Though it is a state-based organization, the Geneva-based South Centre has served this function in relation to CSO actors since its founding in 1995 under the leadership of legendary former Tanzanian president Julius Nyere. The organization emerged in the wake of a pivotal report by the South Commission, *The Challenge to the South*, whose findings evinced the need for southern cooperation at a global level. As the report makes clear, this was particularly evident at the time of its 1990 publication date, as the global trade regime continued to evolve in favor of the global north.[26] In a world of think tanks dominated by northern funding, and clustered in the urban centers of Europe and North America, the Centre functions to reframe these key issues in southern contexts, counterweighing northern intellectual hegemony. The Third World Network, a global consortium of development-related NGOs which began in Malaysia, performs similar functions, producing a great deal of knowledge on north-south power relations while articulating southern interests.

In this regard, non-governmental activity is attuned to the behavior of governmental actors. Key linkages between these actors helped establish and continue to shape non-governmental activities in this area. Nonprofit CSOs are traditional actors in this capacity, utilizing campaigns to affect normative change. By constituting a major part of transnational action networks (which themselves are linked to sympathetic bureaucrats within governments) these groups effectively play a role in the governmental policy making process. Conversely, governments themselves initiate so-called GONGOs—government organized non-governmental organizations—in at times controversial efforts to garner resources aimed at the private sector, or to insert themselves in grassroots-level politics.[27]

In all, these loose knit groups shape policy development by methods that include using exposure tactics such as "naming and shaming," and by utilizing expertise toward issue areas to influence powerful actors. Their analysis is particularly germane to the global public health regime, which has extensive action networks that link civil society with bureaucratic sympathizers.[28] Jonathan Mann, one of the early leaders in the global AIDS effort, pushed for greater integration between the WHO and non-governmental actors with the ability to advance the AIDS cause. This approach later became accepted by the global AIDS movement, one of the most successful in the world at attracting global attention. In the 1990s, following his controversial departure as head of the WHO's Global Program on AIDS, Mann argued the disease had evolved through a series of "frameworks." The most basic of these frameworks was biomedical, focusing strictly on its scientific dimensions. The more complex AIDS frameworks, he argued, were social and human rights oriented. The disease focused, in his words, on *les exclus*, marginalized populations who were at greater risk because of their lack of social choice or power in society.[29]

Mann argued that beyond biomedical efforts, the fight against disease entailed questions of women's status, marriage law, the right to information, and other cultural, governmental, and legal concepts. It stood to reason, in his view, that health advocates like the WHO should "work with those individuals and groups, whether official, nongovernmental, or private, who are already working to promote respect for human rights and dignity within the society."[30] In a letter to the *BMJ* that responded to Fiona Godlee's critical series on the WHO, Mann argued that NGOs have a legitimacy that cannot be attained by governments, who may be "too tied to the benefits of the status quo." Given the apparent stasis of governments and health agencies in the 1990s, he contended that necessary change would most likely be pushed from without. "Nongovernmental organizations," he argued, "can announce boldly and clearly, when the emperor has no clothes."[31] It is legitimacy that is their effective comparative advantage, and this legitimacy orients CSOs toward advocacy. As Keck and Sikkink and other members of the constructivist school argue, these groups are well situated toward influencing outcomes involving actors with far greater "hard" economic power.

The most stunning example of this is the long controversy over HIV/AIDS drug prices, which pitted activists against much more powerful and politically connected pharmaceutical firms. The result was a dramatic drop in prices, growth in the generic market, legal setbacks for the firms, and the emergence of public-private partnerships by which the firms distributed the medicines at little or no cost. None of these things led to the desired goal of universal distribution. However, the confrontation clearly resulted in an unlikely victory for a transnational advocacy network populated by governmental officials, but also weak and often marginalized civil society groups. Three key factors caused the pharmaceutical firms to retreat from their militant stance on frivolous patenting. The first was immense activist pressure. The second was the effort by Brazil and India to produce and distribute the drugs themselves, putting downward pressure on world pricing. These efforts did not occur apart from one another. Activists in Brazil were primary catalysts for the government's efforts. The third factor was UNAIDS's direct negotiations with western ARV manufacturers.

Sell and Prakash contend that NGO networks made strategic use of normative frameworks in order to affect the pharmaceutical debate.[32] NGOs, like their strategic adversaries in business, employ these frameworks to shape world opinion and consequently force the other side to make concessions. For business, this meant intellectual property protection. This normative framework successfully influenced the 1994 Agreement on Trade Related Aspects of Intellectual Property Rights (TRIPS). This normative conception of how international business should be conducted effectively prevailed during the Uruguay round, at least temporarily. It is important to understand, however, that this "normative framework" was backed by economic power—meaning immense economic pressure from developed countries, which largely controlled the proceedings of the Uruguay Round, ultimately leading to the creation of the WTO and TRIPS in their favor. For NGOs the normative agenda centered on access to essential medicines, which won significant victories that helped soften the heavy handed impact of TRIPS on drug duplication efforts.[33] The TRIPS agreement—one of the most controversial multilateral agreements of the 1990s and a harbinger of widespread dissent against the WTO—affirmed patent holders' monopolies on drug products.

The accord, heavily lobbied for by pharmaceutical companies in the United States, called for WTO members to revise domestic laws to establish 20-year patents on both drug products and their manufacturing processes. The Western push for TRIPS provides a strong example of what Raustiala and Victor, among others, call forum shopping or "shifting."[34] Global south countries with an interest in duplicating medicines had strong voices on WIPO and UNCTAD, UN system bodies with more equal representation. Many countries in the developing world at this time had few or no patent restrictions on medicines.[35] For business-backed policymakers in the global north, this encouraged the creation of a new forum—the WTO and with it TRIPS. Though TRIPS was a tremendous victory for the global north, it contains two loopholes. Compulsory licensing allows countries to manufacture the drugs themselves (assuming they are capable) in an emergency. Parallel importing allows countries to import drugs from a third country, where prices may be cheaper, allowing buyers to search for the lowest world price. These prerogatives—emphasized in the 2001 Doha declaration which effectively reinterpreted TRIPS—were the result of significant activist pressure from developing countries in tandem with northern activism.

Still, countries that attempted to take advantage of these loopholes faced stiff legal resistance and, in some cases, the treat of trade retaliation from the United States. Pharmaceutical companies appeared to be unparalleled in their ability to influence governments because of their vast revenues and close ties to the US trade officials who pushed TRIPS. NGOs took on the role of David during this period. But they did so in tandem with governments and drug manufacturers in the global south. Brazil, India, and South Africa sought to reassert their ability to manufacture and distribute life-saving ARV drugs at costs far lower than Western firms' monopoly pricing. Their combined effort changed the normative landscape in global health. It produced a different outcome than that which would have prevailed had these companies continued to dominate the issue. In sum, the campaign to lower drug costs despite international patent norms provides a strong example of what Finnemore and Sikkink call norm emergence and acceptance.[36] Ideational factors are important here, but so is material economic pressure. Ultimately emerging market countries went forward with duplication, putting pressure on brand name drug producers.

Reports of the successful tests of advanced ARV drug regimens were addressed with considerable enthusiasm at the Vancouver conference on AIDS in 1996.[37] The drugs were capable of extending the life of HIV patients dramatically, in some cases dropping the prevalence of the virus to undetectable levels. But these regimens had an annual cost of up to $20,000 per person, far too high for the hardest hit regions, where per capita health spending often does not exceed $10 per person yearly. Most in the development community doubted the financial feasibility of instituting large scale treatment programs in the developing world.[38] Paul Farmer, the founder of Partners in Health and a leading public health advocate, lamented the likelihood that "treatment may be reserved for those in wealthy countries while prevention is the lot of the poor."[39] Many at Vancouver lamented loudly that the emergence of these life sparing drugs meant nothing to the millions of people who could not afford them. Vancouver marked the emergence of a wide NGO coalition that put unrelenting pressure on business and government to make these drugs universally available.

The Brazilian program provides an example of the interplay between activists and governments. As activist groups in urban Brazil pressured the government to expand treatment, the government itself was pushed into the role of global advocate.[40] In 1997, after significant pressure from urban-based gay, lesbian and HIV-positive communities, the Brazilian government developed an initiative to produce generic ARVs and offer them free to any citizens who tested positive. As Davis and Fort note, "The government of Brazil manufactured domestic copies of drugs that were under patent protection in wealthier nations."[41] The World Bank had estimated in 1994 that the number of HIV/AIDS cases in Brazil would top 1.2 million by 2000. Instead, this swift government intervention drastically reduced the number of deaths and new cases, particularly in the disproportionately affected urban slums.[42]

In 2001 the Indian pharmaceutical firm Cipla announced a simplified regimen with a price of $350 per year and has been credited with forcing down world prices. The company offered the drugs to MSF—which was engaged in extensive drug access campaigning—to be distributed for free in the developing world. Cipla's CEO extended the offer to anyone else willing to provide the drugs for free.[43] While taking advantage of existing technologies and patents, Cipla produced innovations of its own. It created a simplified ARV that combined multiple drugs into a single tablet, taken twice daily. Existing regimens at the time entailed as many as 35 pills daily. As Arvind Singhal and Everett M. Rogers noted, "The general reaction was amazement at the ridiculously low price."[44] This movement in the developing world placed downward pressure on world ARV prices. Western companies announced price drops in the immediate wake of Cipla's innovation in duplication. These duplication efforts also helped pressure large patent-holding pharmaceutical firms to the table. In 2000, UNAIDS began its Accelerating Access Initiative (AAI), a plan which brokered deals between governments and pharmaceutical companies for discounted access to ARVs.[45] The program began with pledges from five pharmaceutical firms to offer discounted drugs, and eventually brought 58 countries into direct negotiations with the industry. ARV prices dropped 85 percent on average. In return, governments ensured that the drugs were not sold on the open market for their full retail prices in northern countries.

South Africa provided the most intense point of direct confrontation between activists and pharmaceutical firms. There the government successfully maintained its generic drug program, the South African Medicines Act, despite immense retaliatory pressure from the Clinton administration in support of the US pharmaceutical industry. The United States placed South Africa on its "301 watch list" of countries purportedly in violation of trade norms, and suspended aid. The United States eventually dropped its opposition amidst heavy international outrage, suggesting the durability of the norm of differential pricing—and the sensitivity of the issue during a US election. Much of this pressure was spearheaded by the domestic AIDS activist group ACT UP, which continually protested against Al Gore during the 2000 election year.[46] The Medicines Act continued after the United States dropped its sanctions, although government support for drug distribution in South Africa was disappointingly weak under Thabo Mbeki.

Overall, the price of ARV drugs in the developing world declined 90 percent between 1997 and 2002. The drugs currently cost between $148 and $900 annually, depending on the complexity of the regimen.[47] Clearly, the norm of differential pricing has taken hold, despite the fact that it was deemed a hopeless cause by many in the late 1990s. This has much to do with the continued support of emerging market countries, and their increasing ability to impact the global health discourse through economic pressure. This international norm was followed by the newly emergent Global Fund to Fight HIV/AIDS, Malaria and Tuberculosis, which Kofi Annan announced should "put care and treatment within everyone's reach."[48] The Global Fund ultimately decided to include the funding of AIDS projects that utilize generic drug treatments. The General Assembly's 2001 Declaration of Commitment on HIV/ AIDS effectively enshrined the principle of differential pricing, calling on the international community to provide sustainable access to the drugs worldwide.[49]

Gro Harlem Brundtland, the WHO director general during this time, attributed the drop in prices to an emergent ethical norm of differential pricing. "Popular outrage, political will, market forces and the best science," she argued, "are enabling the pursuit of a fundamental principle of public health—the supply of essential medicines on the basis of need rather than the ability to pay."[50] In sum, non-governmental actors operated according to the humanitarian principle of price differential over patent protection. With governmental help, they were able to establish human rights oriented norms, affecting the behavior of powerful and reluctant firms and their state supporters in the north. Their use of bargaining and pressure forced Western pharmaceuticals to comply with the norm of price differential, despite their considerable advantages in funding and political connections. They were able to articulate an alternative to the profit-based discourse that had prevailed during negotiations over TRIPS.

The ARV case is the starkest (and the most scholarly accepted) example of NGO pressure affecting priorities in global health. Along with this success came two important caveats raised by critics. First, despite the drop in treatment costs, AIDS medications remained out of reach for the vast majority of people living with the disease in the global south, and for most governments to provide them. One health economist estimated that the cost of Highly Active Antiretroviral Therapy (HAART) would have to be $10 per month in Zambia, $20 in Botswana, and $45 in Mozambique in order to be truly affordable for their respective national health care systems.[51] As noted in chapter 1, AIDS remains a leading cause of death among adults in the global south, although the epidemic appears to have leveled off. Moreover significant debate remains over the impact of vertical health programs for AIDS, and the assertion that AIDS funding has effectively siphoned funding for other areas (though, as we have seen, figures for this book are less pessimistic in this regard). For their part, as MSF and other watchdog organizations continue to document, Western pharmaceuticals remain committed to excessive patent protections. As MSF's authoritative 2010 *Untangling the Web* report reveals, "frivolous patenting" remains, while poorer patients are widely left with older off-patent medicines with greater side effects, and uncertain access to second- and third-line regimens.[52] Just as importantly, the normative principles of access to health have advanced more slowly for necessary health products other than AIDS medications. Moreover northern trade negotiators have sought more favorable terms for patent holders in bilateral and regional agreements in a consequential series of forum shifts.[53]

In sum, the non-governmental activism in the case of the ARV drug protests illustrates a traditional linkage between CSO and governmental activity. Non-governmental activists from a wide variety of geographic and social backgrounds identified grievances in government (and corporate) behavior. The movement took advantage of what in most cases were limited resources to foster significant normative changes within the regime. The weight of evidence suggests that non-profit civil society organizations had a major effect in terms of shaping the way the regime collectively thinks about access to medicines. Their strategies were highly attuned to the activities of governmental actors. They responded to what CSOs saw as a key distributional weakness within the regime: the wealth of monopoly rights accruing to a few multinational patent holders while the lower strata were left with no access to vital medicines. Addressing these inefficiencies in distribution required the confluence of a transnational network (initiated largely from below but with the help of states in the global south and generic producing firms) to rectify the power imbalance presented by states and multinationals. The result was a fundamental change in norms and even a restructuring of international law. Under the auspices of a regime complex characterized by overlapping issue spheres, new contestations arise. In this case, we see complex normative interactions between humanitarian understandings of disease and transnational patent law shaping political change.

Philanthropic Foundations

Large philanthropic foundations are playing expanded roles in global health governance. Like multilateral agencies, they face pressure to offer unique contributions to global health or risk decline into irrelevancy. It is difficult to develop new strategies for global health when so many other strategies already exist. One advantage they have over established governmental actors, however, is the luxury of being relatively new. It is easier to develop a niche from scratch than to transition away from a previous approach to global health. As with other major actors, their activities are affected by technological expertise, disease burdens, geographic ties, normative conditions, bureaucratic turf, and increased regime density. Non-governmental as well as governmental actors must consider these factors as they engage public health issues in a very dense, complex international environment. In these ways, large foundations show key equivalencies to their governmental counterparts, fulfilling much of their traditional functions. The vast growth of the largest foundations, particularly the Bill and Melinda Gates foundation, means that governmental organizations are no longer the lone providers of development capital. In 2006, non-state actors provided roughly a quarter of all development assistance for health, up from 13.1 percent in 1990.[54]

This means increasing the number of actors in an already dense global aid regime. Indeed, the emergence of the Bill and Melinda Gates Foundation in this decade has sparked additional fears within the development community. These include that of overlaps, inefficiencies and bureaucratic pressures on local governments seeking to manage the inflow of aid from different actors. As a relatively new player, the Gates Foundation has spent much of its time grappling with this issue, as have other major non-governmental actors. However there are countervailing factors. The activities of these actors are deeply linked to existing networks of governmental activity. Their choices of priorities are greatly affected by what the traditional actors are already doing (or not doing). These groups, like their governmental counterparts, have sought to form unique specializations. A major trend in their activities is to find gaps left by the larger regime, and to address particularly those diseases that have gone ignored by traditional aid financiers. They are also empowered to pursue what they see as riskier approaches not taken by actors that are directly answerable to governments and taxpayers.

Important convergences with norms of specialization are evident among these actors. Like their state and multilateral counterparts, these aid distributors select only a small number of public health issues, and seek to forge distinct approaches. Even the vast Gates organization, which has enough resources to be more broadly based, has adopted this pattern. In that sense we may indulge in comparisons with the United States and other large scale aid distributors. However, these foundations possess significantly different characteristics and logics of action. Their relatively opaque institutional structures also raise concerns over transparency, accountability, and conflicts of interest. Their growing presence raises a corresponding ethical question: Should small groups of wealthy or politically influential individuals be so well positioned to shape policy in the world's poorest areas? In addition, large foundations have drawn scrutiny for investing in corporate activities that serve to undermine public health conditions, thereby acting at cross purposes with their own missions.

The Bill and Melinda Gates Foundation is by far the largest private provider of grants for international health, providing $895 million in 2005. The next largest private US provider that year was the Ford Foundation, at $24 million. Grant levels in public health from the Gates Foundation also exceeded every state aid program except for the United States and Japan.[55] By 2009 the Gates Foundation reported $1.8 billion in funds toward global health alone, making health by far its number one priority.[56] As of 2011, the BMG foundation had a trust in excess of $34 billion according to its own audits.[57] In all, roughly 60 percent of Gates Foundation outlays are devoted to global health.

As noted in the previous chapter, the World Bank's *Investing in Health*—and its emphasis on numerically cost effective, technologically driven interventions—strongly influenced Bill Gates during the Foundation's formative years. As Gates would later tell the *Financial Times*, in a manner strongly reflecting the Bank's ethos after 1993, "We have a very clear criteria of what we fund in global health—having to do with what the other people don't fund, what the burden of disease is and what the scientific choice is. So it's all quite numerical."[58] The BMG global health program, like the entrepreneurial pursuits of its namesakes, takes a technology-based approach that emphasizes partnerships with other entities. It has been particularly active in vaccine development initiatives. It oversees the development of vaccines for "poor diseases" that offer few market incentives for northern research and development—even though much of the research may never pan out. It is also a major supporter of the Global Fund and the GAVI vaccine alliance.

The Gates Foundation specializes in funding scientific advancements geared toward disease burdens in developing countries. It has also been a major source of finance for existing public and private assets in the global health infrastructure, devoting large sums to partnership initiatives. The Global Fund, for instance, has been a large beneficiary, including a 2012 grant for $750 million to help the cash-strapped Fund maintain current grants. Still, patterns in its funding have drawn scrutiny. The Gates Foundation has been criticized for its lack of transparency, making it somewhat less immune to democratic pressures than many of its governmental counterparts. Most of its funding has been channeled through organizations based in the global north, bypassing those in the global south. Its funding has been heavily skewed toward malaria and HIV/AIDS, prompting *The Lancet* to editorialize that "grants made by the foundation do not reflect the burden of disease endured by those in deepest poverty."[59] Two major studies on Gates Foundation grant funding found a relatively poor correlation between its global health financing and disease burdens.[60] Reporting in the *Los Angeles Times* revealed that the BMG Foundation had invested in corporations such as fossil fuel companies whose activities undermine health.[61]

Yet the Gates Foundation does not rely on disease burden as its sole metric. Rather, in keeping with its founder's explicit faith in technology, it takes technological factors into account as it sets priorities. This includes cost-effective measures, but also those that entail high risks of failure (weighed against potentially large successes). This, Gates argues, enables the Foundation to fund projects and make research and development investments that governmental groups sensitive to public accountability could not. It is a "high risk, high return" approach akin to the ethos of venture capitalism that pervades technological sectors in the United States, where Gates accumulated his immense fortune through Microsoft. This underscores the BMG Foundation's emphasis on vaccine development, and Gates's oft-expressed faith in the power of technology driven initiatives to complete the eradication of polio (which currently appears to have been achieved in India). "The pace of innovation keeps getting faster," Gates told the BBC. "The same is true of polio."[62]

The Carter Center has also adopted specific areas of specialization. It has adopted as priorities five diseases that have been relatively neglected by the rest of the global public health regime—guinea worm, trachoma, schistosomiasis, lymphatic filariasis, and river blindness—in addition to malaria. The organization reviews hundreds of diseases in the developing world, selecting as priorities those with a strong chance at being eradicated through low-cost interventions. It seeks to have the highest impact with the fewest resources. Its most prominent triumph was its campaign against guinea worm, an accomplishment evocative of the WHO's historic plan to eliminate smallpox (albeit smaller scale). The Carter Center-led plan to combat the disease through low-cost interventions reduced the number of cases (once 3.5 million) by 99 percent since the campaign began in 1986, the agency claims. The Carter Center's approach is evidence of important structural factors that influence prioritization among foundations. Those without a preponderance of resources may seek to establish credibility by filling gaps, addressing what the larger community has not prioritized. Additionally, resource limitations can lead to innovations in low cost interventions along the lines of those called for by the global health consensus.

The George Soros-founded Open Society Foundations by comparison engage a broad scope of private actor activities, from grant making to political advocacy. With more than $2.7 billion in assets, its grant making powers are formidable, totaling nearly $258 million for all causes in 2011.[63] Focusing on core areas within Europe, Africa, and China, the foundation's central health functions extend to advocacy as well as grant-making and capacity building. The Foundations have particularly engaged issues facing marginalized populations, seeking to address their public health challenges through the broader expansion of rights. For example, the Foundations favor harm reduction strategies to alleviate health problems related to drug use as an alternative to the punitive "war on drugs" approach. They have similarly advocated "sexual rights" for sex workers, alongside stigma reduction, in order to more greatly involve them in health policy.

Public-Private Partnerships

"One key feature of the global health landscape today," argues Carmen Huckel Schneider, "is the apparent proliferation of hybrid forms of governance, where actors of various organizational types (states, intergovernmental organizations, non-governmental organizations, academia and business) work together."[64] For Schneider, public-private partnerships entail joint cooperative action in the production of public goods.[65] For our purposes, this is the kind of formal cooperation we are likely to see in a decentralized, non-hierarchical regime. It constitutes regionally and institutionally specific micro-coordination in a regime famously lacking global macro-coordination. Multilateral forums throughout the UN system, WHO, and World Bank have incubated more extensive, integrated partnerships across sectors during the rise of global health. The World Bank Institute, for its part, organizes forums intended to foster new partnerships in global governance, and to spur the learning process in these undertakings. The Institute itself is an exercise in what it calls "collaborative governance," arguing that "successful development requires building multi-stakeholder coalitions."[66] For the Institute, these partnerships "mobilize private sector resources—technical, managerial, and financial—to deliver essential public services such as infrastructure,

health and education."[67] In the post-Washington Consensus era, partnership and consultation with southern CSOs give the Bank renewed
credibility while retaining key elements of its neoliberal emphasis.

Non-state actors have considerable appeal in terms of knowledge
that outside organizations can tap. As Haas has theorized in the area
of environmental policy, the advice of seemingly powerless groups of
experts can have considerable impact when policy comes to fruition.[68]
Powerful governmental actors lack the knowledge of local communities and often the highly specialized medical expertise needed to carry
out governmental goals. Non-state actors correspondingly have rapidly
expanding roles in governmental activities in global health. Governmental actors have sought CSO partnerships in order to amplify their
messages, gain legitimacy, enhance efficiency, or pool resources. CSOs
provide governments with input on major issues, the dissemination of
services, and advocacy. Powerful intergovernmental organizations have
sought synergies with CSOs in these areas. Jonathan Mann's Global Programme on Aids offered a model for the inclusion of CSOs in advocacy
efforts which has been echoed in the post-Nakajima WHO. Outreach to
CSOs, particularly human rights groups, had been essential to the GPA's
strategy.[69] Mann's interest in human rights prompted his GPA to seek out
briefings from CSOs on how best to approach AIDS from a human rights
perspective. This general view now prevails within the WHO, a change
marked by Gro Harlem Brundtland's tenure as director general. The 2001
Civil Society Initiative sought to institutionalize connections between
the WHO and non-governmental actors. The WHO's own public language toward them is reflective of Mann's. "Evolving concepts about
health and the articulation of its links to poverty, equity and development," the agency noted, "have recently widened the range of WHO's
partners."[70] Global health agencies that have emerged more recently
have constructed institutionalized roles for CSOs from the beginning.
The Global Fund (which funds applicant activities rather than carrying
out its own on-the-ground programming) relies heavily on civil society
organizations and local community groups to run the projects that it
finances. UNAIDS was the first UN agency partially run by civil society
groups, which have active membership in the agency's governing Program Coordinating Board. Five CSOs serve on the PCB on a rotating
basis for up to three years. Three of these are from developing countries.[71]

As aid to health has increased, state and multilateral aid distributors seek CSO channels through which to disseminate development
assistance. Moreover, CSOs fill gaps in the diminished domestic health

programs that were rolled back as part of broader austerity measures (often at the behest of lenders such as the World Bank in the name of "structural adjustment"). As the WHO noted, civil society activity has increased in "response to the perceived weakening of the nation states' authority under globalization."[72] In the WHO's assessment, "The state's role was 'downsized,' either by deliberate policy measures such as structural adjustment programs, by reducing spending or by the declining quality of public services."[73] CSOs and other non-state actors have emerged to fill these gaps, in many cases under the aegis of northern governments and northern dominated IGOs.

Increased non-state involvement (including other non-governmental sectors such as for-profit corporations) has also been encouraged because of a lack of resources by prominent actors in global health. This is the case among the WHO and UNDP which were targets of UN system divestment in the 1990s. As Buse and Walt note, "Negative perceptions of UN effectiveness have provided financial impetus for partnerships in that donors have imposed a policy of zero real growth in UN budgets . . . These funding trends have made [public-private partnerships] attractive to the UN."[74] The UNDP allegedly breached its own funding guidelines in order to court such partnerships.[75] These combined factors are evidence that the historically close relationships between non-governmental and governmental actors in public health will continue. These organizations—from global south civil society groups to major multinational firms—are increasingly central to governmental agendas from international advocacy campaigns to the direct dissemination of public health services.

Governments and multilateral institutions not surprisingly view these relationships as productive.[76] Their activities toward the private sector have corresponded with their rhetoric calling for more private sector involvement, shaping the design of programs and entire institutions. Successful Global Fund grant proposals should, according to Fund guidelines, enable "the development, strengthening, and expansion of government/private/NGO partnership."[77] The World Bank, long a purveyor of private involvement, invests 50 percent of its Multi-Country AIDS Program (MAP) directly into civil society organizations.[78]

While the sheer scale of CSO involvement in development makes it difficult to encapsulate definitively, the rise of CSOs has been met with mixed assessments in scholarly arenas. It sparked a vibrant philosophical debate on the appropriate role for non-state actors in something as elemental to human development as public health. Community-led organizations potentially foster democratic engagement in the policies that affect public health, from road construction to labor conditions, as well as medical infrastructure, social inclusion, and vertical interventions. They promise to give a participatory voice for vulnerable or affected populations, in addition to harnessing their experiences and expertise in the dissemination of basic services. Such partnerships can also convey decision-making power on distant organizations whose priorities many not align with local conditions, thus diminishing decision-making at the local level. They can also provide cover for profit-making MNCs.

Seckinelgin's extensive research on the role of non-governmental groups in Africa's HIV/AIDS governance structures is skeptical of their ability to understand the social underpinnings of local epidemics. NGOs, he argues, lack the institutional flexibility that their protractors laud them for. Their organizational rigidity ultimately undermines the effectiveness of their interventions.[79] While non-state actors make important interventions in public health, their agency is diminished by the overarching governing structure of international aid, and their own characteristics.[80] These flaws undermine their ability to affect deep change over the long term, with the dangers of miscommunication in the field and faulty, culturally inept goal setting. Though he determines that NGOs provide important help, "they do not possess the sort of agency required for sustainable long-term HIV/AIDS interventions."[81]

Seckinelgin sees an overarching governance structure as a constraint on non-governmental action. Much of the rest of the literature in this area differs in that it hinges on the question of conflicts of interest: Does growing enmeshment between CSOs and states undermine CSO independence? This is an essential question because their advocacy functions discussed above derive from their legitimacy. Maintaining legitimacy means maintaining at least perceived independence from presumably self-interested states. As DeChaine estimates, "government funding is the primary factor responsible for the tremendous growth of NGOs in recent times."[82] This creates a delicate balancing act between attracting resources and maintaining political independence, and, if necessary, radical activism directed at states and multinational corporations. These actors may take anti-health stances, but also may extensively fund NGO-led projects. Hence credibility is at stake for CSOs along with financial survival, two forces that may pull civil society groups in opposite directions. DeChaine's study of MSF is illustrative of this dilemma. Many of its country chapters are extensively funded by western governments, yet the organization seeks to maintain fiercely independent stances, as shown most prominently in its early advocacy for price differential in AIDS pharmaceuticals.[83]

By deeply imbedding CSOs into their global south development policies, states seek to make use of the private sector's perceived comparative advantages, particularly efficiency and legitimacy. As Hulme and Edwards contend, "Their relationship with the 'people' is seen as giving them greater public legitimacy than government while their managerial features are seen as permitting private sector levels of cost control and efficiency."[84] Further, CSOs help amplify the reach of states in international regimes. Raustiala's study of expanded non-governmental involvement in the global environmental regime concludes that it amplifies the ability of states to govern despite its potential to cause unwieldy regime density. Their inclusion, he argues, "is based on the confluence of governmental incentives and NGO comparative advantages and resources."[85] Yet Hulme and Edwards articulate the fear that it is exactly this close relationship that can delude non-governmental advantages. Their ability to lobby for progressive social change may diminish under conditions of financial dependence, effectively co-opting previously radical organizations. Their work poses an open question.

> Addressing fundamental inequalities of power and resources by speaking out in favor of particular groups, organizing to defend the interests of poor people, and lobbying governments for policy change, has always been central to the NGO mission. Many of the largest and most respected international NGOs of today (such as Save the Children and Oxfam) were born and raised in opposition to government policy and vested interests at the time. But can this role continue when [northern] NGOs are becoming more and more dependent on government support?[86]

If the independence of such activities diminishes, so may their ability to affect normative change over issue areas such as intellectual property rights described above. This line of criticism of the global health regime is also directed at multilateral institutions such as UNAIDS, the WHO, and UNDP, which due to their perceived legitimacy are comparatively relied upon in the area of advocacy. Each of these organizations has engaged in public-private partnerships with business sectors such as pharmaceuticals, which have routinely found their interests at odds with those of global health. Multinational corporations have much different logics of action than nonprofit CSOs. For these actors, partnerships within the global health regime serve to counteract poor publicity. As we saw in the conflict between MNCs and advocacy-based CSOs, negotiations over drug distribution programs effectively bought time for pharmaceutical firms to maintain high drug prices before generic competition emerged. Profit-motive clearly skews the activities of these actors. In this light, only one percent of the drugs developed between 1975 and 1997 were for tropical diseases.[87] Pharmaceutical firms, in particular, are nevertheless major stakeholders in aid programs that entail the purchase of medical products. Moreover, the ascendant position of global health within international development goals has made conditions ripe for what may at first seem like strange bedfellows in global health partnerships. However as global governance theorists Suerie Moon and Wolfgang Hein optimistically point out, emergent norms including the right to health and access to medicines have fundamentally impacted the strategic behavior of governments and multinational corporations—pressing them to engage global activists.[88]

The dramatic expansion of non-state actors is one of the most significant developments in the rise of global health. The political implication of this reality is correspondingly complex. Does the precipitous increase in the number of non-governmental agencies democratize the public health effort or concentrate power in the hands of unaccountable agencies? There is evidence of both trends. Regarding the latter, public-private partnerships appear at times to usurp the role of the state in decision-making, potentially undermining conventional electoral accountability. But the state is hardly a passive actor, particularly in the global South, often embedding its work under the auspices of private partnerships to hasten political gains. Transnational action networks by their nature take place both inside and outside of government. Hence, non-state actors should not be viewed in isolation from the state. In a domestic context, such organizations were essential to the "inside, outside" strategies underscoring the New Deal, Great Society, and Civil Rights movements that sparked social change in the US. In this light, non-state actors undoubtedly contributed to the dramatic expansion in public health services explored in these pages, and are thus likely catalysts for state-led expansions such as PEPFAR. As the next chapter shows, the emergent global health infrastructure is unlikely to fully reverse itself despite contemporary budget pressures. What are the prospects for this deeply embedded regime complex for global health?

CHAPTER 5

Conclusion

Problems and Prospects for Global Health Governance

This book has explored the problems and prospects of global health governance under conditions of regime complexity. The continual expansion of multilateral infrastructure in the twenty-first century has become a focal point of study within the international relations discipline. This development gives rise to an elemental normative question in political science: Can governance expand effectively, or does its expansion inevitably create grossly suboptimal outcomes? How centrally "governed" does regime activity have to be in order to be effective? The regime complex literature makes an important contribution by applying this question to global governance. It has advanced institutional theory at a time when the world's multilateral infrastructure appears to be in a state of terminal expansion, creating new layers of rules and agencies that overlap with existent ones.

While efficiency must be understood as a means to rather than an end of good governance, the study of regime complexes has raised the timely possibility of unintended consequences resulting from expanded global governance. It has also confronted the political reality that stakeholders investing in new transnational infrastructure are seldom willing to subordinate their activities to existent agencies or central authorities. Raustiala and Victor are likely correct to suggest regime complexes are the wave of the future.[1] International cooperation is in great demand in an unprecedented variety of policy arenas. Even many critics conclude that transnational challenges such as global public health cannot be successfully addressed without it.

The narrative of overexpansion informed by the regime complex literature—as well as by critics of the global health regime and aid more generally—risks inadvertent hostility toward modern global governance at a time when the need for transnational problem solving has never been greater. This interdisciplinary debate should also be careful not to mischaracterize the size and scope of multilateral governance, which does not remotely approach that of domestic bureaucracies. Indeed, essential institutional elements of global governance remain largely neglected by the advanced industrialized countries that lead them, commanding relatively small outlays from states.

As the world's wealthiest countries engage in drastic austerity measures, it is important that the aid-is-futile message does not further condemn the entire project of redistribution through aid before it has fully matured. Health remains at the forefront of the global agenda, reiterated as a priority in 2012 as UN Secretary General Ban Kyi Moon entered his second term. Development assistance is nevertheless in jeopardy amidst austerity. The Global Fund, a key agency in global health's expansion, now struggles to meet ongoing commitments, relying on a $750 million grant from the Bill and Melinda Gates Foundation in 2012 to maintain current projects. In all, international aid targets are likely to remain unreached in the coming years. This comes as the policy tool of development assistance remains essential to the broader global development agenda, figuring centrally in 2009 and 2011 international agreements on climate change.[2]

While acknowledging the inherent risk of failure in expanding funds for global health projects, Paul Farmer, cofounder of Partners in Health, notes the potential advantages of new funding, arguing "aid is not bad in itself, and if managed appropriately it can achieve impressive results. The end of the funding drought has been a tremendous boon, especially for the destitute and sick (and those who provide care to them)."[3] While expanding global governance activities entails varying degrees of risk, it is important to acknowledge that aid can be distributed and implemented effectively. Regime complexes themselves are more than merely the sum of suboptimal institutional development. Indeed, the interconnectedness of global development challenges—from health, to environment, to family planning, to education—often necessitates the blurring of traditional agency roles and require interagency expertise. Elemental regimes may be ill equipped to address these concerns if operating in programmatic isolation. However potentially suboptimal their cross pollinations, regime complexes will be required to meet twenty-first-century challenges. As we saw in chapter 1, this reality has received growing acknowledgment. Robert Keohane, Elinor Ostrom, David Fidler, and other prominent scholars of organizational environments have all in various ways noted the flexibility of decentralized action that may not be available within hierarchical regimes. Regime complexes, they argue, allow for multiple solutions to a complex array of global problems. Overlap within regime complexes leaves contested space for conflict as well as cooperation, resulting in clashes within groups over policy outcomes and norms.

This chapter expounds upon the normative and ethical policy dimensions of the rise of global health. In sum, increases in global aid do not necessarily threaten to "make things worse" by inviting overlap, as Garrett warns. Were Garrett's fears fully warranted, it would make sense for policymakers in rich countries to rethink the entire enterprise of providing expanded development assistance to the global south. That would be a mistake. A failure to adequately finance global health efforts in low-income countries risks widespread public devastation. What the analysis of this book shows is that expanding support for global health efforts—while subject to important efficiency concerns—presents far fewer challenges than would a failure to sufficiently finance a response to the world's disease burdens. The greater danger is of doing too little rather than expanding too much.

This book has tried to avoid using terms such as "donor," and "charity" to describe the largely northern-based aid producers under study, because they imply a certain mythical benevolence on the part of actors who use aid to advance transnational concerns. The notion of development assistance carries no perfect diction, as the intentions and consequences of aid vary greatly. Aid can be deployed to empower participatory, democratic approaches to development, or in ways that curtail state capacity and local autonomy. Through this ethical fog it is important to understand that development assistance remains the most obvious mechanism of global economic redistribution. This includes redressing current and historic extractive relationships between the north and south as well as rich and poor. While the broader causes for global inequality are beyond the scope of this book, labor and raw materials provided by the world's poor continue to play a vital role in maintaining quality of life for the non-poor. Many of the world's poorest regions have been or continue to be destabilized by security and economic policies orchestrated by the world's most powerful nations (thereby impacting health).[4] Truly addressing global inequality requires revising this broad scope of policies, yet aid to health and other issues (notably climate change) are an important part of this picture. These imbalances suggest that redistributive policies from north to south will have to play a key role in a more equitable global economy. Aid will likely be called on to facilitate north-to-south technology transfers including that of medicines and public health infrastructure alongside a broad range of innovations that impact health such as education and climate adaptation.

As austerity places pressure on foreign aid budgets, new actors and new aid channels have emerged to (perhaps) fill much of the potential gap. As we saw in chapter 2, the so-called "BRICS" countries (in addition to other southern actors such as oil producing states) have gradually expanded development funding and thus, potentially, their global influence among smaller low- and middle-income countries.[5] The rise of south-to-south aid distributors could have a fundamental impact on international norms in global health. These remain nascent developments as the DAC still channels most development assistance, but they raise questions over the long-term viability of Western development ideology, and lend themselves to equally important questions on aid effectiveness. Large emerging market countries such as China, India, and Brazil have experience dealing directly with the vastness of their own poverty, as millions have escaped destitution. Yet despite this mutual developing status, power imbalances between "donor" and "recipient" remain. Moreover these countries, while idiosyncratic in their own development models, have assumed many of the most troubling characteristics of extreme capitalism. Their domestic models have also fostered souring economic political imbalances between rich and poor, a dynamic that may well influence development strategies abroad. The remainder of the chapter addresses the implications of regime complexity and the heightened emphasis on cooperation in global public health.

Collective Action as a Means to Health

The input of collective action is necessary for the output of improved global health status. This book focuses on the former but does not confuse it with the latter. More cooperative institutional initiatives, greater communication at (and between) the global and local levels, combined with greater resources, undoubtedly heighten the chances for improved human development outcomes. Ultimate success is rooted—per the WHO constitution—in achieving the highest attainable standards of health. Fully understanding progress toward this requires a complex set of measures including localized health metrics. Achieving optimal health is not resolved simply by greater cooperation. Collective action is a means of implementing the push for the highest attainable health standards. The forms of resource allocation discussed in these pages should not be confused with ends in themselves. This book is about how the global health regime is managed.

The management question is indeed important, and will remain so given the lofty commitments made by this generation toward carrying out emergent health norms. The rise of global health occurs, and is in part a response to, vast global economic inequality. Nearly 40 years separate the societies with the world's longest and shortest life expectancies, according to the World Bank.[6] While debate rages over causality, the rise of global health coincides with incremental improvements in health outcomes. Average global life expectancy increased by five years between 1995 and 2011. During that period, the global maternal mortality rate per 100,000 live births decreased from 360 to 210, while infant mortality fell from 85 per 1,000 live births to 48. The worldwide prevalence of HIV/AIDS, World Bank data show, stabilized in 1999.[7] These outcomes represent meaningful gains, though they remain thoroughly unacceptable in light of today's emergent norms, particularly given disparities between affluent and non-affluent populations. Despite these gains, regression in health outcomes is always possible. For example, the maternal mortality rate in the United States doubled between 1987 and 2006.[8] Persistent economic inequality, the displacement of rural smallholders, global warming, and the decline of aid amidst austerity present threats to the incremental health gains presented here.

These pressures have correspondingly fostered countervailing grassroots organization that inserted itself within the larger regime and pressed it to act. Growing CSO activity, including improved cooperation, emerged in response to social inequalities.[9] What Hein and Moon call the "access norm" for essential medicines has helped shape the activities of even the most powerful stakeholders in the global health regime, including states and multinational corporations.[10]

Yet questions remain over whether collective action is sufficiently ambitious. At the time of this writing, national delegations in New York are replacing the Millennium Development Goals, which mostly expire in 2015. The new goals will likely call for eliminating extreme poverty by 2030. It should be noted, however, that the call to end poverty will only hold world leaders accountable to the low threshold of $1.25 per day unless they have more ambitious national poverty lines. Nor do the no goals in their draft form directly address inequality, a key problem underscoring health disparities.[11] Although the proposed goals heavily emphasize health outcomes, there is no explicit commitment to world-wide universal health care, even though the General Assembly called for this in 2012.[12] Despite clearly emergent norms in international rela-tions emphasizing the right to health, powerful actors remain hesitant to commit to public action on a scale sufficient to eliminate health dis-parities. Nevertheless today's global health regime retains unprecedented networks of actors prepared to marshal resources toward improved health cooperation.

Regime Complexity as the New Normal

It is important to remember how improbable the rise of global health (and of aid more generally) would have seemed even as late as the mid-1990s. Once the Cold War period ended, levels of development assistance dropped off considerably. Yet even as aid declined there were also evident changes in how it was viewed by aid distributors. In ret-rospect, we can look back at this period and see the consensus taking shape. Results-based aid became increasingly important in the 1990s. Africa's economic decline, combined with its exploding AIDS crisis, put this region at the center of attention in international development. Economists and, increasingly, policymakers began to see reversing Afri-ca's decline as germane to the DAC's interests. These issues became particularly pressing as urbanization and globalization in the broader economy created concerns over new vulnerabilities, most glaringly the rapid spread of HIV/AIDS. They also coincided with the securitization of Africa by the United States as newly created AFRICOM found a place in a grander "war on terrorism" scheme. Though the international community backed away from the totality of health as defined by the WHO, potentially transnational epidemics fell under the aegis of global governance. Actors such as the World Bank, the UNDP, and the WHO produced reports that placed health at the center of international devel-opment (most importantly, *Investing in Health*)—reports that would be palatable to an emerging global consensus.

Additionally, the development community faced withering criti-cism associated with the structural adjustment policies of the 80s and 90s. As health conditions worsened, Western creditors and powerful development agencies had pressed for austerity measures that limited governments' roles in public health. During the Washington Consensus years, a "boot straps" policy largely prevailed. In other words, development policy among Western agencies was predicated on incentivizing better decisions on the part of the poor, in part by removing state-led efforts to promote economic security. Poverty was considered a failure of state rather than markets. As Ananya Roy documents in her essential book *Poverty Capital*, this doctrine gradually lost currency as the Washington Consensus failed to fulfill its promise, and as developing countries increasingly resisted the severe austerity policies of the IMF and the World Bank.[13]

In Roy's narrative, the elite neoliberal consensus in Washington begins to look more closely at the human development factors that arguably precede economic growth. This "millennial" era of development coincides with a heighted global conscientiousness of human development issues and, eventually, increased development assistance in the 2000s. This expansive concept of human development emphasizes individual empowerment, personal well-being, education, gender equality, civic participation, and ecological health (alongside traditional liberal understandings of growth). It helped to reframe economic development in the 1990s. This dramatic rethinking was encouraged through the highly influential work of economists Mahbub ul Haq, who pioneered the UNDP's annual human development reports, and Amartya Sen, whose 1999 manifesto *Development as Freedom* (adapted from speeches to the World Bank) gained wide currency.[14] For Sen, poverty is a form of repression limiting the choices of billions of people to maximize their physical well-being and pursue fulfilling human endeavors. Development should alter these repressive structures, thereby promoting freedom. Both of these figures adeptly worked from within the halls of development institutions as well as from without, impacting the broader academic debate for a generation inclined to reinvent itself in the post Washington Consensus years.

The idea of health as central to development was also facilitated by World Bank and WHO efforts to chronicle the economic burden of disease for the purpose of more accurately targeting development aid. The Bank's first massive undertaking to chronicle world health conditions was released in 1996.[15] The follow-up, *Global Burdens of Disease and Risk Factors*, released in 2006 after years of research by the Bank-financed Disease Control Priorities Project, has become the standard for assessing disease burden and is cited widely throughout development agencies.[16] This flurry of activity and norm-entrepreneurship evinces the emergence of an epistemic community that is oriented toward addressing economic burdens of disease. The development of disease burden as a standardized measure is significant because it allowed global need (at least according to the Bank's economics-infused understandings) to be mapped. This resultantly put pressure on development agencies to adapt their policies accordingly. More controversially, these reports, widely presented as magisterial rather than value-laden understandings of disease, emphasize cost-effectiveness and economic productivity rather than health outcomes *per se*. For these reasons, critics see this measure of global disease burden as analytically flawed (see chapter 1). As the discourse changed, and health rose as a central development priority, the line between health and economics blurred.

The global health consensus emerges in this broader context. Contemporary foreign aid patterns reflect a change of thinking that gives health a central place in international development. It is not exactly that human development has replaced raw growth figures as benchmarks for the success of development efforts (though these human development indicators are increasingly important). Rather, human development issues such as global health have become key ingredients for increasing growth. The dominant development narrative sees global health as a cause of growth, not a substitute for it. For these reasons, global health has its own idiosyncrasies within the broader development project. It is among the first of the major development issues to receive heightened attention during the post-Cold War era. This is evident in ODA patterns. Remarkably, aid to health steadily increased as ODA itself was deemed by some to be disappearing. Table 5.1 shows health's growing share of the development assistance pie in the post-Cold War era. While overall development assistance was—recalling the words of Therien and Lloyd—"on the brink," global health funding increased dramatically.[17] The ten-year period from 1991 to 2000 shows health's relative prominence increase as a focus of development efforts. In 1991, as the Cold War receded, overall development assistance (in constant 2005 dollars) topped $65 billion. During that year the total global health outlay was $5.3 billion, less than 9 percent of overall development assistance. By 1993 development assistance declined to below $50 billion overall, not eclipsing that level again until 1996. Health ODA by contrast leaped past $6 billion at mid-decade, reaching $7.8 billion in 1996. By that year aid to health had a 15 percent share of world development assistance, the highest on record in recent decades. By 2000 aid to health

Table 5.1. Health's Share as a Percentage of World Aid 1991–2000

Year	World ODA	Health ODA	Share
1991	$65,393	$5,343	8.17%
1992	55,613	5,800	10.43
1993	49,062	6,389	13.02
1994	49,645	6,033	12.15
1995	49,738	6,696	13.46
1996	54,574	7,887	14.45
1997	52,049	8,190	15.74
1998	60,647	8,585	14.16
1999	67,347	7,449	11.06
2000	72,047	10,069	13.98

Source: CRS Database, in millions of 2005 dollars.

neared $11 billion, foreshadowing the even faster surge in funding that happened later that decade.

If the global recession continues into the indefinite future, miring the global north in a Japan-like period of long term stagnation, we may see OECD states tire of their positions as the global health regime's primary external financiers. This scenario is entirely possible though it is worth noting that health's central position in international development could potentially offset such an occurrence. Even Japan's prolonged recession did not stop global health funding from increasing during the 1990s.[18] Health's central position in international development is very well established among these traditional state actors. Another major factor is the growth in new and nontraditional actors in global health. The number of committed channels for aid to health has increased. Relatively new agencies like the Global Fund provide avenues for funding that did not previously exist, and will likely play a role in continuing high aid volumes. Warren Buffet's $31 billion contribution to the Bill and Melinda Gates Foundation in 2006 ensures that the foundation will retain a palpable presence in global health activity for the foreseeable future. The regime may well benefit from a series of new feedback effects that took shape during the rise of global health. Much of the new resources devoted to health during that expansionary period are path dependent, with influential constituencies across the business, political, and academic tableau.

This book correspondingly makes another critical observation: Specialization is apparent in global aid patterns. This phenomenon has gone understudied by the academic literature, which generally tends to look at global ODA trends rather than those of specific aid producers. The data collected for this book on state and multilateral actors, aforementioned caveats notwithstanding, show very high levels of specialization among virtually all actors. The data for all DAC cases show that this trend is not just limited to our earlier case studies. Beyond the cases we have already looked at, there are a number of important specialization cases. European states, along with the European Union itself, specialize largely in health infrastructure. US specialization in AIDS over other issues has obscured the fact that its European counterparts are investing in health systems infrastructure. This is a key pattern overlooked by critics charging that the international community has turned too sharply toward HIV/AIDS. In reality the AIDS pivot was driven largely by the United States, not the DAC at large. An appendix at the back of this book shows aid patterns for the rest of the DAC membership.

However individuated, specialization comes in the context of ideological conformity that has become apparent across a diversity of actors. States, multilaterals, and NGOs in this study operate in surprisingly similar ways. Highly diverse entities—ranging from the WHO to the World Bank to the Gates Foundation—espouse economism in public health. The World Bank's 1993 development report marked a clear movement away from this more broad-based value in favor of an emphasis on smaller scale, cost-effective interventions aimed at specific disease burdens. It is the latter value that predominates today. Of the bilateral cases explored here, only Sweden maintains serious support for the idea of large publicly financed health systems as an exportable model. This is not to understate the conflict within the regime. Indeed, overlapping spheres of governance are conducive to normative dispute. Norms governing intellectual property enforcement, as we saw in the previous chapter, were altogether at loggerheads with civil society organizations seeking greater drug access. Emphasis on neoliberal efficiency by the World Bank, WTO, and IMF come as the WHO revisits primary care perspectives. Regime complexes also create a new canvas for contestation.

If its critics are correct, we may expect further fragmentation, overlap, inefficiencies, and, generally, wasted resources without the requisite results. Indeed, even though Garrett appears to support the increases in aid, the logical implication of her finding is that policymakers would do well to rethink the vast expansion of aid and bureaucracy devoted to global health. The creation of the Global Fund, Stop TB, the Global Alliance for Vaccine Immunization (GAVI) and PEPFAR could be construed as terrible mistakes that have had the unintended consequences of adding vagaries to the global mission of improving health. In that sense, this book offers a more optimistic analytical perspective, making note of attendant opportunities as well as difficulties. Its logical normative conclusion is that the global public health regime can sensibly expand in size, addressing public health challenges in decentralized, localized patterns rather than through central command. This helps resolve an important conundrum: While there is a large school of thought that believes that aid to health suffers from gaping misallocation, most scholars also realize that the current levels of international aid to health are not yet commensurate to the problem of disease in developing countries. Many of the same critics realize that, in fact, much more aid is needed in order to reverse the tide of avoidable insecurity—physical and mental—that severely impacts the world's poorest countries. Activists, health experts, and communities in these areas are doing much to improve their own conditions, as well as influence global institutions. Well placed development assistance promises to support these efforts.

It is important to reiterate that the purpose of development assistance is not to produce efficiency per se, but to facilitate the right to health. Nevertheless, efficiency has become a constant mantra within the global development project, emphasized at least as loudly as human development concerns. The regime faces crucial questions over how well its expanded funds will be used in light of the increased emphasis on efficiency and effectiveness. Critics such as Laurie Garret, as well as aid-producing agencies themselves, warn that inefficient uses of funds could cause "fatigue" among financiers who see inadequate results.[19] Measures such as improved epidemiology have emerged to pinpoint potential areas in which the global health regime should intervene. An epistemic community of global health experts in the WHO, World Bank, and other institutions has utilized these approaches in order to push aid producers in the direction of using funds effectively. This community has been enlarged by economists, particularly those at the Bank whose influence has increased. Other key institutions, particularly the WHO under Brundtland, have embraced the input of development economists as they strategize how to approach public health. The ascendancy of economically driven institutions has altered the practice of global health.

As funds have grown, official discussion increasingly concerns aid effectiveness. These concerns have emerged vocally in the official discourse on AIDS, which has received the largest amount of new financing. While major aid specialists—most notably the US and World Bank—have committed enormous amounts of new funding, UNAIDS has emerged as a normative purveyor for global AIDS policy. Like other cases we have explored, UNAIDS utilizes its significant expertise and moral credibility to assert itself in a coordinating role. As global financing toward AIDS has increased, UNAIDS has developed systems and procedures designed to make these myriad programs work more efficiently. By the early 2000s these efficiency issues were the subject of official discussion by the agency, as noted in an executive director's report by Peter Piot:

> As the international resource environment changes and new funding becomes available . . . the role of UNAIDS is changing. Greater assistance will be required by countries in refining cost estimates of the expanded response and allocating adequate resources, instituting accountable disbursement mechanisms, developing stronger monitoring and evaluation capacities and strengthening their management capabilities.[20]

Adaptations to this role include a change in the bureaucratic culture at UNAIDS toward a focus on implementation. The five-year evaluation for UNAIDS stressed the need for greater technical support at the country level. In response, UNAIDS has allocated some of its core funding for "Regional Technical Support Facilities," groups of experts who provide technical support and training at the country level.[21]

In 2004 UNAIDS met with wealthy states to come to an agreement on ways to streamline AIDS programs. Within UNAIDS, the move reflected the recent change in thinking that called for enhanced efficiency:

> In the past, AIDS advocacy for developing countries has focused largely on fostering leadership and mobilizing financial resources adequate to the scale of the epidemic. Both of these focuses remain necessary but, now that leadership and financial resources are more in evidence, attention is turning to the urgent question of how to make the money work and how to ensure leadership can be genuinely effective in changing the course of the epidemic.[22]

The result was a worldwide agreement on efficiency standards. The "Three Ones" program seeks to create country-level AIDS policies that are fully unified between local governments, international organizations, DAC states, and civil societies. The agreement calls for these groups to have "one" agreed-upon policy framework that coordinates the efforts of all involved entities, "one" national AIDS coordinating authority that involves all sectors, and "one" agreed-upon country-level monitoring and evaluation system. UNAIDS works with these groups to facilitate this framework. In 2005, the UN created the Global Task Team on Improving AIDS Coordination Among Multilateral Institutions and International Donors (GTT) in order to systematically address problems in implementing the Three Ones. It called on UNAIDS to issue an AIDS support plan that provides a blueprint for dealing with funding bottlenecks and a rational division of labor. The resulting plan enhanced its technical support for states seeking grants from the Global Fund, aiding them in developing and maintaining programs that are eligible for funding.[23]

Additionally, decentralization ensures that reforms take place through independent action (though with a modicum of global standards), raising compliance challenges but also allowing developing countries greater latitude. In late 2012, the UN General Assembly (with surprising north-south support) called for universal health care as the global benchmark, limiting out-of-pocket expenses.[24] At the time of this writing there is still hope that universal health care could in some form appear on the post-MDG agenda currently under discussion. Just how the international community will pursue it remains an open question. The world's poorest regions will require aid. "External financing equally remains an important factor in Zambia's resource mobilization," that country's delegate, Dr. Mwaba Kasese-Bota, told the UK Guardian.[25] The Singaporean delegate noted that countries will ultimately follow their own guidelines: "The path to achieving universal health coverage is complex and there is no universal formula. Instead, member states should adopt different solutions to their unique circumstances."[26] Resolutions in Westphalian bodies of international cooperation set standards, while implementation is polycentric. What is clear is that the regime complex for global health will remain the chessboard upon which future reforms will be carried out.

The corresponding diffusion of the consensus, for all its flaws, indicates that even vast, disperse regimes like public health are capable of articulating paths to reform. The regime complex literature has usefully pointed out caveats to this argument, but risks focusing too heavily on the commonly held stereotypes about international organizations being overly bureaucratic and incapable of taking action to produce discernible results. This book raises the possibility that efficiency can be overemphasized in public health, above and beyond the obvious importance of achieving development outcome at the least possible cost. While recognizing the challenges presented by the narrative of overexpansion, the analysis that we have seen in these pages gives rise to a different set of concerns.

The emphasis on specific diseases, instead of a more holistic approach, has spurred single-issue specialization, but, many argue, has taken specialization too far. This is evidenced by the growing number of single-issue agencies, a development known as verticalization. Critics of the regime argue that the proliferation of these agencies ultimately offsets existent drives for efficiency, threatening to create even greater confusion in recipient countries. Single-issue approaches, they say, siphon away funds from the holistic development of improved general health systems. Moreover the explosion of nongovernmental actors in global health effectively privatizes local health systems, discouraging direct public investments in health. The widespread ideological conformity with the global health consensus is rooted in a neoliberal philosophy that is skeptical of government activism. Yet government activism on the part of developing countries is what will be required if they are to build sustainable health systems. Realizing the right to health ultimately means that local systems will have to be capable of addressing health's holistic challenges rather than addressing single issues piecemeal.

The current push for increased efficiency is driven largely by economists rather than medical personnel. As a result it risks focusing on low cost measures in lieu of large-scale interventions that might be necessary. The reframing of health as a development issue risks ripping the concept of health away from its biomedical and human rights origins, and toward the World Bank's notion of growth at all costs. The current approaches to health focus more on the positive externalities of optimal health—enhanced productivity, reduced drag on growth—than on health itself. This portends a less robust vision of public health. The impetus for low-cost interventions as a factor in producing economic growth is at odds with the WHO's old mantra of "health for all," which emphasized the need for broader government interventions in public health, and for grassroots action. Economic understandings of health doubtlessly attracted more resources to health, but also offer minimalist understandings of health centered on fighting costly epidemics and global vulnerability reduction. The right to health by contrast encompasses environmental and social determinates of health as well as distributive questions such as the right to essential medicines.[27]

The global emphasis on efficiency itself raises persistent ethical challenges that lie at the very foundations of health advocacy: To what extent do economism's notions of "cost-effectiveness" and "replicable" expenditures undermine health's long place as a basic human right? Who is entitled to treatment and who is not? Which epidemics—and which populations—are worthy of international intervention? Does health remain a basic human right at all? More resources than ever are available to address public health challenges, yet there is heightened emphasis on resource maximization and productivity, all of which potentially conflict with the allocation of resources on the basis of socioeconomic need. The dramatic influx of global resources has been accompanied by an ideology of minimalism predicated upon economic logic.

The principle that health is the responsibility of the state is getting short shrift in the neoliberal context of the global health regime's expansion. So while powerful actors in the regime may be more willing and able to address the burden of disease, they may not at all be doing so in a way that promises the long term, stable infrastructure that government provides. Committed advocates for government involvement in health (those voices that had previously been allowed hearing in multilateral agencies) and voices of the global south may be alienated from global health governance. In this sense the regime is less democratic, with ideologically narrow voices such as Gates Foundation carrying disproportionate influence. To understand the patterns of ideological convergence and the process of economization is to better understand these challenges facing the regime.

Aid Priorities Among DAC Bilateral Donors

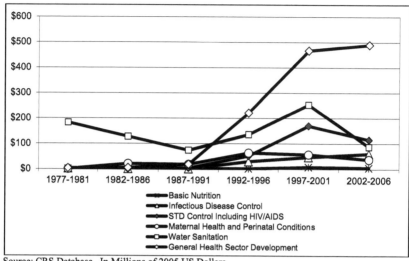

Source: CRS Database. In Millions of 2005 US Dollars.

Figure A.1. Australian Health ODA to Major Issue Areas

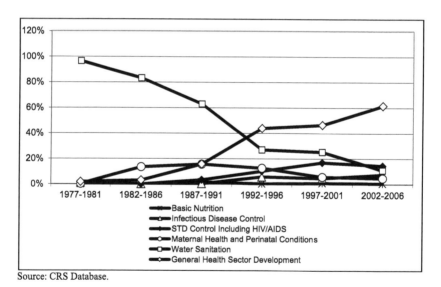

Source: CRS Database.

Figure A.2. Australian Health ODA to Major Issue Areas by Percentage Share

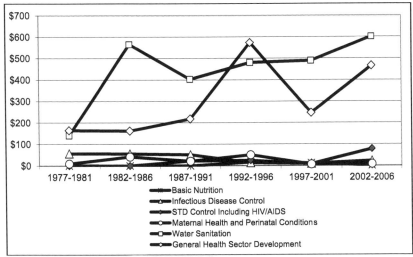

Source: CRS Database. In Millions of 2005 US Dollars.

Figure A.3. Danish Health ODA to Major Issue Areas

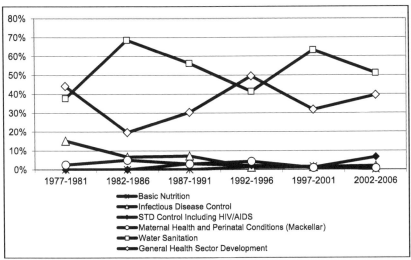

Source: CRS Database.

Figure A.4. Danish Health ODA to Major Issue Areas by Percentage Share

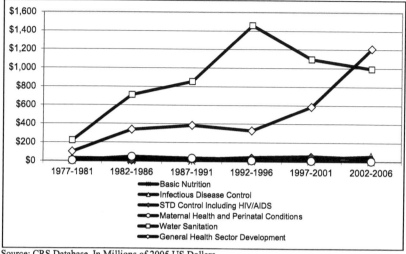

Source: CRS Database. In Millions of 2005 US Dollars.

Figure A.5. French Health ODA to Major Issue Areas

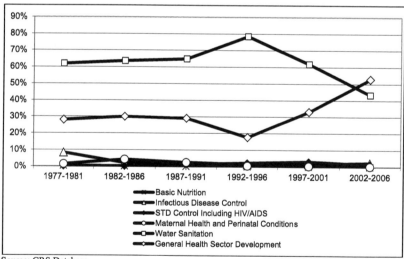

Source: CRS Database.

Figure A.6. French Health ODA to Major Issue Areas by Percentage Share

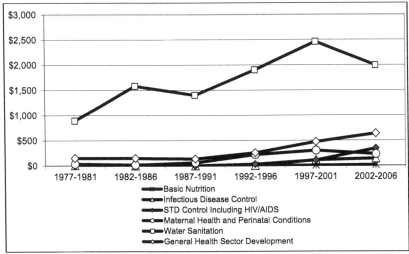

Source: CRS Database. In Millions of 2005 US Dollars.

Figure A.7. German Health ODA to Major Issue Areas

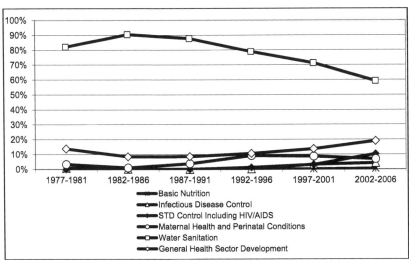

Source: CRS Database.

Figure A.8. German Health ODA to Major Issue Areas by Percentage Share

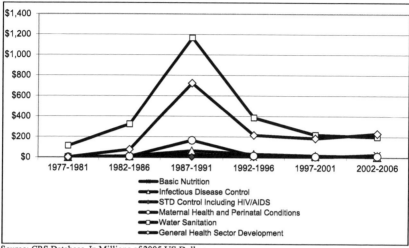

Source: CRS Database. In Millions of 2005 US Dollars.

Figure A.9. Italian Health ODA to Major Issue Areas

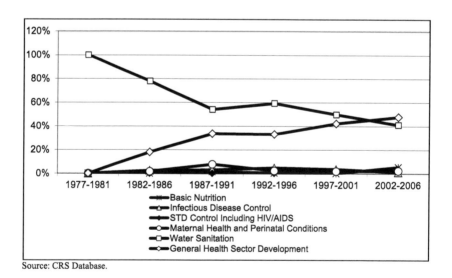

Source: CRS Database.

Figure A.10. Italian Health ODA to Major Issue Areas by Percentage Share

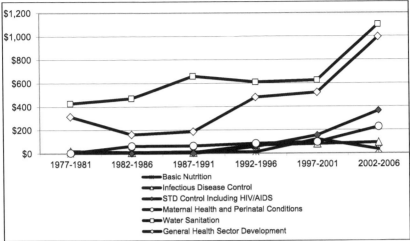

Source: CRS Database. In Millions of 2005 US Dollars.

Figure A.11. Netherlands Health ODA to Major Issue Areas

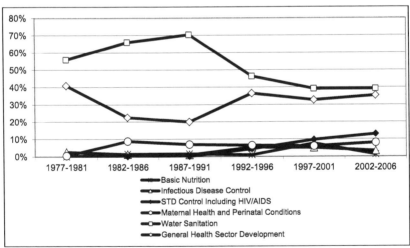

Source: CRS Database.

Figure A.12. Netherlands Health ODA to Major Issue Areas by Percentage Share

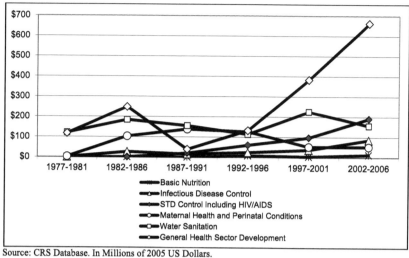

Source: CRS Database. In Millions of 2005 US Dollars.

Figure A.13. Norwegian Health ODA to Major Issue Areas

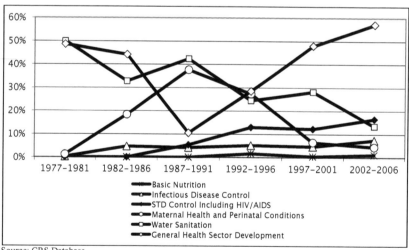

Source: CRS Database.

Figure A.14. Norwegian Health ODA to Major Issue Areas by Percentage Share

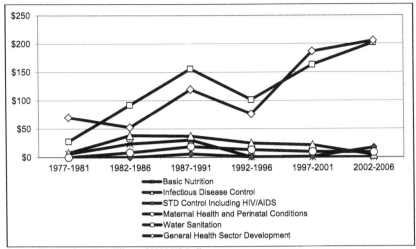

Source: CRS Database. In Millions of 2005 US Dollars.

Figure A.15. Swiss Health ODA to Major Issue Areas

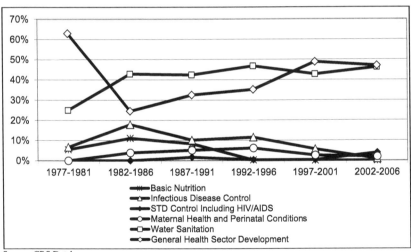

Source: CRS Database.

Figure A.16. Swiss Health ODA to Major Issue Areas by Percentage Share

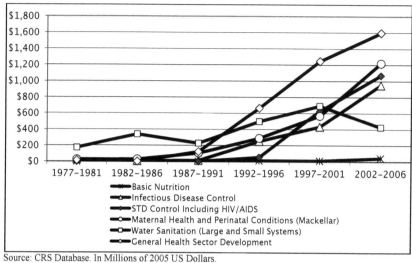

Source: CRS Database. In Millions of 2005 US Dollars.

Figure A.17. United Kingdom Health ODA to Major Issue Areas

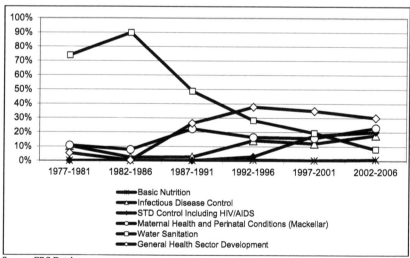

Source: CRS Database.

Figure A.18. United Kingdom Health ODA to Major Issue Areas by Percentage Share

Notes

Chapter 1

1. Karen J. Alter and Sophie Meunier, "The Politics of International Regime Complexity," *Perspectives on Politics* 7 (2009): 13–24.

2. For a discussion on the World Bank's usurpation of some WHO influence, see Kelley Lee, *The World Health Organization (WHO)* (New York: Routledge, 2009), p. 111, and Kamran Abbassi, "The World Bank and World Health: Changing Sides," *BMJ* 318 (1999): 865–69.

3. Laurie Garrett, "The Challenge of Global Health," *Foreign Affairs* 86, no. 1 (2007): 14–38, p. 14.

4. WHO Constitution (1946), available at http://www.who.int/governance/eb/constitution/en/.

5. Kelley Lee, "Understandings of Global Health Governance: The Contested Landscape," in Adrian Kay and Owain David Williams eds., *Global Health Governance: Crisis, Institutions and Political Economy* (New York: Palgrave, 2009), 27–41, p. 29.

6. Lee, "Understandings of Global Health Governance," p. 28.

7. See, for instance, Eibe Riedel, "The Human Right to Health: Conceptual Foundations," in Andrew Clapham, Mary Robinson, Claire Mahon, and Scott Jerbi eds., *Realizing the Right to Health* (Zurich: Swiss Human Rights Book Vol. 3, 2009), 21–39.

8. Karen J. Alter and Sophie Meunier, "Nested and Overlapping Regimes in the Transatlantic Banana Trade Dispute," *Journal of European Public Policy* 13 (2006): 362–82.

9. Alter and Meunier, "Nested and Overlapping Regimes in the Transatlantic Banana Trade Dispute," p. 363.

10. Kal Raustiala and David Victor, "The Regime Complex for Plant Genetic Resources," *International Organization* 58 (2004): 277–309, p. 279.

11. Raustiala and Victor, "The Regime Complex for Plant Genetic Resources," p. 296.

12. Ibid., p. 306.

13. Stephanie C. Hofmann, "Overlapping Institutions in the Realm of International Security: The Case of NATO and ESDP," *Perspective on Politics* 7 (2009): 45–52, p. 46.

14. Judith Kelley, "The More the Merrier? The Effects of Having Multiple International Election Monitoring Organizations," *Perspectives of Politics* 7 (2009): 59–64, p. 62.

15. Robert O. Keohane and David G. Victor, "The Regime Complex for Climate Change," *Perspectives on Politics* 9 (2011): 7–23, p. 7.

16. Keohane and Victor, "The Regime Complex for Climate Change," p. 15.

17. Elinor Ostrom, *Understanding Institutional Diversity* (Princeton: Princeton University Press, 2005), p. 270.

18. Elinor Ostrom, "A Polycentric Approach for Coping With Climate Change," World Bank Policy Research Working Paper 5095 (2009).

19. David Fidler, "Architecture Amidst Anarchy: Global Health Quest for Governance," *Global Health Governance* 1(1) (2007): 1–17, p. 2. In international relations parlance, the term "Westphalian" evokes the Peace of Westphalia that ended the Thirty Years' War in Europe in 1648. The term refers to the norms of domestic sovereignty, centered on the idea of the nation-state that emerged during that time.

20. Fidler, "Architecture Amidst Anarchy," p. 11.

21. Unless otherwise noted, all the data on aid commitments in this book come from the OECD's Creditor Reporting System (CRS) database, which tracks and categorizes aid commitments from all Development Assistance Committee (DAC) members and several major multilateral actors. The data were coded utilizing the following OECD categorizations for aid. "Maternal health and perinatal conditions" combines "reproductive health care" with "family planning." "Water sanitation" combines a variety of water systems categories: "water resources policy and administrative management," "water resources protection," "water supply and sanitation: large systems," "basic drinking water supply and basic sanitation," "river development," "waste management and disposal," and "education and training in water supply and sanitation." "General health sector development," often cited in the book as "health infrastructure," combines "health policy and administration management," "medical education and training," "medical research," "medical services," "basic health care," "basic health infrastructure," "health education," and "health personnel development." Data on AIDS comes from "STD control including HIV/AIDS." Data on communicable diseases comes from the category labeled "infectious disease control." This coding system is similar—though not identical to—those employed in David E. Bloom, "Governing Global Health: How Better Coordination Can Advance Global Health and Improve Value for Money," *Finance and Development* (2007): 31–35, and Landis Mackeller, "Priorities in Global Assistance for Health, AIDS and Population (HAP)" OECD Development Centre, Working Paper no. 244, (2005). Information on the criteria for each OECD category

can be explained, area by area, in Organization for Economic Cooperation and Development, *Reporting Directives for the Creditor Reporting System* (Paris: OECD, 2005), pp. 6–8. Aggregate figures on commitments to global health were calculated by combining the health, population, and water sanitation categories (all subcategories under these headings are shown above in this footnote). The data were reported in 2005 dollars.

22. See WHO Commission on Macroeconomics and Health, *Macroeconomics and Health: Investing in Health for Economic Development* (Geneva: World Health Organization 2001).

23. Jean-Phillipe Therien and Carolyn Lloyd, "Development Assistance on the Brink," *Third World Quarterly* 21 (2000): 21–38.

24. Ibid., p. 21.

25. Sophie Harman, *Global Health Governance* (New York, Routledge, 2012), p. 2.

26. David Fidler, "The Challenges of Global Health Governance," Council on Foreign Relations Working Paper, International Institutions and Global Governance Program (May 2010), p. 9.

27. Jeremy Youde, *Global Health Governance* (Cambridge: Polity, 2012), p. 3.

28. Adrian Kay and Owain Williams, "Introduction: The International Political Economy of Global Health Governance," in Adrian Kay and Owain David Williams eds., *Global Health Governance: Crisis, Institutions and Political Economy* (New York: Palgrave, 2009), 2–23, p. 4.

29. Kay and Williams, "The International Political Economy of Global Health Governance," p. 7.

30. Jennifer Kates, J. Stephen Morrison, and Eric Leif, "Global Health Funding: A Glass Half Full?" p. 187.

31. Garrett, "The Challenge of Global Health," p 23.

32. Jeremy Shiffman, "Has Donor Prioritization of HIV/AIDS Displaced for Other Health Issues?" *Health Policy and Planning* 23 (2008): 95–100.

33. Landis Mackeller, "Priorities in Global Assistance for Health, AIDS and Population (HAP)."

34. William Easterly, *The White Man's Burden: Why the West's Efforts to Aid the Rest Have Done So Much Ill and So Little Good* (New York: Penguin, 2007); Dambisa Moyo, *Dead Aid: Why Aid is Not Working and How There is a Better Way for Africa* (New York: Farrar, Strauss, and Giroux, 2010).

35. This despite the rather undisciplined nature of capital markets in the late 2000s.

36. Financial figures in Table 1.3 are based on expenditures, including operating costs and grants. For the most recent figures available, see President's Emergency Program for AIDS Relief, "PEPFAR Funding: Investments that Save Lives and Promote Security," PEPFAR (June 2011). The reported figure for PEPFAR includes a $1 billion contribution to the Global Fund, and excludes malaria funding. For the Global Fund figure, see The Global Fund to Fight

AIDS Tuberculosis and Malaria, *The Global Fund Annual Report 2010* (Geneva: GFATM, 2010), p. 50. The figure above includes the fund's entire grant portfolio for 2010. Data for GAIN based on expenditures for 2010. See The Global Alliance for Improved Nutrition, *Financial Statements for the Year Ended 2010 and Report of the Statutory Auditor* (Geneva: GAIN 2010), p. 2. Financial data on Stop TB can be found at World Health Organization and Stop TB Partnership, *Stop TB Partnership: Annual Report 2009* (Geneva: WHO, 2009), p. 56. Financial data on the Clinton Foundation available at William J. Clinton Foundation, *Building a Better World: William J. Clinton Foundation Annual Report 2010* (New York: Clinton Foundation, 2011), p. 62. Data on the GAVI alliance found at The GAVI Alliance, *Consolidated Financial Statements and Independent Auditors' Report for the Year Ended 31 December 2009* (Geneva: GAVI Alliance, 2009), p. 4. Reports on the Roll Back Malaria initiative can be found at Roll Back Malaria, *Minutes of the 20th RBM Partnership Board Meeting* (Geneva: RBM, 2011), p. 14. Unlike the other emergent agencies, I make this approximation of the basis of revenue. Information on IAVI reported in International AIDS Vaccine Initiative, Inc., *Consolidated Financial Statements and Other Financial Information Year Ended December 31, 2009* (New York, IAVI, 2009), p. 5. A general overview of the Gates Foundation budget can be found at Bill and Melinda Gates Foundation, "Fact Sheet," *BMG Foundation* (2011). Partners in Health publishes its financial data in html at <http://www.pih.org/annual-report/entry/annual-report-financial-review>. The figure above reports their total expenditures for the fiscal year ending June 30, 2010.

37. Harman, *Global Health Governance*, p. 5.

38. Kelly Lee narrows these perspectives down to "bio-medicine, economism, security, and human rights," see Lee, "Understandings of Global Health Governance," p. 29

39. Fidler, "Architecture Amidst Anarchy," p. 2.

40. The Disease Control Priorities Project (DCPP), sponsored by the World Bank and National Institutes of Health, is the most extensive assessments of global disease patterns. The most recent edition, published in 2006, compiled data for 2001. All disease burden statistics in this book derive from this source unless noted otherwise. Alan D. Lopez, Colin D. Mathers, Majid Ezzati, Dean T. Jamison, and Christopher J. L. Murray, *Global Burden of Disease and Risk Factors* (New York: Oxford University Press, 2006), p. 72.

41. Alan D. Lopez, Colin D. Mathers, Majid Ezzati, Dean T. Jamison, and Christopher J. L. Murray, *Global Burden of Disease and Risk Factors*, p. 8.

42. Alan D. Lopez, et al., *Global Burden of Disease and Risk Factors*, p. 10. This statistic counts only maternal and childhood nutrition, the main beneficiaries in this category. Overall disease burden according to nutritional related risk factors is 29.2 percent in low and middle income countries.

43. As calculated in Mackeller, "Priorities in Global Assistance for Health, AIDS and Population (HAP)."

44. Figures reported in United Nations News Centre, "General Assembly Declares Access to Clear Water and Sanitation is a Human Right," (28 July 2010).

45. Within this cycle, HIV/AIDS received most of these gains in later years, making its gains all the more impressive. Also, although the CRS database combines HIV/AIDS with "STD Control," it is believed that nearly 100 percent of the programs reported are actually for HIV/AIDS. See Shiffman, "Has Donor Prioritization of HIV/AIDS Displaced for Other Health Issues?"

46. For an more complete overview of Neglected Tropical Diseases, see the Center for Disease Control, "Neglected Tropical Diseases," *cdc.gov* <http://www.cdc.gov/globalhealth/ntd/diseases/index.html> (2 November 2012).

47. Harman, *Global Health Governance*, p. 123.

48. Nirmala Ravishankar, Paul Gubbins, Rebecca J. Cooley, Catherine Leach-Kemon, Catherine M. Michaud, Dean T. Jamison, and Christopher J. L. Murray, "Financing of Global Health: Tracking Development Assistance for Health from 1990 to 2007," *The Lancet* 373 (2009): 2113–24, p. 2113.

49. Ravishankar et al., "Financing of Global Health: Tracking Development Assistance for Health from 1990 to 2007," p. 2117.

50. See Christopher J. L Murray, Brent Anderson, Roy Burstein, Katherine Leach-Kemon, Matthew Schneider, Annette Tardif, and Raymond Zhang, "Development Assistance for Health: Trends and Prospects, *The Lancet* 378 (2011): 8–10.

51. Kelley Lee calls this logic "utilitarianism." See Lee, "Understandings of Global Health Governance: The Contested Landscape," pp. 32–33.

52. Fidler, "Architecture Amidst Anarchy," p. 12.

53. United Nations Development Program, *UNDP Strategic Plan, 2008–2011* (New York: UNDP, 2007), p. 10.

54. See The World Bank, *Healthy Development: The World Bank Strategy for Health, Nutrition and Population Results* (Washington, DC: World Bank, 2007), p. 11.

55. These reports are intended to outline the fund's priorities over three year periods.

56. The data below derive from the OECD's CRS database, from 2002–2006, as do all the other cases mentioned in this subsection.

57. It is worth noting that Japan devoted virtually nothing directly to AIDS at this time, though it had made significant contributions to the Global Fund to Fight AIDS, Tuberculosis and Malaria (GFATM).

58. These aid commitments come directly from the European Union itself, excluding individual state donations.

59. Lee, "Understandings of Global Health Goverance: The Contested Landscape," p. 32. Kelley Lee's groundbreaking work explores the role of the World Bank in promoting economism, and influencing other organizations including the WHO. See, especially, Lee, *The World Health Organization (WHO)*, p. 111–228.

60. These landmark agreements greatly emphasize the principles of "donor harmonization," particularly under the banners of "alignment" and "harmonization" among aid producers.

61. Peter Haas, "Do Regimes Matter? Epistemic Communities and Mediterranean Pollution Control," *International Organization* 43 (1989): 377–403.

62. G. John Ikenberry, *After Victory: Institutions, Strategic Restraint, and the Rebuilding of Order After Major Wars* (Princeton, NJ: Princeton University Press, 2001).

63. Paul Pierson, "The New Politics of the Welfare State," *World Politics* 48 (1996): 143–179. Also see Paul Pierson, "The Path to European Integration: A Historical Institutionalist Analysis," *Comparative Political Studies* 29 (1996): 123–63.

Chapter 2

1. Fidler, "Architecture Amidst Anarchy."

2. For a work that makes strong connections between the global trade agenda and health conditions, see Ronald Labonté, Chantal Blouin, and Lisa Forman, "Trade and Health," in Adrian Kay and Owain David Williams eds., *Global Health Governance: Crisis, Institutions, and Political Economy* (New York: Palgrave, 2009): 182–208.

3. In her magisterial book on microfinance, Ananya Roy uses the term "millennial consensus" to define a post-Washington Consensus era in global development characterized by increased aid, an emphasis on human development concerns such as health and education (though not necessarily social or economic equality), and economic liberalism. See Ananya Roy, *Poverty Capital* (New York: Routledge 2010). Also see Josh Leon, "Poverty Capitalism: Interview with Ananya Roy," *Foreign Policy in Focus* (Washington, DC: February 17. 2011).

4. Therien and Lloyd, "Development Assistance on the Brink," p. 21.

5. Convergence refers to the economic theory positing that poorer societies will experience higher growth rates than advanced industrialized countries, over time realizing developmental parity. With unevenness in national growth rates in the global south during the globalization era, economists such as Jeffrey Sachs call for redistributive measures, through foreign aid, to help put poor countries on a convergence path.

6. Jeffrey D. Sachs, "The Development Challenge," *Foreign Affairs* 84 (2005): 78–90, p. 79.

7. In 2005 dollars.

8. However target 6B, universal access to HIV/AIDS treatment, was to be achieved by 2010.

9. These counties are Norway, Luxembourg, Sweden, Denmark, and the Netherlands.

10. See Ravishankar et al., "Financing of Global Health," and Murray et al., "Development Assistance for Health."

11. United States Agency for International Development, *Foreign Aid in the National Interest* (Washington, DC: USAID, 2002), p. 3.

12. United States Agency for International Development, *Child Survival and Health Programs Fund Progress Report* (Washington, DC: USAID, 2004), p. 8.

13. Ibid., p. 19.

14. "AIDS Prevention Possible With Audacious Action," *Canadian Business and Current Affairs Medical Post*, 6 August 2002, 21, and Joint United Nations Programme on HIV/AIDS, *2006 Report on the Global AIDS Epidemic* (Geneva: Switzerland, 2006).

15. "The Self-Interest Case for US Global Health Cooperation," *The Lancet* 349 (1997): 1037.

16. US funding constituted 47 percent of the world's total AIDS funding in 1997, making it the largest donor even when AIDS was a fairly low priority, as reported in Barton Gellman, "The Global Response to AIDS in Africa: World Shunned Signs of the Coming Plague," *Washington Post* (July 5, 2000), A1. The United States currently has 1.2 million people living with HIV or AIDS according to the CIA World Factbook.

17. United States Agency for International Development, *Foreign Aid in the National Interest*, p. 6.

18. Ibid., p. 91.

19. "FACT Sheet: United States Africa Command," *africom.mil* <http://www.africom.mil/getArticle.asp?art=1644> (24 May 2012).

20. See Siri Bjerkreim Hellevik, "'Making the Money Work': Challenges Towards Coordination of HIV/AIDS Programmes in Africa," in Sandra J. MacLean, Sherri A. Brown, and Pieter Fourie eds., *Health for Some: The Political Economy of Global Health Governance* (New York: Palgrave, 2009), 142–61.

21. United States Agency for International Development, *Reducing the Threat of Infectious Diseases of Major Public Health Importance: USAID's Initiative to Prevent and Control Effective Diseases*, (Washington, DC: USAID, 1998), 5.

22. Tuberculosis and Malaria's share of health ODA are included under the "infectious disease control" category in figures 2.4 and 2.5. PEPFAR also addresses both of these epidemics.

23. "Health Overview," *usaid.gov* <http://www.usaid.gov/our_work/global health/> (3 December 2008).

24. "Coping With AIDS in Africa: Three Years into the WHO Program on AIDS," Hearing Before the Subcommittee on Africa of the House Committee on Foreign Affairs," (June 14, 1989), p. 68.

25. The reauthorization includes funds for the Global Fund for AIDS, Tuberculosis and Malaria. United States Agency for International Development, "Fast Facts: HIV/AIDS," (Washington, DC: USAID, 2008).

26. Claire Provost, "Anti-Prostitution Pledge in US AIDS Funding 'Damaging' HIV Response," UK Guardian (24 July 2012).

27. See The US President's Emergency Program For AIDS Relief, "Comprehensive HIV Prevention for People Who Inject Drugs, Revised Guidance," (Washington, DC: July 2010)

28. Siri Bjerkreim Hellevik, "'Making the Money Work': Challenges Towards Coordination of HIV/AIDS Programmes in Africa," p. 155.

29. Ibid., p. 156.

30. This is followed by "Joint Planning Countries," where aid resources are capable of making a significant but "lesser" global impact, and "Special Circumstance Countries," which have considerable political or economic significance, or are in a particular crisis.

31. United States Agency for International Development, Report to Congress: Child Survival and Health Programs Progress Report (Washington, DC: USAID, 2004), p. 4.

32. For an excellent concise discussion on the GHI and aid effectiveness see, especially, Amanda Glassman and Denizhan Duran, "Global Health Initiative 2.0: Effective Priority Setting in a Time of Austerity," Center for Global Development (30 January, 2012).

33. The Henry J. Kaiser Family Foundation, "US Global Health Policy: 2012 Survey on the US Role in Global Health, (May 2012), p. 5.

34. Rodney Loeppky, "The Accumulative Nature of the US Health Complex," in Sandra J. MacLean, Sherri A. Brown, and Pieter Fourie eds., Health for Some: The Political Economy of Global Health Governance (New York: Palgrave, 2009), 39–52, p. 39.

35. Japan Ministry of Foreign Affairs, "Japan's Official Development Assistance Charter," (Tokyo: MOFA, 2003), p. 3.

36. Junichiro Koizumi, "Statement by Prime Minister Junichiro Koizumi, Africa: The Home of Self-Endeavor," Mofa.go.jp May 1, 2006 <http://www.mofa.go.jp/region/africa/pmv0605/state.html/> (December 12, 2006).

37. Japan International Cooperation Agency, Second Study on International Cooperation for Population and Development (Tokyo: Institute for International Cooperation, 2003), p. 12.

38. Masahiko Koumura, "Global Health and Japan's Foreign Policy—From Okanawa to Toyako," mofa.go.jp November 25, 2007 <http://mofa.go.jp/policy/health_c/address0711.html/> (12 December, 2008).

39. Japan Ministry of Foreign Affairs, "Japan's Contribution in Achieving the Health Related MDGs," (Tokyo: MOFA, 2005).

40. Howard Lehman, "Japan's Foreign Aid Policy to Africa Since the Tokyo International Conference on African Development," Pacific Affairs 78 (2005): 423–42.

41. See, for example, Steven W. Hook and Guang Zang, "Japan's Aid Policy Since the Cold War: Rhetoric and Reality," Asian Survey 38 (1998): 1051–1066; Alan Rix, Japan's Economic Aid: Policy-Making and Politics (New York: St. Martin's

Press, 1980), p. 268; and Xiaoming Zhou, "Japan's Official Development Assistance Program: Pressures to Expand," *Asian Survey* 31 (1991): 341–50.

42. Justin McCurry, "Monitoring Japan's Aid Commitments," *The Lancet* 368 (2006): 1561–62.

43. Japan Ministry of Foreign Affairs, *Japan's Official Development Assistance Charter*, p. 2.

44. Mitsuya Araki, "Japan's Official Development Assistance: The Japan ODA Model That Began Life in Southeast Asia," *Asia-Pacific Review* 14, no. 2 (2007): 17–29.

45. This area of specialization also reflects a deficiency in the face-to-face field presence required by "soft" interventions such as education, personnel training and other knowledge-based practices that characterize agencies such as USAID. For ample discussion on Japan's capital intensive approach to development, see David Arase's edited volume, *Japan's Foreign Aid: Old Continuities and New Directions* (Abingdon: Routledge, 2005).

46. Figure cited in Kevin Morrison, "The World Bank, Japan, and Aid Effectiveness," in *Japan's Foreign Aid: Old Continuities and New Directions* ed. David Arase (Abingdon: Routledge, 2005), 23–40, p. 26.

47. Japan International Cooperation Agency, *Second Study on International Cooperation for Population and Development: New Insights from the Japanese Experience*, p. 1.

48. Japan International Cooperation Agency, "Japan's Efforts in ODA," (Tokyo: JICA, 2006). This is larger than the second and third largest aid distributors (the United States and Germany at 15 percent of water aid each).

49. Marie Soderberg, "Swedish Perceptions of Japanese ODA," p. 92.

50. Japan International Cooperation Agency, *Approaches for Systemic Planning of Development Projects: Water Resources*, p. xiv.

51. Government of Japan, "Water Sanitation Broad Partnership Initiative (WASABI)," (Tokyo: JICA, 2006), p. 2.

52. Japan International Cooperation Agency, *Approaches for Systemic Planning of Development Projects: Water Resources*, p. xii.

53. Ibid., p. 8.

54. Ibid., p. 10.

55. Ibid., p. 10.

56. Japan International Cooperation Agency, *Approaches for Systematic Planning of Development Projects: Basic Education, Anti-HIV/AIDS Measures, Promotion of Small and Medium Enterprises, Rural Development* (Tokyo: JICA, 2003), p. 1.

57. Ibid., p. 82.

58. Japan International Cooperation Agency, *Approaches for Systematic Planning of Development Projects: Basic Education, Anti-HIV/AIDS Measures, Promotion of Small and Medium Enterprises, Rural Development*, p. 82.

59. Junichiro Koizumi, "Statement by Prime Minister Junichiro Koizumi, Africa: The Home of Self-Endeavor."

60. Swedish International Development Agency, *Health Is Wealth* (Stockholm: SIDA, 2002), p. 4.

61. "While we can appreciate this recognition," said Minister for International Development Cooperation Gunilla Carlsson, in response Sweden's place at the top of the CDG's donor ratings, "it is the total commitment of the world that is crucial. Sweden is not only proactive in development efforts, it is also proactive in getting other donors to increase their commitments." "Sweden Best at Development Assistance," *Sweden.gov.se*, 9 December 2008 <http://www.sweden.gov.se/sb/d/11214/a/117202> (12 December 2009).

62. See Soderberg, "Swedish Perceptions of Japanese ODA." Soderberg contends that Swedish aid may favor recipients with strong social democratic presences.

63. "Sweden's New Development Cooperation Policy," *Sweden.gov.se* 20 September 2007 <http://www.sweden.gov.se/sb/d/9439/a/88669> (12 December 2008).

64. "Sweden's New Development Cooperation Policy," *Sweden.gov.se*.

65. Gunilla Carlsson, "Speech By Gunilla Carlsson at the ABCDE-Conference 2010," *Government.se*, 31 May 2010 <http://www.government.se/sb/d/7953/a/146942> (18 December 2012).

66. Swedish International Development Cooperation Agency, *Health Is Wealth*, p. 16.

67. Sweden Ministry of Foreign Affairs, "Focused Bilateral Development Cooperation," (Stockholm: MOFA, 2008), p. 1.

68. Ibid., p. 5.

69. Ibid., p. 5.

70. Swedish International Development Cooperation Agency, *Health Is Wealth*, p. 9.

71. Ibid., p. 31.

72. Ibid., p. 30.

73. Swedish Ministry for Foreign Affairs, *Investing for Future Generations: Sweden's International Response to HIV/AIDS* (Stockholm: SMFA, 1999), p. 7.

74. Ibid., p. 40.

75. Ibid., p. 10.

76. Ibid., p. 46.

77. Kim Richard Nossal, "Mixed Motives Revisited: Canada's Interest in Development Assistance," *Canadian Journal of Political Science* 21, no. 1 (1988): 35–56. Nossal argues that Canada mainly ascribes to the foreign policy model, contending that "Canada's development assistance program is designed primarily to benefit the interests of Canadian foreign policy makers; other beneficiaries, whether in Canada or in underdeveloped countries, are of distinctly secondary importance," p. 38. Also see Ryan Macdonald and John Hoddinott, "Determinates of Canadian Bilateral Aid Allocations: Humanitarian, Commercial or Political?" *Canadian Journal of Economics* 37 (2004): 294–312. Macdonald and

Hoddinotts' study of Canadian ODA patterns between 1984 and 2000 see the humanitarian cause as more prominent, calling its program "moderately altruistic," p. 296.

78. See David R. Morrison's magisterial *Aid and Ebb Tide: A History of CIDA and Canadian Development Assistance*, particularly chapter 2 for the Cold War origins of Canadian development assistance.

79. See Macdonald and Hoddinott, "Determinates of Canadian Bilateral Aid Allocations: Humanitarian, Commercial or Political?" Macdonald and Hoddinott contend that Canada's commercial motives saw increasing importance to Canadian ODA in the later years under study.

80. Parliamentary Information and Research Service, "Official Development Assistance Spending," (Ottawa: Library of Parliament, 2007).

81. This despite spearheading a major initiative in 2010 to address maternal and infant health, an ambitious pledge during Canada's G8 Presidency that year.

82. Janet Davison, "Does Cutting Foreign Aid Threaten Canada's Reputation in the World?" *CBC News* (3 April 2012).

83. Colleen O'Manique, "Palliative Interventions: Canadian Foreign Policy, Security, and Global Health Governance," in Sandra J. MacLean, Sherri A. Brown, and Pieter Fourie eds., *Health for Some: The Political Economy of Global Health Governance* (New York: Palgrave, 2009), 53–66, p. 57.

84. *Canada in the World* is available in html format; "VI. International Assistance," *Foreign Affairs and International Trade Canada* <http://www.dfait-maeci.gc.ca/foreign_policy/cnd-world/chap6-en.asp/> (12 December 2008).

85. *Canada in the World*, "VI. International Assistance," *Foreign Affairs and International Trade Canada*.

86. Ministerial Council on HIV/AIDS, *Meeting the Challenge: Canada's Foreign Policy on HIV/AIDS: With a Particular Focus on Africa* (Ottawa: CIDA, 2003), p. 26.

87. Micheline Beaudry-Somcynsky, "Japanese ODA Compared to Canadian ODA," in *Japan's Foreign Aid: Old Continuities and New Directions* ed. David Arase (Abingdon: Routledge, 2005), 133–151, p. 133.

88. Canadian Public Health Association, *Leading Together: Canada Takes Action on HIV/AIDS (2005–2010)* (Ottawa: CPHA, 2005), p. 7.

89. Ibid., p. 31. In this sense, influential policy documents such as *Leading Together* reflect earlier documents circulated within the Canadian government, calling for these same measures to confront Canada's epidemic. See Theodore de Bruyn, *A Plan for Action to Reduce HIV/AIDS-related Stigma and Discrimination*, available at <http://aidslaw.ca/Maincontent/issues/discrimination.htm>.

90. The debate over public health approaches versus punitive ones within Canada is beyond the scope of this book, although this dynamic political contestation certainly informs the design of foreign aid programs. A fuller account of this debate in Canada is provided in Gabor Maté, *In the Realm of Hungry Ghosts:*

Close Encounters With Addiction (Berkeley: North Atlantic Books, 2010). Maté, a Vancouver based physician, pioneers health-based approaches to drug addiction.

91. Canadian Public Health Association, *Leading Together*, p. 17.

92. Public Health Agency of Canada, *Strengthened Leadership: Taking Action, Canada's Report on HIV/AIDS 2005* (Ottawa: PHAC, 2005), p. 12.

93. *Canada in the World* is available in html format; "VI. International Assistance," *Foreign Affairs and International Trade Canada* <http://www.dfait-maeci.gc.ca/foreign_policy/cnd-world/chap6-en.asp/> (12 December 2008).

94. Canadian International Development Agency, "Canada Helps Save Lives in Tanzania by Improving Health Management," (Ottawa: CIDA, 2008).

95. Brazil's economy grew by 5.1 percent in 2008. That same year Venezuela's expanded by nearly 5 percent. China and India grew by a whopping 7.4 percent and 9 percent respectively. The United States, European Union, and Japan saw little or no growth during that year, according to the CIA World Factbook. As this book goes to press, however, emerging economies are on shakier ground.

96. Barney Jopson and Jamil Anderlini, "China Pledges $10 Billion in Low Cost Loans to Africa," *The Washington Post* (9 November 2009).

97. Naim, "Help Not Wanted," the *New York Times* (15 February 2007).

98. Ngaire Woods, "Whose Aid? Whose Influence? China, Emerging Donors and the Silent Revolution in Development Assistance," *International Affairs* 84 (2008): 1205–21, p. 1205.

99. Ibid., p. 1206.

100. For a full discussion of these failures, see Woods, *The Globalizers: The IMF, World Bank and Their Borrowers*, Stiglitz, *Globalization and its Discontents*; and Naomi Klein, *The Shock Doctrine: The Rise of Disaster Capitalism* (New York: Metropolitan Books, 2007).

101. Many non-BRIC countries including Zimbabwe, Thailand, and South Africa were instrumental in expanding what Wolfgang Hein and Surie Moon call the "access norm." As we'll see in later chapters, and as Hein and Moon also show, Civil Society Organizations (CSOs) in these countries were instrumental in fostering these norms at the national and global levels. See Wolfgang Hein and Surie Moon, *Informal Norms in Global Governance* (Surrey, England: Ashgate, 2013), particularly chapter 6.

102. The founding members were Brazil, Chile, France, Norway, and the United Kingdom. The membership has since expanded to include Benin, Burkina Faso, Cameroon, Central African Republic, Congo, Cote d'Ivoire, Cyprus, Gambia, Guinea, Jordan, Liberia, Luxembourg, Madagascar, Mali, Mauritius, Morocco, Namibia, Niger, South Korea, Sao Tome and Principe, Senegal, South Africa, Spain, and Togo, with additional partnerships with non-state actors, particularly the Bill and Melinda Gates Foundation, which provides direct financial support alongside select state members.

103. "Innovative Financing," *Unitaid.eu* <http://www.unitaid.eu/en/how/innovative-financing> (13 January 2014).

104. See The Brandt Commission, *Common Crisis North-South* (Cambridge, MA: MIT Press, 1983).

Chapter 3

1. Dani Rodrik, "Why Is There Multilateral Lending?" in *World Bank Annual Conference on Development Economics 1995* (Washington: World Bank 1996).

2. In constant 2005 dollars.

3. This may understate the share of ODA distributed through multilateral channels, since data collected from multilaterals by the OECD is generally less complete than that from bilateral agencies.

4. Helen V. Milner, "Why Multilateralism? Foreign Aid and Domestic Principle-Agent Problems." In Darren G. Hawkins, David A. Lake, Daniel L. Nielson, and Michael J. Tierney (eds.), *Delegation and Agency in International Organizations* (New York: Cambridge University Press, 2006), 107–139, p. 112.

5. World Health Organization, "High Level Forum on the Health Millennium Development Goals," *Who.int* <http://www.who.int/hdp/hlf/en/> (6 January 2014).

6. World Health Organization, "About the Health Metrics Network," *Who.int* <http://www.who.int/healthmetrics/about/en/> (6 January 2014).

7. International Health Partnership, *Scaling Up for Better Health: Work Plan for the International Health Partnership and Related Initiatives* (Geneva: IHP, 2008).

8. Charles E. Allen, "World Health and World Politics," *International Organization* 4 (1950): 27–43.

9. "WHO Constitution," (1946), available at <http://www.who.int/governance/eb/constitution/en/>.

10. Results from the latter have been mixed. Its long campaign against malaria, for instance, has not rolled back the disease, though its campaign against smallpox, which included vaccinations, has gone down in history as one of the organization's greatest successes.

11. See Kelley Lee, "The Pit and the Pendulum: Can Globalization Take Health Governance Forward?" *Development* 47(2): 11–17; Also see Caroline Thomas and Martin Weber, "The Politics of Global Health Governance: What Happened to Global Health for All by the Year 2000?" *Global Governance* 10 (2004), 187–205. The Alma Ata Declaration is available at <http://www.who.int/hpr/NPH/docs/declaration_almaata.pdf>.

12. Lee, *The World Health Organization (WHO)*, p. 75.

13. "Declaration of Alma Ata" (1978), available at <http://www.paho.org/english/dd/pin/alma-ata_declaration.htm>.

14. For perspective on this debate, see Ananya Roy, *Poverty Capital.*

15. United Nations Children's Fund and World Health Organization, *Alternative Approaches to Meeting Basic Health Needs in Developing Countries* (Geneva: World Health Organization, 1975).

16. "Declaration of Alma Ata," Article II.

17. Ibid., Article III.

18. Ibid., Article IV.

19. See, especially, Kelley Lee's probing discussion of the WHO's budgetary challenges in *World Health Organization (WHO)*, pp. 38–44.

20. Werner has written several critiques of the move away from PHC, including David Werner, "Elusive Promise, Whatever Happened to 'Health for All'?" *New Internationalist* 331 (January/February 2001), and David Werner, "Who Killed Primary Health Care?" *New Internationalist* 272 (October 1995).

21. For an overview of the SPHC movement, see J. A. Walsh and K. S. Warren, "Selective Primary Health Care: An Interim Strategy for Disease Control in Developing Countries," *New England Journal of Medicine* 301 (1979): 967–74. For critical perspectives, see Oscar Gish, "Selective Primary Health Care: Old Wine in New Bottles," *Social Science and Medicine* 22(10) (1982): 1049–63 and Evelyne Hong, "The Primary Health Care Movement Meets the Free Market," in Meredith Fort, Mary Anne Mercer and Oscar Gish, eds., *Sickness and Wealth: The Corporate Assault on Global Health* (Cambridge: South End Press, 2004), pp. 27–36.

22. For Farmer's views in this area, see especially Paul Farmer, *Pathologies of Power: Health, Human Rights and the New War on the Poor* (Berkeley: UC Press, 2005), and Paul Farmer, *Infections and Inequalities: The Modern Plagues* (Berkeley: UC Press, 2001).

23. For an extensive discussion on how the WHO's struggles with the issue of HIV/AIDS ultimately culminated in the creation of UNAIDS, see Joshua K. Leon, "Confronting Catastrophe: Norms, Efficiency, and the Evolution of the AIDS Battle in the UN," *Cambridge Review of International Affairs* 24(3) (2011): 471–91.

24. The program was initially known as the Special Program on AIDS (SPA).

25. Jonathan M. Mann, "Human Rights and AIDS: The Future of the Pandemic," in Jonathan M. Mann, Sofia Gruskin, Michael A. Grodin, and George J. Annas eds., *Health and Human Rights* (New York: Routledge, 1999), p. 223.

26. Jonathan Mann, "Health Promotion Against AIDS: A Typology," in Jaime Sepulveda, Harvey Fineberg and Jonathan Mann, *AIDS: Prevention Through Education: A World View* (Oxford: Oxford University Press, 1992), p. 31.

27. Shalala was an advocate for an expanded response and a leading supporter of creating UNAIDS in particular. "As long as Hiroshi Nakajima was at the helm," reported journalist Greg Berhman, she believed that the WHO's response "would be feckless." Greg Behrman, *The Invisible People: How the US has Slept Through The Global AIDS Pandemic, the Greatest Humanitarian Catastrophe of Our Time* (New York: Simon and Schuster, 2006), p. 76.

28. In particular, Elizabeth Reid, the founder of the UNDP's HIV and Development Program, was critical of the GPA for its apparently unidimensional approach to AIDS. See this chapter's subsection on the UNDP for further discussion on these tensions. Barton Gellman, "The Global Response to AIDS in Africa: World Shunned Signs of the Coming Plague."

29. For an overview on UN activities during the later years of the GPA, see Lisa Garbus, "The UN Response," in Jonathan M. Mann and Daniel J. M. Tarantola eds., *Aids in the World II: Global Dimensions, Social Roots and Responses* (Oxford: Oxford University Press, 1996), p. 372.

30. Gellman, "The Global Response to AIDS in Africa: World Shunned Signs of the Coming Plague."

31. The Americans, British, and Dutch expressed a lack of confidence in Nakajima's approach to AIDS. Behrman, *The Invisible People*, pp. 166–67. Additionally, it is important to note that, despite its expanded mandates, UNAIDS faced significant challenges that hindered its ability to generate an expanded response. Contributions declined considerably after the dissolution of the GPA. The United States let its contribution decline by 50 percent from its previous GPA allocation. Additionally, bureaucratic turf struggles stalled the efforts of UNAIDS to enhance efficiency and reduce overlap, with few officials in sponsoring agencies willing to cede budgetary authority. The transition years were thus frustrating for AIDS advocates. This delay, marked by fierce debate over bureaucratic turf and power over the eventual funding, helped enable public health conditions to worsen in AIDS impacted regions.

32. Gill Walt, "WHO Under Stress: Implications For Health Policy," *Health Policy* 24 (1993): 125–44.

33. Fiona Godlee, "WHO in Retreat: Is It Losing Its Influence?" *BMJ* 309 (1994): 1491–95. Also see Fiona Godlee, "The World Health Organization: WHO in Crisis," *BMJ* 309 (1994): 1424–28.

34. Theodore M. Brown, Marcos Cueto, and Elizabeth Fee, "The World Health Organization and the Transition from International to Global Public Health," *American Journal of Public Health* 96 (2006): 62–72, p. 64.

35. Gro Harlem Brundtland, "Address to Permanent Missions in Geneva," World Health Organization (10 November, 1998).

36. The program fell well short of this target, but was credited for spurring a big push in ARV distribution. It also helped establish its progenitor, Jim Yong Kim, as a leading public health activist.

37. Gro Harlem Brundtland, "Presentation to the Development Assistance Committee of the OECD," World Health Organization (9 November 2000).

38. See WHO Commission on Macroeconomics and Health, *Macroeconomics and Health: Investing in Health for Economic Development*. Also see Howard Waitzkin, "Report of the WHO Commission on Macroeconomics and Health: A Summary and Critique," *Lancet* 361: 523–26.

39. Gro Harlem Brundtland, "Address to Permanent Missions in Geneva."

40. Gro Harlem Brundtland, "Presentation to the Development Assistance Committee of the OECD."

41. It is also important to remember that the WHO had gone through extreme budgetary pressure, with its regular budget having been frozen for years.

42. Cited in Lee, *The World Health Organization (WHO)*, p. 108.

43. These were communicable and non-communicable diseases, sustainable development, health systems, health information, health technology, mental health, external relations and management reform.

44. World Health Organization, *Engaging for Health: Eleventh General Program of Work: 2006–2015, A Global Health Agenda* (Geneva: WHO, 2006), p. 23.

45. For example, the WHO has played an important role in assisting with applications to the Global Fund.

46. See Gavin Yamey, "WHO in 2002: Why Does the World Still Need WHO?" *BMJ* 325 (2002): 1294–98.

47. The IHRs were known as the International Sanitary Regulations until 1956.

48. World Health Organization, "International Health Regulations" (2005), available at <http://www.who.int/ihr/en/>.

49. Sophie Harman, *Global Health Governance*, p. 37.

50. World Health Organization, "Framework Convention on Tobacco Control," (2003), available at <http://www.who.int/fctc/en>/. For analysis on specific provisions, see Simon Barraclough, "Chronic Diseases and Global Health Governance, in Adrian Kay and Owain David Williams eds., *Global Health Governance: Crisis, Institutions and Political Economy* (New York: Palgrave, 2009), 102–28, p. 113.

51. Harman, *Global Health Governance*, p. 38.

52. World Health Organization, *A Safer Future: Global Public Health Security in the 21ˢᵗ Century* (Geneva: WHO, 2007), p. 11.

53. Ibid., p. 11.

54. Ibid., *A Safer Future*, p. 13.

55. World Health Organization, *Programme Budget 2012–2013* (Geneva: WHO, 2011), p. 11.

56. Ibid., p. 4.

57. Global Health and Knowledge Network, *Toward Health-Equitable Globalization: Rights, Regulation, and Redistribution* (Ottawa: University of Ottawa, 2007), p. 73.

58. Ibid., p. 74.

59. World Health Organization, *Primary Health Care: Now More Than Ever* (Geneva: WHO, 2008).

60. For extensive discussion on the ethics of drug research and development, see Harriet Washington, *Deadly Monopolies: The Shocking Corporate Takeover of Life Itself—and the Consequences for your Health and Our Medical Future* (New York, Anchor Books, 2012).

61. Agreement on Trade-Related Aspects of Intellectual Property Rights (TRIPS), available at <http://www.wto.org/english/tratop_e/trips_e/t_agm0_e.htm>.

62. World Health Organization, *Report of the Commission on Public Health, Innovation, and Intellectual Property Rights* (Geneva: WHO, 2006), p. 83.

63. Ibid., p. 83.

64. Ibid., p. 84.

65. Ibid., p. 148.

66. For extensive discussion of the creation of the WTO, and on the influence of the United States and European Union on this process, see John H. Barton, Judith L. Goldstein, Timothy E. Josling, and Richard H. Steinberg, *The Evolution of the Trade Regime: Politics, Law and Economics of the GATT and WTO* (Princeton: Princeton University Press, 2006).

67. For a full survey of the power struggle between southern and northern countries in international forums, including the north's insistence that matters of great economic consequence not be handled within WIPO, see Vijay Prashad, *The Poorer Nations: A Possible History of the Global South* (London: Verso, 2012). Specific discussion on WIPO is on p. 106 and p. 192.

68. Doha Declaration (2001), available at <http://www.wto.org/english/thewto_e/minist_e/min01_e/mindecl_e.htm>.

69. World Health Organization, *Report of the Commission on Public Health, Innovation, and Intellectual Property Rights*, p. 91.

70. Ibid., p. 149.

71. World Health Assembly, "Global Strategy and Plan of Action on Public Health, Innovation, and Intellectual Property," WHA Resolution 61.21 (24 May, 2008).

72. The World Bank's exact time of entry into the global health regime is debatable, but scholars generally argue that its foray into health began during Robert McNamara's tenure as president. Harman argues that "the role of the Bank in global health really came to the fore in the 1970s with the appointment of Robert McNamara (1968–81) who shifted the Bank's approach and policy lending profile towards a more holistic approach to development that addresses the social determinants of poverty." Harman, *Global Health Governance*, p. 46.

73. "New IBRD/IDA Health Sector Commitments by Sector and Region" *worldbank.org*, September 8, 2011<http://go.worldbank.org/IP0NBIFK70> (13 February 2013).

74. A number of studies have sought to articulate the deep consequences of neoliberal free trade and structural adjustment on health. See Global Health and Knowledge Network, *Toward Health-Equitable Globalization: Rights, Regulation, and Redistribution.* Also see Ronald Labonté, Chantal Blouin, and Lisa Forman, "Trade and Health."

75. Ngaire Woods, *The Globalizers: The IMF, World Bank, and Their Borrowers* (Ithaca, NY: Cornell University Press, 2007).

76. See Kamran Abbasi, "The World Bank and World Health: Changing Sides," *BMJ* 318 (1999): 865–69 and Kamran Abbasi, "The World Bank and World Health: Under Fire," *BMJ* 318 (1999): 1003–06.

77. Lee, *World Health Organization (WHO)*, p. 112.

78. Kelley Lee contends that the growing presences of the Bank and IMF, and the attendant influence of their economic personnel, impacted the work within the WHO during this period. Lee, *World Health Organization (WHO)*, p. 128.

79. Peter Haas, "Do Regimes Matter? Epistemic Communities and Mediterranean Pollution Control."

80. The World Bank, *World Development Report 1993: Investing in Health* (Washington, DC: World Bank, 1993), p. iii.

81. Ibid., p. 3.

82. Ibid., p. 108.

83. Ibid., p. 11.

84. Ibid., p. 108. Indeed this had been occurring globally as a part of World Bank designed structural adjustment packages.

85. Ibid., p. 156.

86. Ibid., p. 17.

87. Ibid., p. 7.

88. Ibid., p. 5.

89. Among other accounts, see Gates' interview with PBS host Bill Moyers. "Transcript: Bill Moyers Interviews Bill Gates," *NOW* (9 May 2003). Available at <http://www.pbs.org/now/transcript/transcript_gates.html>.

90. These landmark agreements greatly emphasize the principles of "donor harmonization," particularly under the banners of "alignment" and "harmonization" among actors.

91. For this critical perspective, see Evelyne Hong, "The Primary Health Care Movement Meets the Free Market," p. 34.

92. Sophie Harman, "The World Bank and Health," in Adrian Kay and Owain David Williams eds., *Global Health Governance: Crisis, Institutions, and Political Economy* (New York: Palgrave, 2009): 227–44.

93. See Harman, "The World Bank and Health," and Abbasi, "The World Bank and World Health: Changing Sides."

94. This put Stiglitz under considerable pressure from the US Treasury. Its head, Lawrence Summers reportedly called for his departure. For insights into Stiglitz's thought processes during this time, see Robert Wade, "Showdown at the World Bank," *New Left Review* 7 (2001): 124–37, and Joseph Stiglitz, *Globalization and its Discontents* (New York: W. W. Norton, 2002).

95. Harman, "The World Bank and Health," p. 236.

96. Ibid., p. 240.

97. It is an overstatement, however, to say that *all* funds coming from the IDA are transfers from rich to poor. In addition to wealthy country contributions to the pool, a substantial minority of IDA funds come from borrowers' repayments. In this regard, the World Bank runs much like a business.

98. GAVI is the Global Alliance for Vaccines and Immunization, GAIN is the Global Alliance for Improved Nutrition. The World Bank, *Healthy Development: The World Bank Strategy for Health, Nutrition and Population Results*, p. 11.

99. The World Bank, *Healthy Development: The World Bank Strategy for Health, Nutrition and Population Results*, p. 11.

100. The World Bank, "IDA 14, Report from the Executive Directors of the International Development Association to the Board of Governors," (Washington, DC: World Bank, 2005), p. 5.

101. The World Bank, "Health: Supporting Systemic Change in a New Global Context," (Washington, DC: World Bank, 2007).

102. The World Bank, "IDA 15, Report from the Executive Directors of the International Development Association to the Board of Governors," (Washington, DC: The World Bank, 2008), p. 16.

103. The World Bank, "IDA 13, Report from the Executive Directors of the International Development Association to the Board of Governors," (Washington, DC: The World Bank, 2002), p. 5.

104. Barton Gellman, "The Global Response to AIDS in Africa: World Shunned Signs of the Coming Plague."

105. Craig N. Murphy, *The United Nations Development Programme: A Better Way?* (Cambridge: Cambridge University Press, 2006), p. 324.

106. Ibid., p. 324.

107. Ibid., p. 299.

108. Ibid., p. 303.

109. Richard Jolly, Louis Emmerij, and Thomas G. Weiss, "The UN and Human Development," *United Nations Intellectual History Project*, Briefing Note no. 8 (July 2009).

110. Murphy, *The United Nations Development Programme: A Better Way?* p. 300.

111. United Nations Development Program, *UNDP Strategic Plan, 2008–2011*, p. 10.

112. For further discussion on how it builds upon these advantages, see United Nations Development Program, *UNDP Strategic Plan, 2008–2011*, p. 19.

113. United Nations Development Program, *Human Development Report 2003: Millennium Development Goals: A Compact among Nations to End Human Poverty* (New York: UNDP, 2003), p. 15.

114. Ibid., p. 15.

115. Ibid., p. 18.

116. For discussion on the politics of its budgetary processes, see Ngaire Woods, *The Globalizers*, chapter. 1.

117. On the UNDP's relative big tent, see Murphy, *The United Nations Development Programme: A Better Way?* chapter 1.

118. Figure cited in Stephen Dearden, "The Future Role of the European Union in Europe's Development Assistance," *Cambridge Review of International Affairs* 16 (2003): 105–16.

119. Frederick Nixson, "Aid, Trade and Economic Development: The EU and the Developing World," in *The Economics of the European Union*, 4th ed.,

eds., Mike Artis and Fredrick Nixson (Cambridge: Cambridge University Press, 2007), 322–53, p. 340.

120. Dearden, "The Future Role of the European Union in Europe's Development Assistance," p. 115.

121. Quoted in Hein and Moon, *Informal Norms in Global Governance*, p. 108.

122. The agreement, in the EU's official language, entails the expiration of preferences. See European Union "The Cotonou Agreement," *Ec.europa. edu* <http://ec.europa.eu/europeaid/where/acp/overview/cotonou-agreement/> (7 January 2014). Preferential or "non-reciprocal" trading standards were included in the earlier Lomé Conventions. European Union, "From Lomé I to IV," *Ec.europa.edu* <http://ec.europa.eu/europeaid/where/acp/overview/lome-convention/lomeitoiv_en.htm> (7 January 2014).

123. European Commission, *Second Revision of the Cotonou Agreement* (Brussels: European Union, 2010), p. 13

124. Ibid., p. 24.

125. Ibid., p. 27.

126. European Commission, "The European Consensus on Development," (2006/C 46/01).

127. Dearden, "The Future Role of the European Union in Europe's Development Assistance," p. 106.

128. European Commission, *An EU Aid Effectiveness Roadmap to Accra and Beyond* (Brussels: European Union, 2008), p. 28.

129. See European Commission, "Council Conclusions on the EU Code of Conduct on Complementarity and Division of Labor in Development Policy," (15 May 2007). Available at <http://register.consilium.europa.eu/pdf/en/07/st09/st09558.en07.pdf>.

130. European Commission, *An EU Aid Effectiveness Roadmap to Accra and Beyond*, p. 8.

131. European Commission, *Aid Effectiveness After Accra: Where Does the EU Stand and What More Do We Need to Do?* (Brussels: European Union, 2009), p. 6.

132. Ibid., p. 10.

133. European Commission, *European Commission on Development Cooperation Strategies* (Brussels: European Union, 2007), p. 29.

134. Ibid., p. 31.

135. European Commission, *Aid Effectiveness After Accra*, p. 22.

136. European Commission, *An EU Aid Effectiveness Roadmap to Accra and Beyond*, p. 9.

Chapter 4

1. Garrett, "The Challenge of Global Health."

2. These data were retrieved from the Foundation Center, which tracks the activities of US foundations, on January 10, 2014, and are available at <foundationcenter.org>. The figures cited above do not fully capture health's centrality to the national philanthropic enterprise. For example, the Foundation's "human services" category contains subcategories that directly relate to health, as does its "international affairs" category.

3. Fidler, "Architecture Amidst Anarchy," p. 7.

4. Ibid., p. 8.

5. David Hulme and Michael Edwards report that NGOs registered in the global north increased from 1,600 in 1980 to nearly 3,000 in 1993. Their spending also more than doubled during this period. David Hulme and Michael Edwards, "NGOs, States and Donors: An Overview," in *NGOs, States and Donors: Too Close for Comfort?* eds. David Hulme and Michael Edwards (New York: St. Martin's Press, 1997), 3–22, p. 4.

6. Garrett, "The Challenge of Global Health," p. 21.

7. Teju Cole, "The White Savior Industrial Complex," *The Atlantic* (21 March 2011).

8. John Garrison, "A New Social Contract with Civil Society?" <blogs. worldbank.org> (27 April 2011).

9. The World Bank, "Defining Civil Society," *worldbank.org* 4 August 2010 <http://web.worldbank.org/WBSITE/EXTERNAL/TOPICS/CSO/ 0,,contentMDK:20101499~menuPK:244752~pagePK:220503~piPK:220476~the SitePK:228717,00.html> (6 February 2013).

10. World Health Organization, "Civil Society," *who.int* <http://www.who. int/trade/glossary/story006/en/index.html> (6 February 2013).

11. Sonia Bartsch, "Southern Actors in Global Public-Private Partnerships: The Case of the Global Fund," in Sandra J. MacLean, Sherri A. Brown, and Pieter Fourie eds., *Health for Some: The Political Economy of Global Health Governance* (New York: Palgrave, 2009), 130–143.

12. The WSF is intended as a more progressive, democratic alternative to the World Economic Forums held annually in Davos, Switzerland. It emphasizes what it sees as a broader development agenda, featuring alternatives to neoliberalism. Yet WSF meetings can be contentious. See <http://www.forumsocialmundial.org.br>.

13. The PHM seeks to advance the principles of the Alma Ata declaration. It has also persistently engages the WHO, see <http://www.phmovement.org/>.

14. <http://www.joinred.com/>.

15. See, especially, the work of Helmut K. Anheier.

16. Cited in Jean-Loup Motchane, "Health for All or Riches for Some: WHO Responsible?" *Le Monde Diplomatique* (July 2002). Available at <http:// mondediplo.com/2002/07/17who/>.

17. Ananya Roy, *Poverty Capital*, p. 26.

18. For more on these distinctions, see Ananya Roy, *Poverty Capital*.

19. For extended discussion on the relationship (and potential conflicts of interest) between states and NGOs, see Hulme and Edwards, *NGOs, States and Donors: Too Close for Comfort?*

20. Figures cited in Wolfgang Hein, Sonja Bartsch, and Lars Kohlmorgen, eds., *Global Health Governance and the Fight Against HIV/AIDS* (New York: Palgrave, 2007). See pp. 92, 102, 103, and 110, respectively.

21. Ann Swidler, "Syncretism and Subversion in AIDS Governance: How Locals Cope With Global Demands," *International Affairs* 82 (2006): 269–84, p. 273.

22. Kamal Malhotra, "NGOs Without Aid: Beyond the Global Soup Kitchen," *Third World Quarterly* 21 (2000), 665–68.

23. See Laurie Garrett, *Betrayal of Trust: The Collapse of Global Public Health* (New York: Hyperion, 2000). The movement to clean up New York, Garrett argues, was a founding moment in modern public health.

24. <http://www.brettonwoodsproject.org/index.shtml>.

25. <http://aidspan.org/page/our-history>.

26. South Commission, *The Challenge to the South* (Oxford: Oxford University Press, 1990), p. 16. For a more complete overview of the fascinating story behind the report, and the debates which surrounded its creation, see Prashad, *The Poorer Nations*, p. 89, p. 103, and p. 118.

27. Contradictory terminology notwithstanding, GONGOs are widely used but by no means limited to the Global South. For critical viewpoints on them, see Anthony J. Spires, "US Foundations Boost Chinese Governments, Not NGOs," *Yale Global* (28 March 2012) and Moisés Naim, "What is a GONGO? How Government Sponsored Groups Masquerade as Civil Society," *Foreign Policy* (13 January 2012).

28. Margaret E. Keck and Kathryn Sikkink, *Activists Beyond Borders*. See, in particular, the broad array of actors that they incorporate into their concept of TANS, on p. 9.

29. Mann argued passionately for a human rights-based approach to HIV/AIDS until his untimely death in a plane crash in 1998. His view that NGOs should take a central position in this advocacy role was arguably helped by his disenchantment with the WHO, then headed by the bureaucratic and very biomedically oriented Hiroshi Nakajima.

30. Jonathan M. Mann, "Human Rights and AIDS: The Future of the Pandemic," p. 223.

31. J. Mann, "Non-Government Organizations Should Be Catalysts for Change," *BMJ* 310 (1996).

32. Susan K. Sell and Aseem Prakash, "Using Ideas Strategically: The Contest Between Business and NGO Networks in Intellectual Property Rights," *International Studies Quarterly* 48 (2004): 143–75. Sell and Prakash use the term NGO rather than CSO, the term favored throughout this chapter unless other common designations are appropriate.

33. Susan K. Sell and Aseem Prakash, "Using Ideas Strategically"

34. Raustiala and Victor, "The Regime Complex for Plant Genetic Resources." Other works that play a central role in understanding forum shopping or "shifting" include Sell and Prakash, "Using Ideas Strategically," and John Braithwaite and Peter Drahos, *Global Business Regulation* (Cambridge:

Cambridge University Press, 2000). For an overview of northern dissatisfaction with WIPO and UNCTAD, see Wolfgang Hein, "Global Health Governance and WTO/TRIPS: Conflicts Between 'Global Market Creation' and 'Global Social Rights,'" in Wolfgang Hein, Sonja Bartsch and Lars Kohlmorgen, *Global Health Governance and the Fight Against HIV/AIDS* (New York: Palgrave, 2007): 38–66. Also see Mark W. Zacher and Tania J. Keefe, *The Politics of Global Health Governance: United by Contagion* (New York: Palgrave, 2008).

35. Paul Davis and Meredith Fort, "The Battle Against Global AIDS," in Meredith Fort, Mary Anne Mercer, and Oscar Gish, *Sickness and Wealth* (Cambridge: South End Press, 2004): 145–57.

36. Martha Finnemore and Kathryn Sikkink, "International Norm Dynamics and Political Change," *International Organization* 52, no. 4 (1998): 887–917. According to the authors, "norm emergence," is sparked by norm entrepreneurs through advocacy, and requires an organizational platform. The second phase is the norm's acceptance, called "cascade," which occurs through socialization—leaders (the primary mechanism in this phase) persuade other leaders to adhere.

37. It should be noted that this enthusiasm wasn't unanimous. The drugs' potentially painful side effects were also discussed at the conference.

38. Bernhard Schwartlander, Ian Grubb, and Jas Perriens, "The 10-Year Struggle to Provide Antiretroviral Treatment to People With HIV in the Developing World," *The Lancet* 368 (2006): 541–46.

39. Davis and Fort, "The Battle Against Global AIDS," p. 152.

40. See Jamila Headley and Patricia Siplon, "Roadblocks on the Road to Treatment: Lessons from Barbados to Brazil," *Perspectives on Politics* 4 (2006): 655–61 and Davis and Fort, "The Battle Against Global AIDS."

41. Davis and Fort, "The Battle Against Global AIDS," p. 153.

42. Ibid., p. 153.

43. See Arvind Singal and Everett M. Rogers, *Combating AIDS: Communication Strategies in Action* (Thousand Oaks: Sage, 2003), p. 152.

44. Ibid.

45. This initiative was the latest and largest phase in a series of negotiations that began in the mid-1990s. In 1997 UNAIDS launched the Drug Access Initiative (DAI), a pilot program which offered ARV drugs in four lesser developed countries. Participating pharmaceutical companies offered the drugs at subsidized rates. The program helped the organizations involved gain experience in drug distribution and demonstrated the possibility for an expanded effort in the future. Additionally, it marked the first signs of differential pricing in ARV distribution among Western firms.

46. Al Gore was shocked at the regular infiltrations and disruptions of his 2000 campaign rallies and meetings. The Clinton administration grew fearful of the negative press during an election year. For a full account, see Greg Behrman, *The Invisible People.*

47. As reported by UNAIDS. Joint United Nations Programme on HIV/AIDS, "Report of the Executive Director to the Programme Coordinating Board 2000–2001," p. 32–33.

48. Schwartlander et al., "The 10-Year Struggle to Provide Antiretroviral Treatment to People With HIV in the Developing World."

49. The declaration nevertheless stopped short of calling for universal access, a goal often called for by UNAIDS. Joint United Nations Programme on HIV/AIDS, "Keeping the Promise: Summary of the Declaration of Commitment on HIV/AIDS" (Geneva, Switzerland: 2001).

50. "UN Call for 'New Deal' On AIDS Drug Supply," *Pharma Marketletter*, 21 February 2001.

51. See Rebecca Voelker, "Setting Priorities and Budgets to Fight Against Global AIDS," *Journal of the American Medical Association* 21 (2000): 2709–10.

52. See Medecins Sans Frontieres, *Untangling the Web of Antiretroviral Price Reductions* 13th ed. (July 2010). MSF has been out front on the issue of ARV drug distribution since the early years of these drugs' development.

53. See, especially, discussion on the evolution of the "access norm" in Hein and Moon, *Informal Norms in Global Governance*. Hein and Moon also raise the issue of forum shifting.

54. Ravishankar et al., "Financing of Global Health: Tracking Development Assistance for Health from 1990 to 2007," p. 2117.

55. Data provided by Bloom, "Governing Global Health," p. 32. For states, Bloom uses a calculation similar to mine, taking into account the health, population and water sanitation categories in the OECD's DAC database. His data on foundations derives from the Foundation Center.

56. Bill and Melinda Gates Foundation, *2008 Annual Report: Progress and Pressing Needs* (Seattle: BMG Foundation, 2009), p. 23.

57. KMPG, "Bill and Melinda Gates Foundation Trust: Financial Statements," (31 December 2011), p. 2.

58. Gideon Rachman, "Inside the Gates Foundation," *Financial Times* (12 November, 2010).

59. "What Has the Gates Foundation Done for Global Health?" *The Lancet* 373 (2009): 1577.

60. See Devi Sridhar and Rajaie Batniji, "Misfinancing Global Health: A Case For Transparency in Disbursements and Decision-making," *The Lancet* 372 (2008): 1185–91; and David McCoy, Gayatri Kembhavi, Jinest Patel, and Akish Luintel, "The Bill and Melinda Gates Foundation's Grant-Making Programme for Global Health," *The Lancet* 373 (2009): 1645–53.

61. Charles Piller, Edmund Sanders, and Robyn Dixon, "Dark Cloud Over Good Works of Gates Foundation," *Los Angeles Times* (7 January 2007).

62. Fergus Walsh, "Bill Gates: The World Can Defeat Polio," BBC (27 January 2013).

63. Figures derive from the Foundation Center.

64. Carmen Huckel Schneider, "Global Public Health and Innovation in Governance: The Emergence of Public Private Partnerships," in Sandra J. MacLean, Sherri A. Brown, and Pieter Fourie eds., *Health for Some: The Political*

Economy of Global Health Governance (New York: Palgrave, 2009), 105–17, p. 105.

65. Carmen Huckel Schneider, "Global Public Health and Innovation in Governance," p. 106.

66. The World Bank Institute, "About WBI," *worldbank.org* <http://wbi.worldbank.org/wbi/about> (8 February 2013).

67. The World Bank Institute, "Public-Private Partnerships," *worldbank.org* <http://wbi.worldbank.org/wbi/about/topics/public-private-partnerships> (8 February 2013).

68. Peter M. Haas, "Do Regimes Matter? Epistemic Communities in Mediterranean Pollution Control."

69. Christer Jonsson and Peter Soderholm, "IGO-NGO Relations and HIV/AIDS: Innovation or Stalemate?" in Thomas G. Weiss and Leon Gordenker, *NGOs, the UN and Global Governance* (London: Lynne Rienner, 1996): 121–38.

70. World Health Organization, *WHO and Civil Society: Linking for Better Health: Civil Society Initiative* (Geneva: WHO, 2002), p. 2.

71. However they do not have voting status. For an overview of UNAID's membership policies, see <http://www.unaids.org/en/aboutunaids/unaidsprogrammecoordinatingboard/>.

72. World Health Organization, *Strategic Alliances: The Role of Civil Society and Health,* (Geneva: WHO, 2001), p. 4.

73. Ibid., p. 5.

74. K. Buse and G. Walt, "Global Public-Private Partnerships: Part I—A New Development In Health?" *Bulletin of the World Health Organization* 4 (2000), p. 6.

75. K. Buse and G. Walt, "Global Public-Private Partnerships: Part II—What Are The Health Issues For Global Governance?" *Bulleting of the World Health Organization* 5 (2000): 699–709.

76. See Department for International Development, *Assessing the Impact of Global Health Partnerships* (London: DFID, 2004). The report summarizes a number of studies on GPPP impacts in public health and reflects, in my view, the general consensus on the issue.

77. See The Global Fund to Fight AIDS, Tuberculosis and Malaria, "Guidelines for Proposals," (Geneva: GFATM, 2002).

78. Hakan Seckinelgin, "Who Can Help People With HIV/AIDS in Africa? Governance of HIV/AIDS and Civil Society," *Voluntas: International Journal of Voluntary and Nonprofit Organizations* 15 (2004): 287–304, p. 293.

79. Seckinelgin, "Who Can Help People With HIV/AIDS in Africa? Governance of HIV/AIDS and Civil Society."

80. Hakan Seckinelgin, "A Global Disease and its Governance: HIV/AIDS in Sub-Saharan Africa and the Agency of NGOs," *Global Governance* 11 (2005): 351–68.

81. Seckinelgin, "A Global Disease and its Governance: HIV/AIDS in Sub-Saharan Africa and the Agency of NGOs," p. 352.

82. D. Robert DeChaine, *Global Humanitarianism: NGOs and the Crafting of Community* (Lanham, MD: Lexington Books, 2005), p. 77.

83. See DeChaine, *Global Humanitarianism*.

84. Hulme and Edwards, "NGOs, States and Donors: An Overview," p. 6.

85. Kal Raustiala, "States, NGOs, and International Environmental Institutions," *International Studies Quarterly* 41 (1997): 719–40, p. 720.

86. David Hulme and Michael Edwards, "Too Close to the Powerful, Too Far from the Powerless?" in *NGOs, States and Donors: Too Close for Comfort?* eds. David Hulme and Michael Edwards (New York: St. Martin's Press, 1997): 275–84, p. 280.

87. Youde, *Global Health Governance*, p. 83.

88. Hein and Moon, *Informal Norms in Global Governance*.

Chapter 5

1. Raustiala and Victor, "The Regime Complex for Plant Genetic Resources," p. 306.

2. Commitments to use aid to finance climate adaptation and technology transfers came about at Copenhagen and Durban, respectively, though the willingness of the global north to redress "climate debt" is questionable.

3. This was part of a web-based roundtable in response to Garrett's critical piece "The Challenge of Global Health" in *Foreign Affairs*, available at <http://www.foreignaffairs.com/discussions/roundtables/how-to-promote-global-health>.

4. See Global Health and Knowledge Network, *Toward Health-Equitable Globalization: Rights, Regulation, and Redistribution*.

5. The term BRICS is used to describe the large states whose characteristics include fast emerging markets and generally high levels of economic growth. It is also used to describe a high-level international forum intended to serve as an alternative to the north-led G8 (in which Russia is also a member). The BRICS partners are Brazil, Russia, India, and China, with the recent inclusion of South Africa.

6. Sierra Leone had the world's lowest life expectancy that year, at 45 years of age from birth. A number of developed countries have life expectancies reaching 83 years of age. These data can be found at <http://data.worldbank.org/topic/health>.

7. This is among people between the ages of 15 and 49, which now stands at 0.8%.

8. Amnesty International, *Deadly Delivery: The Maternal Health Care Crisis in the USA* (London: Amnesty International, 2010), p. 1.

9. Hein and Moon, *Informal Norms in Global Governance*, p. 25.

10. Ibid., p. 5.

11. United Nations, *A New Global Partnership: Eradicate Poverty and Transform Economies Through Sustainable Development* (New York: United Nations, 2013). This report summarizes the recommendations of the High Level Panel of Eminent Persons for the post-2015 development agenda. As of this writing a new set of goals has yet to be finalized.

12. United Nations General Assembly Resolution A/67/L.36 (6 December 2012).

13. Roy, *Poverty Capital: Microfinance and the Making of Development.*

14. See Amartya Sen, *Development As Freedom* (New York: Anchor Books, 1999) and Mahbub ul Haq, *Reflections on Human Development* (Oxford: Oxford University Press, 1995).

15. Christopher J. L. Murray and Alan D. Lopez, *The Global Burden of Disease* (Washington, DC: World Bank 1990). This volume estimated the global burden of disease for the year 1990.

16. Lopez et al., *Global Burden of Disease and Risk Factors.*

17. Therien and Lloyd, "Development Assistance on the Brink."

18. CRS database. Japan's total aid to health was $6.3 billion during its roaring 1980s. This figure increased to $11.6 billion in the stagnant 1990s.

19. See Garrett, "The Challenge of Global Health."

20. Joint United Nations Programme on HIV/AIDS, "Report of the Executive Director to the Program Coordinating Board 2000–2001," p. 10.

21. For an overview, see Joint United Nations Programme on HIV/AIDS, "From Advocacy to Action: A Progress Report on UNAIDS at the Country Level" (Geneva, Switzerland: 2005), p. 68.

22. Joint United Nations Programme on HIV/AIDS, "The 'Three Ones' in Action: Where We Are and Where We Go From Here" (Geneva, Switzerland: 2005), p. 12.

23. Joint United Nations Programme on HIV/AIDS, "Making the Money Work Through Greater UN Support for AIDS Responses: The 2006–2007 Consolidated UN Technical Support Plan for AIDS" (Geneva, Switzerland: 2005).

24. United Nations General Assembly Resolution A/67/L.36.

25. Mark Tran, "UN Adopts 'Momentous' Resolution on Universal Health Care," *UK Guardian* (13 December 2012).

26. Tran, "UN Adopts 'Momentous' Resolution on Universal Health Care."

27. The right to health is enshrined in numerous international agreements. For an overview, see World Health Organization, "The Right to Health," *who.int* November 2012 <http://www.who.int/mediacentre/factsheets/fs323/en/index.html> (13 February 2013).

References

Abbasi, Kamran. "The World Bank and World Health: Changing Sides." *British Medical Journal* 318 (1999): 865–869.

———. "The World Bank and World Health: Under Fire." *British Medical Journal* 318 (1999): 1003–1006.

"AIDS Prevention Possible With Audacious Action." *Canadian Business and Current Affairs Medical Post* 6 August 2002.

Allen, Charles E. "World Health and World Politics." *International Organization* 4 (1950): 27–43.

Alter, Karen J., and Sophie Meunier. "Nested and Overlapping Regimes in the Transatlantic Banana Trade Dispute." *Journal of European Public Policy* 13 (2006): 362–382.

———. "The Politics of International Regime Complexity." *Perspectives on Politics* 7 (2009): 13–24.

Amnesty International. *Deadly Delivery: The Maternal Health Care Crisis in the USA*. London: Amnesty International, 2010.

Araki, Mitsuya. "Japan's Official Development Assistance: The Japan ODA Model That Began Life in Southeast Asia." *Asia-Pacific Review* 14, no. 2 (2007): 17–29.

Arase, David ed. *Japan's Foreign Aid: Old Continuities and New Directions*. Abingdon: Routledge, 2005.

Barraclough, Simon. "Chronic Diseases and Global Health Governance." In *Global Health Governance: Crisis, Institutions and Political Economy*. Edited by Adrian Kay and Owain David Williams, 102–128. New York: Palgrave, 2009.

Barton, John H., Judith L. Goldstein, Timothy E. Josling, and Richard H. Steinberg. *The Evolution of the Trade Regime: Politics, Law and Economics of the GATT and WTO*. Princeton, NJ: Princeton University Press, 2006.

Bartsch, Sonia. "Southern Actors in Global Public-Private Partnerships: The Case of the Global Fund." In *Health for Some: The Political Economy of Global Health Governance*. Edited by Sandra J. MacLean, Sherri A. Brown, and Pieter Fourie, 130–143. New York: Palgrave, 2009.

Beaudry-Somcynsky, Micheline. "Japanese ODA Compared to Canadian ODA." In *Japan's Foreign Aid: Old Continuities and New Directions*. Edited by David Arase, 133–151. Abingdon: Routledge, 2005.

Behrman, Greg. *The Invisible People: How the US has Slept Through The Global AIDS Pandemic, the Greatest Humanitarian Catastrophe of Our Time*. New York: Simon and Schuster, 2006.

Bill and Melinda Gates Foundation. *2008 Annual Report: Progress and Pressing Needs*. Seattle: BMG Foundation, 2009.

———. "Fact Sheet," *BMG Foundation* (2011).

Bloom, David E. "Governing Global Health: How Better Coordination can Advance Global Health and Improve Value for Money." *Finance and Development* (2007): 31–35.

Braithwaite. John, and Peter Drahos. *Global Business Regulation*. Cambridge: Cambridge University Press, 2000.

Brandt Commission. *Common Crisis North-South*. Cambridge, MA: MIT Press, 1983.

Brown, Theodore M., Marcos Cueto, and Elizabeth Fee. "The World Health Organization and the Transition from International to Global Public Health." *American Journal of Public Health* 96 (2006): 62–72, p. 64.

Brundtland, Gro Harlem. "Address to Permanent Missions in Geneva." World Health Organization, 10 November, 1998.

———. "Presentation to the Development Assistance Committee of the OECD." World Health Organization, 9 November 2000.

Buse, K., and G. Walt. "Global Public-Private Partnerships: Part I—A New Development In Health?" *Bulletin of the World Health Organization* 4 (2000)

———. "Global Public-Private Partnerships: Part II—What Are the Health Issues for Global Governance?" *Bulleting of the World Health Organization* 5 (2000): 699–709.

Canadian International Development Agency. "Canada Helps Save Lives in Tanzania by Improving Health Management." Ottawa: CIDA, 2008.

Canadian Public Health Association. *Leading Together: Canada Takes Action on HIV/AIDS (2005–2010)*. Ottawa: CPHA, 2005.

Carlsson, Gunilla. "Speech By Gunilla Carlsson at the ABCDE-Conference 2010." *Government.se* 31 May 2010 <http://www.government.se/sb/d/7953/a/146942> 18 December 2012.

Center for Disease Control. "Neglected Tropical Diseases." *cdc.gov* <http://www.cdc.gov/globalhealth/ntd/diseases/index.html> 2 November 2012.

Cole, Teju. "The White Savior Industrial Complex." *The Atlantic* (21 March 2011).

"Coping With AIDS in Africa: Three Years into the WHO Program on AIDS." Hearing Before the Subcommittee on Africa of the House Committee on Foreign Affairs." June 14 1989.

Davis, Paul, and Meredith Fort. "The Battle Against Global AIDS." In *Sickness and Wealth*. Edited by Meredith Fort, Mary Anne Mercer, and Oscar Gish, 145–157. Cambridge: South End Press, 2004.

Davison, Janet. "Does Cutting Foreign Aid Threaten Canada's Reputation in the World?" *CBC News* (3 April 2012).

Dearden, Stephen. "The Future Role of the European Union in Europe's Development Assistance." *Cambridge Review of International Affairs* 16 (2003): 105–116.

de Bruyn, Theodore. *A Plan for Action to Reduce HIV/AIDS-related Stigma and Discrimination*. Available at <http://aidslaw.ca/Maincontent/issues/discrimination.htm>.

DeChaine, D. Robert. *Global Humanitarianism: NGOs and the Crafting of Community*. Lanham MD: Lexington Books, 2005.

Department for International Development. *Assessing the Impact of Global Health Partnerships*. London: DFID, 2004.

Easterly, William. *The White Man's Burden: Why the West's Efforts to Aid the Rest Have Done So Much Ill and So Little Good*. New York: Penguin, 2007.

European Commission. *Aid Effectiveness After Accra: Where Does the EU Stand and What More Do We Need to Do?* Brussels: European Union, 2009.

European Commission. *An EU Aid Effectiveness Roadmap to Accra and Beyond*. Brussels: European Union, 2008.

———. "Council Conclusions on the EU Code of Conduct on Complementarity and Division of Labor in Development Policy" 15 May 2007.

———. *European Commission on Development Cooperation Strategies*. Brussels: European Union, 2007.

———. "The European Consensus on Development" (2006/C 46/01).

———. *Second Revision of the Cotonou Agreement*. Brussels: European Union, 2010.

European Union. "The Cotonou Agreement." *Ec.europa.edu* <http://ec.europa.eu/europeaid/where/acp/overview/cotonou-agreement/> (7 January 2014).

———. "From Lomé I to IV." *Ec.europa.edu* <http://ec.europa.eu/europeaid/where/acp/overview/lome-convention/lomeitoiv_en.htm> (7 January 2014).

"FACT Sheet: United States Africa Command." *africom.mil* <http://www.africom.mil/ getArticle.asp?art=1644> 24 May 2012.

Farmer, Paul. *Infections and Inequalities: The Modern Plagues*. Berkeley: UC Press, 2001.

———. *Pathologies of Power: Health, Human Rights and the New War on the Poor*. Berkeley: UC Press, 2005.

Fidler, David. "Architecture Amidst Anarchy: Global Health Quest for Governance." *Global Health Governance* 1(1) (2007): 1–17.

———. "The Challenges of Global Health Governance." Council on Foreign Relations Working Paper, International Institutions and Global Governance Program (May 2010).

Finnemore, Martha, and Kathryn Sikkink. "International Norm Dynamics and Political Change." *International Organization* 52, no. 4 (1998): 887–917.

———. "Taking Stock: The Constructivist Research Program in International Politics and Comparative Politics." *Annual Review of Politics Science* 4 (2001): 391–416.

Garbus, Lisa. "The UN Response." In *Aids in the World II: Global Dimensions, Social Roots and Responses.* Edited by Jonathan M. Mann and Daniel J. M. Tarantola. Oxford: Oxford University Press, 1996.

Garrett, Laurie. *Betrayal of Trust: The Collapse of Global Public Health.* New York: Hyperion, 2000.

————. "The Challenge of Global Health." *Foreign Affairs* 86, no. 1 (2007): 14–38.

————. "The Song Remains the Same." *Foreign Affairs,* 23 January 2007. <http://www.foreignaffairs.com/discussions/roundtables/how-to-promote-global-health> (11 November 2009).

Garrison, John. "A New Social Contract with Civil Society?" <blogs.worldbank.org>. 27 April 2011.

GAVI Alliance. *Consolidated Financial Statements and Independent Auditors' Report for the Year Ended 31 December 2009.* Geneva: GAVI Alliance, 2009.

Gellman, Barton. "The Global Response to AIDS in Africa: World Shunned Signs of the Coming Plague." *Washington Post* (July 5, 2000), A1.

Gish, Oscar. "Selective Primary Health Care: Old Wine in New Bottles." *Social Science and Medicine* 22(10) (1982): 1049–1063.

Glassman, Amanda, and Denizhan Duran. "Global Health Initiative 2.0: Effective Priority Setting in a Time of Austerity." *Center for Global Development* (30 January, 2012).

Global Alliance for Improved Nutrition. *Financial Statements for the Year Ended 2010 and Report of the Statutory Auditor.* Geneva: GAIN 2010.

The Global Fund to Fight AIDS Tuberculosis and Malaria. *The Global Fund Annual Report 2010.* Geneva: GFATM, 2010.

————. "Guidelines for Proposals." Geneva: GFATM, 2002.

Global Health and Knowledge Network. *Toward Health-Equitable Globalization: Rights, Regulation, and Redistribution.* Ottawa: University of Ottawa, 2007.

Godlee, Fiona. "WHO in Retreat: Is It Losing Its Influence?" *British Medical Journal* 309 (1994): 1491–1495.

————. "The World Health Organization: WHO in Crisis." *British Medical Journal* 309 (1994): 1424–1428.

Government of Japan. "Water Sanitation Broad Partnership Initiative (WASABI)." Tokyo: JICA, 2006.

Haas, Peter. "Do Regimes Matter? Epistemic Communities and Mediterranean Pollution Control." *International Organization* 43 (1989): 377–403.

Harman, Sophie. *Global Health Governance.* New York, Routledge, 2012.

————. "The World Bank and Health." In *Global Health Governance: Crisis, Institutions and Political Economy.* Edited by Adrian Kay and Owain David Williams, 227–244. New York: Palgrave, 2009.

Headley, Jamila, and Patricia Siplon. "Roadblocks on the Road to Treatment: Lessons from Barbados to Brazil." *Perspectives on Politics* 4 (2006): 655–661.

Hecht, Robert, and Raj Shah. "Recent Trends and Innovations in Development Assistance for Health." In *Disease Control Priorities in Developing Countries,*

2nd ed. Edited by Dean T. Jamison, Joel G. Bremen, Anthony R. Measham, George Alleyne, Mariam Cleason, David. B. Evans, Prabhat Jha, Anne Mills, and Philip Musgrove, 243–257. Oxford: Oxford University Press, 2006.

Hein, Wolfgang. "Global Health Governance and WTO/TRIPS: Conflicts Between 'Global Market Creation and Global Social Rights." In *Global Health Governance and the Fight Against HIV/AIDS*. Edited by Wolfgang Hein, Sonja Bartsch, and Lars Kohlmorgen, 38–66. New York: Palgrave, 2007.

Hein, Wolfgang, Sonja Bartsch, and Lars Kohlmorgen, eds. *Global Health Governance and the Fight Against HIV/AIDS*. New York: Palgrave, 2007.

Hein, Wolfgang, and Surie Moon. *Informal Norms in Global Governance*. Surrey, England: Ashgate, 2013.

Hellevik, Siri Bjerkreim. "'Making the Money Work': Challenges Towards Coordination of HIV/AIDS Programmes in Africa." In *Health for Some: The Political Economy of Global Health Governance*. Edited by Sandra J. MacLean, Sherri A. Brown, and Pieter Fourie, 142–161. New York: Palgrave, 2009.

Henry J. Kaiser Family Foundation. "US Global Health Policy: 2012 Survey on the US Role in Global Health." May 2012.

Hoadley, Stephen, J. "Small States as Aid Donors." *International Organization* 34, no. 1 (1980): 121–137.

Hoffman, Stephanie C. "Overlapping Institutions in the Realm of International Security: The Case of NATO and ESDP." *Perspective on Politics* 7 (2009): 45–52.

Hong, Evelyne. "The Primary Health Care Movement Meets the Free Market." In Meredith Fort, Mary Anne Mercer, and Oscar Gish, eds., *Sickness and Wealth: The Corporate Assault on Global Health*, 27–36. Cambridge: South End Press, 2004.

Hook, Steven W., and Guang Zang. "Japan's Aid Policy Since the Cold War: Rhetoric and Reality." *Asian Survey* 38 (1998): 1051–1066

Hulme, David, and Michael Edwards. "NGOs, States and Donors: An Overview." In *NGOs, States and Donors: Too Close for Comfort?* Edited by David Hulme and Michael Edwards, 3–22. New York: St. Martin's Press, 1997.

———. "Too Close to the Powerful, Too Far from the Powerless?" In *NGOs, States and Donors: Too Close for Comfort?* Edited by David Hulme and Michael Edwards, 275–284. New York: St. Martin's Press, 1997.

Ikenberry, G. John. *After Victory: Institutions, Strategic Restraint, and the Rebuilding of Order After Major Wars*. Princeton, NJ: Princeton University Press, 2001.

International AIDS Vaccine Initiative, Inc. *Consolidated Financial Statements and Other Financial Information Year Ended December 31, 2009*. New York, IAVI, 2009.

International Health Partnership. *Scaling Up for Better Health: Work Plan for the International Health Partnership and Related Initiatives*. Geneva: IHP, 2008.

Japan International Cooperation Agency. *Approaches for Systematic Planning of Development Projects: Basic Education, Anti-HIV/AIDS Measures, Promotion of Small and Medium Enterprises, Rural Development*. Tokyo: Japan International Cooperation Agency, 2003.

———. *Approaches for Systemic Planning of Development Projects: Water Resources*. Tokyo: Japan International Cooperation Agency, 2003.

———. "Japan's Efforts in ODA." Tokyo: Japan International Cooperation Agency, 2006.

———. *Second Study on International Cooperation for Population and Development*. Tokyo: Institute for International Cooperation, 2003.

Japan Ministry of Foreign Affairs. "Japan's Contribution In Achieving the Health Related MDGs." Tokyo: Ministry of Foreign Affairs, 2005.

———. "Japan's Official Development Assistance Charter." Tokyo: Ministry of Foreign Affairs, 2003.

Joint United Nations Programme on HIV/AIDS. *2006 Report on the Global AIDS Epidemic*. Geneva: Switzerland, 2006.

———. "From Advocacy to Action: A Progress Report on UNAIDS at the Country Level." Geneva, Switzerland: 2005.

———. "Keeping the Promise: Summary of the Declaration of Commitment on HIV/AIDS." Geneva, Switzerland: 2001.

———. "Making the Money Work Through Greater UN Support for AIDS Responses: The 2006–2007 Consolidated UN Technical Support Plan for AIDS." Geneva, Switzerland: 2005.

———. "Report of the Executive Director to the Program Coordinating Board 2000–2001." Geneva, Switzerland, 2002.

———. "The 'Three Ones' in Action: Where We Are and Where We Go From Here." Geneva, Switzerland: 2005.

Jolly, Richard, Louis Emmerij, and Thomas G. Weiss, "The UN and Human Development," *United Nations Intellectual History Project*. Briefing Note no. 8, July 2009.

Jonsson, Christer, and Peter Soderholm. "IGO-NGO Relations and HIV/AIDS: Innovation or Stalemate?" In Thomas G. Weiss and Leon Gordenker, *NGOs, the UN and Global Governance*, 121–138. London: Lynne Rienner, 1996.

Jopson, Barney, and Jamil Anderlini. "China Pledges $10 Billion in Low Cost Loans to Africa," *The Washington Post*. 9 November 2009.

Kates, Jennifer J., Stephen Morrison and Eric Leif. "Global Health Funding: A Glass Half Full?" *The Lancet* 368 (2006): 187–188.

Kay, Adrian, and Owain Williams. "Introduction: The International Political Economy of Global Health Governance." In *Global Health Governance: Crisis, Institutions and Political Economy*. Edited by Adrian Kay and Owain David Williams, 2–23. New York: Palgrave, 2009.

Keck, Margaret E., and Kathryn Sikkink. *Activists Beyond Borders: Advocacy Networks in International Politics.* Ithaca, NY: Cornell, 1998.

Kelley, Judith. "The More the Merrier? The Effects of Having Multiple International Election Monitoring Organizations." *Perspectives of Politics* 7 (2009): 59–54, p. 62.

Keohane Robert O., and David G. Victor. "The Regime Complex for Climate Change." *Perspectives on Politics* 9 (2011): 7–23.

Klein, Naomi. *The Shock Doctrine: The Rise of Disaster Capitalism.* New York: Metropolitan Books, 2007.

KMPG. "Bill and Melinda Gates Foundation Trust: Financial Statements." 31 December 2011.

Koizumi, Junichiro. "Statement by Prime Minister Junichiro Koizumi, Africa: The Home of Self-Endeavor." *Mofa.go.jp* May 1, 2006. <http://www.mofa.go.jp/region/africa/pmv0605/state.html/> (12 December 2006).

Koumura, Masahiko. "Global Health and Japan's Foreign Policy—From Okanawa to Toyako." *mofa.go.jp* November 25, 2007. <http://mofa.go.jp/policy/health_c/address0711.html/> (12 December, 2008).

Labonté, Ronald, Chantal Blouin, and Lisa Forman. "Trade and Health." In *Global Health Governance: Crisis, Institutions and Political Economy.* Edited by Adrian Kay and Owain David Williams, 182–208. New York: Palgrave, 2009.

Lai, Brian. "Examining the Goals of US Foreign Assistance in the Post Cold War Period, 1991–96." *Journal of Peace Research* 40, no. 1 (2003): 103–128.

Lebovic, James H. "Donor Positioning: Development Assistance from the US, Japan, France, Germany and Britain." *Political Research Quarterly* 58, no. 1 (2005): 119–126.

Lee, Kelley. "The Pit and the Pendulum: Can Globalization Take Health Governance Forward?" *Development* 47(2): 11–17

———. "Understandings of Global Health Governance: The Contested Landscape." In *Global Health Governance: Crisis, Institutions and Political Economy.* Edited by Adrian Kay and Owain David Williams, 27–41. New York: Palgrave, 2009.

———. *The World Health Organizaton (WHO).* New York: Routledge, 2009.

Lehman, Howard. "Japan's Foreign Aid Policy to Africa Since the Tokyo International Conference on African Development." *Pacific Affairs* 78 (2005): 423–442.

Leon, Josh. "Poverty Capitalism: Interview with Ananya Roy." *Foreign Policy in Focus.* Washington, DC: February 17. 2011.

Leon, Joshua K. "Confronting Catastrophe: Norms, Efficiency, and the Evolution of the AIDS Battle in the UN." *Cambridge Review of International Affairs* 24(3) (2011): 471–491.

Loeppky, Rodney. "The Accumulative Nature of the US Health Complex." In *Health for Some: The Political Economy of Global Health Governance.* Edited by Sandra J. MacLean, Sherri A. Brown, and Pieter Fourie, 39–52. New York: Palgrave, 2009.

Lopez, Alan D., Colin D. Mathers, Majid Ezzati, Dean T. Jamison, and Christopher J. L. Murray. *Global Burden of Disease and Risk Factors*. New York: Oxford University Press, 2006.

Macdonald, Ryan, and John Hoddinott. "Determinates of Canadian Bilateral Aid Allocations: Humanitarian, Commercial or Political?" *Canadian Journal of Economics* 37 (2004): 294–312, p. 296.

Mackeller, Landis. "Priorities in Global Assistance for Health, AIDS and Population (HAP)" OECD Development Centre, Working Paper no. 244, (2005).

Malhotra, Kamal. "NGOs Without Aid: Beyond the Global Soup Kitchen." *Third World Quarterly* 21 (2000), 665–668.

Mann, J. "Non-Government Organizations Should Be Catalysts for Change." *British Medical Journal* 310 (1996).

Mann, Jonathan. "Health Promotion Against AIDS: A Typology." In *AIDS: Prevention Through Education: A World View*. Edited by Jonathan Mann. Oxford: Oxford University Press, 1992.

Mann, Jonathan M. "Human Rights and AIDS: The Future of the Pandemic." In *Health and Human Rights*. Edited by Jonathan M. Mann, Sofia Gruskin, Michael A. Grodin and George J. Annas. New York: Routledge, 1999.

Maté, Gabor, *In the Realm of Hungry Ghosts: Close Encounters With Addiction*. Berkeley: North Atlantic Books, 2010.

McCoy, David, Gayatri Kembhavi, Jinest Patel, and Akish Luintel. "The Bill and Melinda Gates Foundation's Grant-Making Programme for Global Health." *The Lancet* 373 (2009): 1645–1653.

McCurry, Justin. "Monitoring Japan's Aid Commitments." *The Lancet* 368 (2006): 1561–1562.

McKinlay, R. D,. and R. Little. "A Foreign Policy Model of US Bilateral Aid Allocation." *World Politics* 30, no. 1 (1977): 58–86.

Medecins Sans Frontieres. *Untangling the Web of Antiretroviral Price Reductions* 13th ed. (July 2010).

Milner, Helen V. "Why Multilateralism? Foreign Aid and Domestic Principle-Agent Problems." In *Delegation and Agency in International Organizations*. Edited by Darren G. Hawkins, David A. Lake, Daniel L. Nielson, and Michael J. Tierney, 107–139. New York: Cambridge University Press, 2006.

Ministerial Council on HIV/AIDS. *Meeting the Challenge: Canada's Foreign Policy on HIV/AIDS: With a Particular Focus on Africa*. Ottawa: CIDA, 2003.

Morrison, David R. *Aid and Ebb Tide: A History of CIDA and Canadian Development Assistance*. Waterloo: Wilfrid Laurier, 1998.

Motchane, Jean-Loup. "Health for All or Riches for Some: WHO Responsible?" *Le Monde Diplomatique* (July 2002).

Moyers, Bill. "Transcript: Bill Moyers Interviews Bill Gates." *NOW* 9 May 2003.

Moyo, Dambisa *Dead Aid: Why Aid is Not Working and How There is a Better Way for Africa* (New York: Farrar, Strauss, and Giroux, 2010).

Murphy, Craig N. *The United Nations Development Programme: A Better Way?* Cambridge: Cambridge University Press, 2006.

Murray, Christopher J. L, Brent Anderson, Roy Burstein, Katherine Leach-Kemon, Matthew Schneider, Annette Tardif, and Raymond Zhang. "Development Assistance for Health: Trends and Prospects." *The Lancet* 378 (2011): 8–10.

Murray, Christopher J. L., and Alan D. Lopez, *The Global Burden of Disease*. Washington, DC: World Bank, 1990.

Murray, Christopher J. L., Alan D. Lopez, Robert Black, Colin D. Mathers, Kenji Shibuya, Majid Ezzati, Joshua A. Salomon, Catherine M. Michaud, Neff Walker, and Theo Vos. "Global Burden of Disease 2005: Call for Collaborators." *The Lancet* 370: 109–110.

Musgrove, Philip, and Julia Fox-Rushby. "Cost-Effective Analysis for Priority Setting." In *Disease Control Priorities in Developing Countries*, 2nd ed. Edited by Dean T. Jamison, Joel G. Bremen, Anthony R. Measham, George Alleyne, Mariam Claeson, David. B. Evans, Prabhat Jha, Anne Mills, and Philip Musgrove, 217–285. Washington, DC: The World Bank, 2006.

Naim, Moisés. "Help Not Wanted." *New York Times*. 15 February 2007.

———. "What is a GONGO? How Government Sponsored Groups Masquerade as Civil Society." *Foreign Policy* 13 January 2012.

Neumayer, Eric. "The Determinants of Aid Allocation by Regional Multilateral Development Banks and United Nations Agencies." *International Studies Quarterly* 47 (2003): 101–122.

"New IBRD/IDA Health Sector Commitments by Sector and Region." *worldbank.org* September 8, 2011,< http://go.worldbank.org/IP0NBIFK70> 13 February 2013.

Nixson, Frederick. "Aid, Trade and Economic Development: The EU and the Developing World." In *The Economics of the European Union*, 4th ed. Edited by Mike Artis and Fredrick Nixson, 322–353. Cambridge: Cambridge University Press, 2007.

Nossal, Kim Richard. "Mixed Motives Revisited: Canada's Interest in Development Assistance." *Canadian Journal of Political Science* 21, no. 1 (1988): 35–56, p. 38.

O'Manique, Colleen. "Palliative Interventions: Canadian Foreign Policy, Security, and Global Health Governance." In *Health for Some: The Political Economy of Global Health Governance*. Edited by Sandra J. MacLean, Sherri A. Brown, and Pieter Fourie, 53–66. New York: Palgrave, 2009.

Organization for Economic Cooperation and Development. "Recent Trends in Official Development Assistance to Health." Prepared by the DAC Secretariat for the Third Meeting on Macroeconomics and Health (November, 2000).

————. *Reporting Directives for the Creditor Reporting System*. Paris: OECD, 2005.

Ostrom, Elinor. "A Polycentric Approach for Coping With Climate Change." World Bank Policy Research Working Paper 5095 (2009).

————. *Understanding Institutional Diversity*. Princeton, NJ: Princeton University Press, 2005.

Parliamentary Information and Research Service. "Official Development Assistance Spending." Ottawa: Library of Parliament, 2007.

Pierson, Paul. "The New Politics of the Welfare State." *World Politics* 48 (1996): 143–179.

————. "The Path to European Integration: A Historical Institutionalist Analysis," *Comparative Political Studies* 29 (1996): 123–163.

Piller, Charles, Edmund Sanders, and Robyn Dixon. "Dark Cloud Over Good Works of Gates Foundation." *Los Angeles Times*, 7 January 2007.

President's Emergency Program for AIDS Relief. "Comprehensive HIV Prevention for People Who Inject Drugs, Revised Guidance." Washington, DC, July 2010.

————. "PEPFAR Funding: Investments that Save Lives and Promote Security," PEPFAR (June 2011).

Provost, Claire. "Anti-Prostitution Pledge in US AIDS Funding 'Damaging' HIV Response." *UK Guardian* 24 July 2012.

Prashad, Vijay. *The Poorer Nations: A Possible History of the Global South*. London: Verso, 2012.

Public Health Agency of Canada. *Strengthened Leadership: Taking Action: Canada's Report on HIV/AIDS 2005*. Ottawa: PHAC, 2005.

Raustiala, Kal. "States, NGOs, and International Environmental Institutions." *International Studies Quarterly* 41 (1997): 719–740.

Raustiala, Kal, and David G. Victor. "The Regime Complex for Plant Genetic Resources." *International Organization* 58 (2004): 277–309.

Ravishankar, Nirmala, Paul Gubbins, Rebecca J. Cooley, Catherine Leach-Kemon, Catherine M. Michaud, Dean T. Jamison, and Christopher J. L. Murray. "Financing of Global Health: Tracking Development Assistance for Health from 1990 to 2007." *The Lancet* 373 (2009): 2113–2124

Riedel, Eibe. "The Human Right to Health: Conceptual Foundations." In *Realizing the Right to Health*. Edited by Andrew Clapham, Mary Robinson, Claire Mahon and Scott Jerbi, 21–39. Zurich: Swiss Human Rights Book, vol. 3, 2009.

Rix, Alan. *Japan's Economic Aid: Policy-Making and Politics*. New York: St. Martin's Press, 1980.

Rodrik, Dani. "Why Is There Multilateral Lending?" in *World Bank Annual Conference on Development Economics 1995*. Washington: World Bank 1996.

Roll Back Malaria. *Minutes of the 20th RBM Partnership Board Meeting*. Geneva: RBM, 2011.

Roy, Ananya. *Poverty Capital: Microfinance and the Making of Development*. New York: Routledge, 2010.

Sachs, Jeffrey. "The Development Challenge." *Foreign Affairs* 84 (2005): 78–90.

Sachs, Jeffrey D. *Common Wealth: Economics for a Crowded Planet*. New York: Penguin, 2008.

Schneider, Carmen Huckel. "Global Public Health and Innovation in Governance: The Emergence of Public Private Partnerships." In *Health for Some: The Political Economy of Global Health Governance*, 105–117. Edited by Sandra J. MacLean, Sherri A. Brown, and Pieter Fourie, 53–66. New York: Palgrave, 2009.

Schwartlander, Bernhard, Ian Grubb, and Jas Perriens. "The 10-Year Struggle to Provide Antiretroviral Treatment to People with HIV in the Developing World." *The Lancet* 368 (2006): 541–546.

Seckinelgin, Hakan. "A Global Disease and its Governance: HIV/AIDS in Sub-Saharan Africa and the Agency of NGOs." *Global Governance* 11 (2005): 351–368.

———. "Who Can Help People With HIV/AIDS in Africa? Governance of HIV/AIDS and Civil Society." *Voluntas: International Journal of Voluntary and Nonprofit Organizations* 15 (2004): 287–304.

"The Self-Interest Case for US Global Health Cooperation." *The Lancet* 349 (1997): 1037.

Sell, Susan K., and Aseem Prakash. "Using Ideas Strategically: The Contest Between Business and NGO Networks in Intellectual Property Rights." *International Studies Quarterly* 48 (2004): 143–175.

Sen, Amartya. *Development As Freedom*. New York: Anchor Books, 1999.

Shiffman, Jeremy. "Has Donor Prioritization of HIV/AIDS Displaced for Other Health Issues?" *Health Policy and Planning* 23 (2008): 95–100.

Singal, Arvind, and Everett M. Rogers. *Combating AIDS: Communication Strategies in Action*. Thousand Oaks: Sage, 2003.

Soderberg, Marie. "Swedish Perceptions of Japanese ODA." In *Japan's Foreign Aid: Old Continuities and New Directions*. Edited by David Arase, 81–94. Abingdon: Routledge, 2005.

South Commission. *The Challenge to the South*. Oxford: Oxford University Press, 1990.

Spires, Anthony J. "US Foundations Boost Chinese Governments, Not NGOs." *Yale Global* (28 March 2012).

Sridhar, Devi, and Rajaie Batniji. "Misfinancing Global Health: A Case for Transparency in Disbursements and Decisionmaking." *The Lancet* 372 (2008): 1185–1191.

Stiglitz, Joseph. *Globalization and its Discontents*. New York: W. W. Norton, 2003.

"Sweden Best at Development Assistance." *Sweden.gov.se* 9 December 2008 <http://www.sweden.gov.se/sb/d/11214/a/117202> (12 December 2009).

Sweden Ministry of Foreign Affairs. "Focused Bilateral Development Cooperation." Stockholm: Ministry of Foreign Affairs, 2008.

———. *Investing For Future Generations: Sweden's International Response to HIV/AIDS*. Stockholm: Ministry of Foreign Affairs, 1999.

"Sweden's New Development Cooperation Policy." *Sweden.gov.se* 20 September 2007 <http://www.sweden.gov.se/sb/d/9439/a/88669> (12 December 2008).

Swedish International Development Agency. *Health Is Wealth*. Stockholm: Swedish International Development Agency, 2002.

Swidler, Ann. "Syncretism and Subversion in AIDS Governance: How Locals Cope With Global Demands." *International Affairs* 82 (2006): 269–284.

Therien, Jean-Phillippe, Carolyn Lloyd, and Caroline Lloyd. "Development Assistance on the Brink." *Third World Quarterly* 21, no. 1 (2000): 21–38.

Thomas, Caroline, and Martin Weber. "The Politics of Global Health Governance: What Happened to Global Health For All by the Year 2000?" *Global Governance* 10 (2004), 187–205.

Tran, Mark. "UN Adopts 'Momentous' Resolution on Universal Health Care." *UK Guardian* 13 December 2012.

ul Haq, Mahbub. *Reflections on Human Development*. Oxford: Oxford University Press, 1995.

"UN Call for 'New Deal' On AIDS Drug Supply." *Pharma Marketletter* 21 February 2001.

UNITAID. "Innovative Financing." *Unitaid.eu.* <http://www.unitaid.eu/en/how/innovative-financing> (13 January 2014).

United Nations. *A New Global Partnership: Eradicate Poverty and Transform Economies Through Sustainable Development*. New York: United Nations, 2013.

United Nations Children's Fund and World Health Organization. *Alternative Approaches to Meeting Basic Health Needs in Developing Countries*. Geneva: World Health Organization, 1975.

United Nations Development Program. *Human Development Report 2003*. New York: United Nations Development Program, 2003.

———. *UNDP Strategic Plan, 2008–2011*. New York: United Nations Development Program, 2007.

United Nations General Assembly Resolution A/67/L.36. 6 December 2012.

United Nations News Centre. "General Assembly Declares Access to Clear Water and Sanitation is a Human Right." (28 July 2010).

"UN Millennium Development Goals." *UN.org*, 7 July 2008, <http://un.org/millenniumgoals/> (8 July 2008).

United States Agency for International Development. *Child Survival and Health Programs Fund Progress Report*. Washington, DC: United States Agency for International Development, 2004.

———. "Fast Facts: HIV/AIDS." Washington, DC: United States Agency for International Development, 2008.

———. *Foreign Aid in the National Interest.* Washington, DC: United States Agency for International Development, 2002.

———. "Health Overview." *usaid,gov* <http://www.usaid.gov/our_work/global health/> 3 December 2008.

———. *Reducing the Threat of Infectious Diseases of Major Public Health Importance: USAID's Initiative to Prevent and Control Effective Diseases.* Washington, DC: United States Agency for International Development, 1998.

———. *Report to Congress: Child Survival and Health Programs Progress Report.* Washington, DC: United States Agency for International Development, 2004.

Voelker, Rebecca. "Setting Priorities and Budgets to Fight Against Global AIDS." *Journal of the American Medical Association* 21 (2000): 2709–2710.

Wade, Robert. "Showdown at the World Bank." *New Left Review* 7 (2001): 124–137.

Waitzkin, Howard. "Report of the WHO Commission on Macroeconomics and Health: A Summary and Critique." *Lancet* 361: 523–26.

Walsh, Fergus. "Bill Gates: The World Can Defeat Polio." *BBC* 27 January 2013.

Walsh, J. A., and K. S. Warren. "Selective Primary Health Care: An Interim Strategy for Disease Control in Developing Countries." *New England Journal of Medicine* 301 (1979): 967–74.

Walt, Gill. "WHO Under Stress: Implications For Health Policy." *Health Policy* 24 (1993): 125–144.

Washington, Harriet. *Deadly Monopolies: The Shocking Corporate Takeover of Life Itself—and the Consequences for your Health and Our Medical Future.* New York, Anchor Books, 2012.

Werner, David. "Elusive Promise, Whatever Happened to 'Health for All'?" *New Internationalist* 331 (January/February 2001).

Werner, David. "Who Killed Primary Health Care?" *New Internationalist* 272 (October 1995).

"What Has the Gates Foundation Done for Global Health?" *The Lancet* 373 (2009): 1577.

WHO Commission on Macroeconomics and Health. *Macroeconomics and Health: Investing in Health for Economic Development.* Geneva: World Health Organization 2001.

William J. Clinton Foundation. *Building a Better World: William J. Clinton Foundation Annual Report 2010.* New York: Clinton Foundation, 2011.

Woods, Ngaire. *The Globalizers: The IMF, World Bank and Their Borrowers.* Ithaca: Cornell, 2006.

Woods, Ngaire. "Whose Aid? Whose Influence? China, Emerging Donors and the Silent Revolution in Development Assistance." *International Affairs* 84 (2008): 1205–1221.

The World Bank, "Defining Civil Society." *worldbank.org* 4 August 2010 <http://web.worldbank.org/WBSITE/EXTERNAL/TOPICS/CSO/0,,contentM

DK:20101499~menuPK:244752~pagePK:220503~piPK:220476~theSite
PK:228717,00.html> 6 February 2013.

———. "Health: Supporting Systemic Change in a New Global Context."
Washington, DC: World Bank, 2007.

———. *Healthy Development: The World Bank Strategy for Health, Nutrition and
Population Results.* Washington, DC: World Bank, 2007.

———. "IDA 13, Report from the Executive Directors of the International
Development Association to the Board of Governors." Washington, DC:
The World Bank, 2002.

———. "IDA 14, Report From the Executive Directors of the International
Development Association to the Board of Governors." Washington, DC:
World Bank, 2005.

———. "IDA 15, Report from the Executive Directors of the International
Development Association to the Board of Governors." Washington, DC:
The World Bank, 2008.

———. *World Development Report 1993: Investing in Health.* Washington, DC:
World Bank, 1993.

The World Bank Institute. "About WBI." *worldbank.org* < http://wbi.worldbank.
org/wbi/about> 8 February 2013.

———. "Public-Private Partnerships." *worldbank.org* <http://wbi.worldbank.org/
wbi/about/topics/public-private-partnerships> 8 February 2013.

World Health Assembly. "Global Strategy and Plan of Action on Public Health,
Innovation, and Intellectual Property." WHA Resolution 61.21 (24 May,
2008).

World Health Organization. *A Safer Future: Global Public Health Security in the
21st Century.* Geneva: WHO, 2007.

———. "About the Health Metrics Network." *Who.int* <http://www.who.int/
healthmetrics/about/en/> (6 January 2014).

———. "Civil Society." *who.int* <http://www.who.int/trade/glossary/story006/en/
index.html> 6 February 2013.

———. *Engaging for Health: Eleventh General Program of Work: 2006–2015, A
Global Health Agenda.* Geneva: World Health Organization, 2006.

———. "High Level Forum on the Health Millennium Development Goals."
Who.int <http://www.who.int/hdp/hlf/en/> (6 January 2014).

———. *Primary Health Care: Now More Than Ever.* Geneva: WHO, 2008.

———. *Programme Budget 2012–2013.* Geneva: WHO, 2011.

———. *Report of the Commission on Public Health, Innovation, and Intellectual
Property Rights.* Geneva: WHO, 2006.

———. "The Right to Health." *who.int* November 2012 <http://www.who.int/
mediacentre/factsheets/fs323/en/index.html> 13 February 2013.

———. *Strategic Alliances: The Role of Civil Society and Health.* Geneva: World
Health Organization, 2001.

———. *WHO and Civil Society: Linking for Better Health: Civil Society Initiative.*
Geneva: World Health Organization, 2002.

World Health Organization and Stop TB Partnership. *Stop TB Partnership: Annual Report 2009*. Geneva: WHO, 2009.

Yamey, Gavin. "WHO in 2002: Why Does the World Still Need WHO?" *BMJ* 325 (2002): 1294–1298.

Youde, Jeremy. *Global Health Governance*. Cambridge: Polity, 2012.

W. Zacher, Mark and Tania J. Keefe. *The Politics of Global Health Governance: United by Contagion*. New York: Palgrave, 2008.

Zhou, Xiaoming. "Japan's Official Development Assistance Program: Pressures to Expand." *Asian Survey* 31 (1991): 341–350.

Index

79163264R00145

Made in the USA
Lexington, KY
18 January 2018